The Autobiography

The Autobiography

SEÁN ÓG Ó hAILPÍN

PENGUIN BOOKS

PENGUIN BOOKS

Published by the Penguin Group
Penguin Books Ltd, 80 Strand, London WC2R ORL, England
Penguin Group (USA) Inc., 375 Hudson Street, New York, New York 10014, USA
Penguin Group (Canada), 90 Eglinton Avenue East, Suite 700, Toronto, Ontario, Canada M4P 2Y3
(a division of Pearson Penguin Canada Inc.)
Penguin Ireland, 25 St Stephen's Green, Dublin 2, Ireland
(a division of Penguin Books Ltd)
Penguin Group (Australia), 707 Collins Street, Melbourne, Victoria 3008, Australia
(a division of Pearson Australia Group Pty Ltd)
Penguin Books India Pvt Ltd, 11 Community Centre,
Panchsheel Park, New Delhi – 110 017, India
Penguin Group (NZ), 67 Apollo Drive, Rosedale, Auckland 0632, New Zealand
(a division of Pearson New Zealand Ltd)
Penguin Books (South Africa) (Pty) Ltd, Block D, Rosebank Office Park,
181 Jan Smuts Avenue, Parktown North, Gauteng 2193, South Africa

Penguin Books Ltd, Registered Offices: 80 Strand, London WC2R ORL, England

www.penguin.com

First published by Penguin Ireland 2013
Published in Penguin Books 2014
001

Copyright © Seán Óg Ó hAilpín, 2013
All rights reserved

The moral right of the author has been asserted

Typeset by Palimpsest Book Production Limited, Falkirk, Stirlingshire
Printed in Great Britain by Clays Ltd, St Ives plc

Except in the United States of America, this book is sold subject
to the condition that it shall not, by way of trade or otherwise, be lent,
re-sold, hired out, or otherwise circulated without the publishers
prior consent in any form of binding or cover other than that in
which it is published and without a similar condition including this
condition being imposed on the subsequent purchaser

ISBN: 978-0-241-95591-8

www.greenpenguin.co.uk

MIX
Paper from
responsible sources
FSC™ C018179

Penguin Books is committed to a sustainable
future for our business, our readers and our planet.
This book is made from Forest Stewardship
Council™ certified paper.

To Teu, Sarote, Setanta, Aisake and Étaoin.
To Öhon and Öfa.
To Siobhán.

I.

You may feel as though you know me.

That wouldn't be surprising. After all, I've been giving interviews for almost twenty years: newspapers, radio, TV, websites. I've been asked for my opinion a thousand times, and I've always given an honest answer. This game, that opponent; in English, as Gaeilge.

It's probably what's created that image in your head of me. Hurler. Gaeilgeoir. Corkman. Wing-back. Captain. Brother. Striker.

No one is a collection of labels, though. There are shades to all of those impressions.

I was a hurler who for years didn't want to hurl.

An Irish speaker who didn't know a word of the language until I was eleven.

A Corkman who wished he was still in Sydney.

In fact, most people don't even know my real name.

Part of my motivation for writing this book has been to flesh out those contradictions.

After reading it I hope you'll know me a little better.

Father from Fermanagh. Mother from Fiji. Neither a hurling stronghold. You've heard it often enough, and it was a good line from Micheál Ó Muircheartaigh all those years ago.

It's something that gives me a lot of pride: that as a child I came to Ireland, picked up a sport relatively late in life and managed to do well at it.

When you're at the height of your career, you're living it from day to day, from week to week: preparation, matches, recovery; you don't have a moment to stand back and look at what was involved.

Now I can appreciate it a bit more. The adventure. The journey. And not just mine, either.

If Micheál had had more information, he could have been even more specific: father from Rosslea and mother from Rotuma.

I understand people's curiosity about the two of them. Even now, with Irish kids heading for Thailand and Australia and all points east as a matter of course, it'd be a pretty unusual connection to make; almost forty years ago it was unheard of.

My mother, Emeli, is Fijian by nationality, but she's actually from Rotuma, a tiny island about 400 miles north of the Fijian archipelago.

On Rotuma they grow fruit and cassava and taro. Each family has an allotment in the interior of the island. Most would also have chickens and pigs and goats, and there's always plenty of fish to supplement the diet, though it's not like industrial fishing out of Castletownbere. They use little boats like currachs. Those who are looking for a life involving something other than farming or fishing tend to leave Rotuma – for Suva, the capital of Fiji, or further afield.

One side of the island is Methodist and the other is Roman Catholic. Mum is from the Catholic side where – small world – she was taught by two Irish missionaries of the Marist Order, Fr Johnson and Fr Maguire, from whom she got some vague impression about Ireland.

Most Rotuman families would be the same size as families in Ireland thirty or forty years ago. My mum is the second youngest of thirteen – five boys and eight girls. Seven of them stayed on the island (Kerera, Apao, Sarote, Taito, Tivaknoa, Vamarase, Teu) while the other six (Uraria, Tifare, Atfoa, Mua, Mum, Viki) left the island and eventually made homes in mainland Fiji, New Zealand, Australia, Canada and Ireland.

Mum was nineteen years of age when she hopped on the government boat to Suva in 1972 to start working as a receptionist in Nadi.

★

That story, of leaving your home place in search of opportunity, is my dad's story too.

He's from a place called Rosslea in south Fermanagh, a strongly nationalist spot very close to the Monaghan border, between Clones and Scotstown. There were six of them in his family: Pat, Dad and James, who were non-identical twins, Eddie, Denis and Mary.

His father was from Scotstown, but his mother, my gran, was from Kilgarvan in Kerry. They met while working in London and came back to Fermanagh to raise their kids.

I never knew my grandfather, but I knew my grandmother well – Peggy 'Cooper' O'Sullivan. She was the person who showed me the way Kerry people think about football. When she'd ring us in Australia, maybe once a year, we'd go on the line and be told to ask if Kerry would win the All-Ireland, and she'd say, 'Ah, I suppose they will.' As in, it'd be a shock if they didn't.

Obviously there wasn't a lot of work in a tiny village in Fermanagh, and my father's sister Mary was the only one who didn't emigrate. The boys all went to Belfast for work, and then they headed further afield. Pat ended up in Sydney, running a construction company, while Denis, James and Eddie all worked in construction in London.

Dad went to Glasgow, where he became a huge Celtic supporter. For years he treasured a book about Celtic's European Cup win in 1967 that included a photograph of him thumbing his way down to Lisbon for the final.

When visas for Australia were advertised in the early 1970s, he decided to head down under. He worked in Brisbane, Darwin, Melbourne and Sydney. He also put in a spell working in Papua New Guinea.

When he fancied a holiday, he headed out of the country. While on a break in Fiji, he met Mum. She went with him to Australia and they got married there, but when she was expecting me she went back to Rotuma for the birth.

I was born in Ahau, the capital of Rotuma, in a small hospital. When I went back there in December 2006 for the making of the documentary *Tall, Dark and Ó hAilpín*, they showed me the tiny room

I was born in. Medical care is pretty basic on Rotuma. If you survive a serious injury they either ship you out to Suva for surgery or you heal slowly and painfully on Rotuma.

I've told people over the years that it was a cultural thing, that Rotumans liked their first-born to be born on the island of their ancestors, and it is; but the real story's a bit more prosaic. Five or six months into her pregnancy, Mum wasn't feeling at all well. Her parents visited, and my grandmother wanted to know if it was OK for Mum to come back to Rotuma. My grandmother helped out as a midwife on the island and was a bit of a herbalist, so she'd have been well equipped to look after Mum. It was my grandmother who delivered me in that little room in the hospital.

A month after I was born Mum was ready to bring me back to Australia, but my grandfather suddenly passed away. As heartbroken as Mum was, she always says that at least she was there for the funeral, which wouldn't have been possible for her if she'd had me in Australia. In Rotuma funerals are held the day after a person dies because there are no morgues to hold bodies in; she wouldn't have got back in time.

My mother and I stayed on the island for three months. Then we moved to Brisbane, where Dad was working at the time. In 1979 we moved to Sydney, because Dad had picked up new work there.

My mother and I – and my siblings, when they came along – spoke Rotuman at home. We'd eat Rotuman delicacies – corned beef wrapped in spinach leaves and cooked in coconut milk, or taro, a starchy vegetable, or the Rotuman version of *fulacht fiadh*, cooking a pig underground with hot stones. We'd meet Mum's relatives regularly, too. But for the most part I was a little Australian. I have very happy memories of Sydney. Walking around barefoot. Wearing shorts. The sun beating down. All the clichés come true.

We lived at 25 Waterloo Road in Greenacre, a suburb to the west of central Sydney. It was a timber house, with two bedrooms and an outside toilet. It didn't take long for the kids' bedroom to get crowded. Teu was born while we were still in Brisbane, a year after me. Sarote, Setanta and Aisake were born in Sydney, while Étaoin was born later, in Cork.

The house wasn't luxurious, but there was one obvious attraction for a family with small kids: a half-acre of garden. A high timber fence surrounded the garden, which was no harm because the house was on a busy road. I've never forgotten the sound of the bus: there was a stop right outside the house, so all day long you'd hear the bus stopping and starting.

There was a primary school at the top of the hill and when we were very small Mum walked us up that hill to school. (She'd also slather us in baby oil every morning before we left the house. For our skin, or our hair – don't ask me why!) As we got older we went off to school ourselves, and on the way home after school Teu and I would head to the public park and the Rugby League field, Roberts Park, halfway up the hill, to play on the swings and kick the ball around. Mum would go up there with us every now and again – she'd jog to keep her weight in check, and we'd fall in for a couple of laps of the field alongside her before heading off to play on our own.

There was a fifty-metre public pool in the neighbourhood. My star turn there was to dive into the deep end, swim down and touch the bottom, and then kick for the surface again. That was fine until the day I kicked off and caught my foot on a toy someone had thrown in, slashing it open. It was bad enough getting a few stitches afterwards but when the doctor took out a needle for a tetanus jab . . .

Going past the house in the other direction there was a huge fruit market, and myself and Teu would head down there to slog a few apples from time to time. Beyond that again was Punchbowl railway station, where you caught the train to central Sydney. The journey took under an hour, but as a young kid it seemed a very long way.

The school on the hill and the train station beyond the house: they were the two poles of our little world in Sydney.

Sport was a huge part of our lives from a very early stage. Dad had represented Queensland in Gaelic football in the GAA State championships in Australia, and he always had an interest in sport. And there was a huge focus on sport in primary school. There were sports days for the entire school, and a big deal was made out of representing the school in Rugby League, for instance, which was a huge attraction for me. We played backyard cricket as well.

Most Sundays Dad would bring us to the old GAA centre in Auburn, Sydney. At that stage he'd retired from playing himself, but he and the other Irish fellas would bring along their kids and there'd be a big crowd of us playing Gaelic football on the side pitch while a senior game was going on on the main field. We were all Australian kids, most of us with Irish parents, and we'd be listening to 'Kerry' Murphy, a Knocknagoshel native who was a legendary character in Australian GAA circles, as he coached us in the skills, though 'coaching' might be stretching the definition. Basically we ran around in a gang after the ball.

One Sunday I played a match, and afterwards, when I got into the car to go home with Dad, he was fuming. Raging. We drove off down the road but after a couple of minutes he pulled over and told me to get out. When I did, he drove off and left me there, standing on the side of the road.

The reason he was angry? A guy had passed me in the game and I hadn't chased back. I'd given up. That drove him mad.

I didn't know where I was. I was just a small kid, maybe seven years of age, alone on a strange road somewhere in Sydney, wondering what was going to happen. After twenty minutes or so he came back and I was still there. That was one thing that amazed him, he said later, that I hadn't moved from the spot.

For a full week after that he had me doing sprints in the evening, every evening, in the back garden. Wall to wall, over and over. You can imagine how I did the following Sunday out in Auburn. I chased fellas all over the field, from start to finish.

As far back as I can remember, if we were running, sprinting, playing with a ball or throwing on a pair of boots, Dad was never too far away. He pushed us hard from an early age. Sometimes he pushed us so hard that he took the fun out of sport.

I like my food, always have. As a kid I was pudgy enough. Incredible Rotuman delicacies like *ikou* and *puatkau*, *tarhoro* and *iá fekei*, and of course good old ice cream, were my downfall, and Mum was my facilitator.

As a way of sorting that out, Dad enrolled us both for the big fun run in Sydney, the *Sun-Herald* City2Surf race.

Good bonding? I was seven. It's a 14-km run.

We went running every second day to train for it, pounding the footpaths around Greenacre. I can recall dreading the beep from the car as he pulled in after work, because it meant we'd be heading out for a run.

But it prepared me. I'd feel the same tingle, the little kick from the nerves, years later when we'd be going out to play a championship game.

Ireland? It might as well have been on Mars.

I remember a few different, unrelated impressions. When I was a kid we had a sign on the kitchen wall which said '*Sláinte*', and if Dad had friends over, they'd open beers and say '*Sláinte*' before having a drink.

Or the fact that Dad had a brother, Pat, in Sydney, so he'd be over the odd time and they'd talk about Ireland, or they'd read the *Irish Press*, which Dad subscribed to.

Or getting woken up after midnight in 1986 for the radio broadcast of the All-Ireland final, Dad getting excited because as an Ulsterman he enjoyed hearing about Tyrone doing well for a while, before Kerry eventually reeled them in.

The other annual event that reminded us of Ireland was the St Patrick's Day parade in Sydney, when Dad had us togged out in

green, white and orange. When we moved to Ireland, I was surprised
by the fact that people weren't dressed like little leprechauns, the way
we were, back in Sydney.

There was another interaction with Ireland: when an International Rules team goes to Australia there's a tradition that they
play a local selection, Irish lads who play football in Sydney. In 1986
I was at Parramatta Stadium and played in the curtain-raiser, the
kids' game, before the Rules-versus-locals match. Afterwards we all
got autographs from the Irish players. Who were they? We didn't
have a clue. I remember distinctly, though, that I had Adidas boots
with yellow stripes and a yellow sole, and one of the Irish players
signed the sole.

When we got home I finally deciphered the writing. It was one of
the men we'd been hearing about on that late-night radio broadcast:
Pat Spillane.

That was Ireland. Did I see myself living there? Not in a million
years.

In real terms life was in Greenacre, and that meant Rugby League.

The local team was the Canterbury Bulldogs, and they were our
heroes. Getting a new Bulldogs jersey at a sports shop would have
made a fair dent in the family finances, but I remember Mum getting
me a Bulldogs top in a second-hand shop, and I wore it for years.
Blue and white – the same as the colours I'd later wear at North Mon,
and the reason I follow Everton to this day.

During the eighties the Bulldogs dominated the sport; themselves
or Parramatta won the Grand Final most years. Bulldogs players went
around to the schools, conducting clinics for kids. They were the
sportspeople you wanted to emulate – the likes of Steve Mortimer,
Peter Tunks and Terry Lamb.

Australian Rules football wasn't a popular sport in Sydney, but we
had a neighbour in Greenacre called Bob Carlton, who followed
Carlton Football Club because he shared the same name. Once when
myself and Teu went next door he had a game on, a Grand Final

between Carlton and Hawthorn. Because he was for Carlton we decided to support Hawthorn, and I've supported them since.

Sydney was an outdoor society more or less all year round – the only difference in winter was that it got darker a little earlier – and a multi-ethnic one. I was in school with Italians, Lebanese, Greeks, Croats, Serbs; I don't remember any Irish. As it happens, most people didn't see us as Irish

Then Dad changed our names.

That's something people don't know about me.

The name on my birth certificate, and the name by which I was known until I was seven, is Seán Halfpenny. Apparently my father's father had tried to register his children's name in Irish, but he wasn't allowed to do so. After my father's sister Mary died, and Dad came back from the funeral in Fermanagh, he was very strong on wanting our names registered in Irish, and he got a solicitor in Sydney to look into it. That was a lengthy process, but eventually the solicitor succeeded in getting permission for it in 1984, so our surnames were changed to Ó hAilpín. Dad, who had been John Halfpenny, became Seán Ó hAilpín. And I, having been Seán, became Seán Óg.

I went into school the following day with a new name. I imagine the Australian school system was well accustomed to challenging names, but people who didn't know would, quite naturally, call me Seán. My father would say, 'Your name's not Seán, it's Seán Óg.' He was very insistent on that. (Sarote and Teu got off easily because there was no way to translate their first names into Irish, but I had the last laugh when we came to Cork: everyone could pronounce Seán Óg, but their names were more of a challenge . . .)

Dad also got us Irish passports, rather than holding an Australian passport with the Union Jack on it. But that didn't make me feel any more Irish.

Neither did a souvenir or two from home.

After my Aunt Mary's death in 1983, Dad stayed on in Ireland for a few weeks after the funeral to look after some business. When he came back after the funeral he had two hurleys in his bag, and a sliotar. That was the first time I saw a hurley.

Myself and Teu, having no concept of how to puck around, tried to use the hurleys like tennis rackets: Wimbledon was on at the time and we thought we could use these weird sticks for the odd overhand smash.

It wasn't long before the novelty wore off, the hurleys were stashed away, and we went back to the important stuff: the Rugby League ball.

One evening, after getting home from work, Dad told us all to sit down because he had some news.

'We're going back to Ireland,' he said.

I'm sure I asked questions, but I can't remember.

Our destination was Cork. Why Cork? He and his brothers had had to clear out of Rosslea because there was no work there, so that wasn't a viable destination. A large urban area offered employment, but Dublin didn't appeal to him. He saw Cork as having a particularly strong Irish identity. (I remember a later brief flirtation with the notion of moving to Baile Bhuirne in the west Cork Gaeltacht.) He worked with a few Cork lads in Sydney who were big into their GAA, and they helped him fix on Cork as our destination.

There were no big arguments, but I wasn't happy. I was resentful. My attitude was, 'It's OK for him to want to go back, that's where he's from, but we're happy here.' Dad probably thought I'd snap out of it.

The next thing I remember was boxes being delivered to the house, and packing them up with our stuff.

I played a bit of soccer with the local club and they presented me with a jersey and ball before I left, but that was about it in terms of big send-offs.

If we'd stayed, the ultimate dream would have been a career in

Rugby League, maybe. But Dad was very set on the Gaelic games. He'd have been happy enough with us watching Rugby League on television, but he wouldn't have been bringing us to games.

I didn't understand everything that was going on at the time, at only ten years of age, but Dad had had the idea in his head ever since he'd met Mum: that eventually he would come back to Ireland with us. We'd have been back long before 1988, only Mum kept putting it off. She always thought it was a crazy idea to bring your family to the other side of the world, particularly as there were more Irish people going out to Australia than the other way round.

Everything she was hearing from Dad's circle of friends about the economic situation in Ireland at that time strengthened her opinion; several friends of Dad's who'd tried to make it back in Ireland had had to go back out to Australia. For Mum, if there was a move to be made from Australia, it would have been back to Rotuma. Dad was making good money working in Sydney; Mum had her sister Atfoa – and five cousins – living near us; Fiji was obviously easier to reach if you were living in Australia . . . she didn't want to leave Australia at all, but the line was drawn, and Dad was insistent.

There was a particular reason why we left late in 1987. One thing that irked Dad about living in Australia was the link to the Commonwealth, because he's very republican in his views. If we were watching the FA Cup Final, for instance, he'd always mute the television for half a minute before the kick-off, and it was only years later I realized that the purpose of this was to avoid hearing 'God Save the Queen' when it was sung before the game. The bicentenary of Captain Cook discovering Australia was to fall in 1988, and he didn't want to be around all the hullabaloo celebrating the link to Britain, so in November 1987 we headed off on our travels, starting with Rotuma, Mum's island, in Fiji.

My most vivid memory of that time was being at the airport in Sydney and saying goodbye to Mum's sister and her family. The reality dawned then: up to that point we were almost laughing and joking about it; I think on some level we thought it would never really happen.

By the time we got through security and were making our way to the gate, all of us kids were bawling.

We flew to Nadi, a six-hour flight from Sydney, and then crossed the main island of Fiji to Suva. We stayed there with Mum's sister Uraria for two weeks before catching the government boat out to Rotuma for a visit, before moving halfway across the world.

The govenment boat drops supplies at the islands governed by Fiji, and people use it too, but it's not luxurious. The focus is on getting provisions to the far-flung islands, not providing comfort for passengers – people crash together in communal areas on board. At that time the government boat only went out around the islands once every six weeks or so, and if you missed your lift back to one of the distant islands, you had a long wait for the next trip.

It was a journey of three days and three nights to Rotuma by the government boat if the seas were rough – and they're always rough. Our sea-legs weren't great, so the Ó hAilpín kids spent much of the voyage puking over the side of the ship into the Pacific.

When we got to the island, we met relatives we didn't really know, and headed on to Juju, Mum's village. Life there was – and is – pretty basic. The houses have brick walls and corrugated-iron roofs, and the toilet is outside. On the other hand, you're only ten yards from the beach. We enjoyed that immensely for the six weeks we were there – running around the island, up and down to the beach. Fantastic fun.

As the day of our departure approached, we spotted the government boat in the distance – it took a couple of hours for it to come around to the wharf on the other side of the island, and as we were getting ready it sailed right past Juju. We threw everything into my Uncle Taito's jeep and headed down to the wharf. Mum was distraught. Bawling.

I didn't appreciate it fully at the time, but from talking to her later

I came to understand that when she walked down to the wharf that day with her own mum, my grandmother, she knew she was on a one-way ticket. My grandmother was almost eighty at that time and both of them understood that this was the last goodbye. Granny had been to Sydney a few times and had found those journeys taxing enough – never mind going to the other side of the world.

Her last words to Mum were: 'If anything happens to you and John, make sure the kids get back here to Rotuma, and they'll be looked after no matter what.'

Because so few people come to Rotuma, everyone makes a big deal out of visitors, and everyone makes a big deal out of their departure. Everyone in the village goes down to the wharf when someone's heading away, whether they're related to the person or not.

Mum had told her family she was going to Ireland and that she wouldn't see them again. She'd say it herself: a piece of her died that day. I can still see her standing on the concrete of the wharf, holding her own mum's hand, the two of them crying, until the moment when she had to get on the boat before it pulled away. When Mum got on board, that was the end of Rotuma for her as she knew it.

(In 1994, Fr Maguire and Fr Johnson, the two Irish priests who were still working on Rotuma, were at home on holidays, and they drove to Cork to give Mum the news that her mother had died. I came home from school that day and found Mum upset: they had given her a long, detailed letter from her sister, my aunt Viki, about her mum's passing.)

From Rotuma we went back to Suva, back to Nadi, and then we got a flight to Vancouver, where my mother's brother Tifare was living.

In Vancouver, for the first time we encountered snow, and cold – unbelievable cold. It was a shock. I'd wear four or five layers of clothes, with a jacket on top.

Tifare lived down by Stanley Park, a tourist area, and we moved in with him for three weeks. He was great. One of my strongest memories of Vancouver is his boss's car, a flashy Japanese job with a built-in voice message to remind you to fasten your seatbelt.

I know Tifare tried to talk Mum out of the move to Cork, but they weren't going to turn around at that stage. We flew on to Amsterdam, and from there to Dublin.

I remember staying in a bed and breakfast around Parnell Square, somewhere near the Wax Museum. Dad needed to collect stuff he'd sent on ahead to a friend of his.

Then we were on a train to Cork.

My first impression of Cork? I didn't want to be there.

We got off the train at Kent Station on a wet, overcast February afternoon. I can clearly remember standing on the footpath, looking at Dad in a phone-box, going through the ads in that day's *Cork Examiner*, trying to find somewhere we could stay that night.

No pre-booking on the Internet then. No Skyping with a pal to sort out accommodation before getting on the flight in Sydney. We watched as he started making phone calls – me, aged ten, my brother Teu, nine, and sister Sarote, seven, with Setanta and Aisake, four and two, standing close to Mum, who was expecting my youngest sister, Étaoin. In those days everyone headed for town on Saturday to do their shopping, rather than going to out-of-town shopping centres, and I remember throngs of people stepping around the little crowd of strangers waiting by the phone-box.

After a while Dad got off the phone and we all piled into a cab. I remember heading out around Carrigaline to see a house, but Mum said it wouldn't suit us. On with the search and back to the city. More phone calls.

It was getting dark when Dad finally got a lead on a place: a guy was gone to America for a while and his house, up in the northside of the city, would be vacant. We arrived at 44 Park Drive, in the Parklands estate off the Commons Road, around teatime. Mum and Dad went looking for the nearest shop for something to feed us, and fuel for the fire, while we explored our new house, a three-bed semi-detached.

You might think that that experience, that uncertainty, would be traumatic for kids, but not us. Not at that point.

By the time we landed up in Parklands, we'd already been travelling for nearly three months.

44 Park Drive was our home for a few months. That first night I wouldn't say I was frightened, just anxious to get into a routine, to settle down after months of travelling. Deep down I expected that we'd be going back to Sydney sooner or later. That this was an adventure I'd be telling pals in Australia about in years to come, the time we travelled around the world.

I never expected that I'd still be in Cork twenty-five years on. Not for a second.

2.

Nowadays when I leave Na Piarsaigh after a game or a training session, I often see the small kids milling around the clubhouse or the pitch, nine- and ten-year-olds heading out to play a game themselves or just pucking around at one of the goals, billowing the net with the odd shot.

I see them having fun, enjoying themselves, and I hope they always get the same kick out of the game. When I was their age, I didn't.

There were obvious enough reasons for this, some of the time. I was identifiably different, certainly different enough to be singled out by the ignorant. I am glad to see non-white faces among the kids in Na Piarsaigh jerseys now, and Asian and eastern European names on the team sheets. I certainly hope they don't have to listen to the sort of things I had to as a child on the playing fields of Cork.

But there were other reasons why I didn't enjoy playing as much as I should have as a child. Reasons which were far less obvious.

When we landed in Parklands, a collection of big housing estates that overlook the road to Limerick, word went around pretty fast that a new family had arrived, and that they were different. The fact that I was carrying a pretty strong Australian accent at the time probably made me even more unusual.

At that age you just want to fit in. There are green areas in front of the houses in Parklands and I could see boys out playing soccer on them every day, and I was mad to join in.

And in fairness, they were grand. I fell in after a couple of weeks. I don't recall any racism; I don't remember being told to fuck off or anything – it was 'Yeah, come on so, you play with that team' and we were off and away.

I got pally in particular with Gary Sheehan, who's now the senior football coach in Na Piarsaigh, and Barry Sheehan (no relation), who lives in Philadelphia these days.

They asked me if I wanted to join the local GAA club, Na Piarsaigh, which they played for, and my first visit to the place which would become so important for me – the first time I walked in through the gates – was when Dad brought me up to see if I could join.

Abie Allen was the man who looked after the team the Sheehans played for. He ran the underage section of the club, like a thousand fellas in a thousand clubs all over the country. When Dad asked if I could join, he said there was no problem, and when he asked if I had football boots Dad said he'd get me a pair.

Abie said to hang on. At that time, Tom and Mary Walsh lived upstairs in the club; they'd been involved since the foundation of Na Piarsaigh, back in the 1940s. Abie went up the stairs to Tom, got a pair of boots from him, came back down and threw them to me. They were two sizes too big for me, but I didn't care. I got them on me and I was ready for action.

School was a bit trickier. The Sheehans, who were like a two-man integration committee, brought me up to Scoil Íosagán, the primary school at the top of Farranree, for a day; but in the end I went to another school – the North Monastery, maybe half a mile further away.

Because it was February and halfway through a school year, they decided to put me in fifth class for the remaining months of the term so I could get acclimatized with the school and curriculum. I could start fifth from scratch the following September.

When I was put into the class the first day, the teacher asked me where I was from. I said we'd come from Australia. One of the kids jumped up and ran over to a map of Europe hanging on the wall: 'That's where you're from, look, there!'

Austria.

That's when it dawned on me: tough days ahead.

It was uncomfortable enough. A different environment. That's no fault of the teachers and kids in the Mon, but Cork was so different from where I'd been.

Take the climate. Torture. Ireland in February compared to Sydney? When I started to play hurling and football, the experience of mud and rain on a field in March was more than a shock to me. I'd be running around the boggy field thinking, 'I don't belong here.'

Food? Growing up in Sydney, I'd never seen a stew – but that became a staple in Cork soon enough. Mum can recall finding fruit very expensive in Cork compared to Australia, and the selection was very narrow. Apples and oranges, fine, but no papaya, mango, passion fruit, watermelon or rock melon, which we were used to back in Sydney. Mum and Dad were basically living off their savings until he got established with a job, and so my beloved ice creams were a thing of the past.

Hand-me-downs were the norm and nothing was thrown out, as one of the smaller ones might use it. Nowadays we all look at photographs from the early years in Cork and slag each other off about our fashion choices, but the truth was there wasn't much choice involved. Luxuries were off the table: that's just the way it was.

There were other little differences. I spent those first few weeks wrapped up in clothes – we all did. The walk to school was about a mile, compared to a few hundred metres up the hill back in Greenacre.

We had no car (though we wouldn't have been the only family in the estate, or in Cork, in the eighties in that situation), and we walked everywhere. To town. To Na Piarsaigh. To school.

After a year and a half living in the north side we moved out to Blarney – or at least in the general direction of Blarney. We lived three miles from the village and there was no bus line passing the house. Dad eventually got a car, but if he wasn't around we went on foot. For training and matches that wasn't an issue, because if you had a hurley or gearbag, someone would be bound to stop for you.

I remember being out in the schoolyard in my first days at the Mon and kids just coming over to look at me as though I'd landed from Mars.

What helped me, though, was that I seemed to be physically bigger than most of the kids my own age. That probably prevented fights.

Because of the disruption, the upheaval, I withdrew into myself. I was already a shy enough kid, and the new environment didn't encourage me to open up. I went along with the kids in the class: if someone cracked a joke and I didn't get it, which was most of the time, I just laughed along.

Educationally I was way behind. The Irish system I landed into was far ahead of the Australian school in terms of what was being done in maths, for instance. The homework load came as a bit of a rude awakening, too; what we got in Australia was nothing in comparison to the work you had to do in Ireland.

In Sydney it was home, dash off a few quick exercises the teacher had given you, and out into the fresh air to play; in Cork, by the time you had the homework finally done, particularly in winter, it was pitch dark.

Then there was the new language. I was sent down to Denis Burns, the remedial teacher, to try to get me up to speed with the *Gaeilge*, and it was basic stuff.

Picture of an egg: *ubh*.

Picture of a bottle of milk: *bainne*.

The other kids were writing sentences in Irish and studying grammar and so on, while I was doing kindergarten-level stuff, but Denis was very good, very understanding – and an All-Ireland winner with the Cork hurlers, too. Getting to grips with Irish was hard going for me in the early years. Teu and Sarote, being younger, had an easier introduction to the language. They were enrolled in the Modh Scoil, the all-Irish school across from the fire station in Cork, but I was too old for that.

Sport was the way to integrate. Because I'd played back in Sydney at the GAA centre, at least I knew how to play Gaelic football. And I only played Gaelic football when I first came to Cork – no hurling. The game was alien to me, and as a kid the last thing you want is to make a fool of yourself in front of the others.

The problem was the way games were organized and scheduled: there'd be a series of football games for maybe three weeks, and then there'd be a series of hurling games for three weeks. If I wasn't playing hurling I was left on my own, and if a kid doesn't want to make a fool of himself, he certainly doesn't want to be left alone. I had a choice: either take up hurling or be left out entirely.

Abie's persistence helped hugely. He said he'd help if I wanted to give it a go, and I needed a lot of help. Basically, I started off playing hurling with a Rugby League outlook: tackle everything that moves. With a stick in my hand, it was not a pretty sight. One of the lads who played with me then, John Twomey, still reminds me of the time I nearly decapitated him. He wouldn't have been the only one.

Abie gave me my game, though. He kept picking me. He put me in to full-forward, which was difficult; you had your back to the goal and had to turn with the ball to attack, whereas in Rugby League it was a matter of going forward more or less all the time.

In Gaelic football, by contrast, I was a wing-back, which was grand because I was facing the ball and coming on to it, going forward nearly all the time. Not that there weren't issues with the big ball. Soloing was a bit of a novelty for me, so I was routinely blown for overcarrying as I charged up the field. The fact that I brought over a tasty hand-off from Rugby League didn't help either: it's one thing in Gaelic football to push someone away, but a straight-arm hand-off into someone's face is inclined to make the referee reach for the whistle.

*

Treats came after games. If you did well in a match Dad might slip you a Kit-Kat, which was a fair incentive to impress. He had a bicycle and used to bring me down on the crossbar of his bike to Páirc Uí Chaoimh to watch National League games.

At that time the leagues resumed after a Christmas break and I remember hearing on the radio about a Dublin guy called Barney Rock playing football against Cork. Then I remember the name 'English' being mentioned when Tipperary played Cork, and I couldn't make head or tail of that. In our house the Union Jack, England, Britain, all of that was a no-no, so as a kid I couldn't get it straight in my head how English could be the name of a guy playing GAA. I remember thinking, small as I was, 'Dad probably doesn't like that guy.'

Rock? English? What kind of Irish names were they?

Myself, Teu and Dad were in Páirc Uí Chaoimh for the Munster football final in 1988, at the City End, near the covered stand. It was absolutely packed. There was my old pal Pat Spillane, from the International Rules visit a couple of years before, and here was I, shouting for my new team, Cork. Maurice Fitzgerald announced himself at senior intercounty level for Kerry, scoring a goal and eight points, but Cork won. They had a great team.

The Bulldogs were gone. Hawthorn – gone. Cork were the team now. The footballers made it to the All-Ireland final that year, and the hype drew you in.

Even then I was the kind of person who would put everything into trying to master a challenge. But hurling was desperately hard to get to grips with.

Lifting the ball I was able to manage, but I struggled hugely with striking the ball. To be honest, I wasn't fully confident in my striking until halfway through my senior career.

Abie and Paddy Moore didn't give up on me. They gave me extra training sessions and didn't call a halt even when the basics were a problem. Their first job was to stop me using a cricket-style grip,

where you hold the bat square on with your knuckles facing out; I'd
have the sliotar and throw it up to strike, and my hands would be
swinging the hurley as though I was trying to hit a six at the Melbourne Cricket Ground.

In front of them I'd try to use an orthodox hurling grip, but when
they weren't looking I'd revert to the cricket grip, and I'd hear Paddy
Moore roaring across the field: 'Seán Óg! What did I tell you!'

It was all for my benefit, though, and the pair of them went above
and beyond the call of duty. Seeing as I was just down the road from
the club, they said, why didn't I come up the odd Friday night and
they'd help me work on my skills? There were no ball alleys in the
area at the time, so that was a good option.

The two lads would drive balls down at me for an hour, two hours,
easy, and eventually they'd say 'Last ball' and I'd be saying 'No, no,
one more'. This would be ten, half ten at night in the summer, and
the lads would want to lock up and head home, and here was this kid
shouting 'One more, one more', trying to keep them there. To keep
improving.

The games themselves were an eye-opener. You were marking lads
who'd had a hurley in their hands since they were five or six, who
were alive to all the nuances. They knew when to go, when to stick;
when to contest a breaking ball, when to stay out. It was all instinct-
ive with them, not learned behaviour, as it was with me.

Was there a particular low point as I learned the games? There were a
lot of them: games in which I felt completely out of my depth.
Cleaned out totally by an opponent.

I was split a few times, though I wore a helmet; I have a mark on
my cheek which was the result of having mis-timed a hook, but I
didn't suffer anything serious. I wasn't nervous of getting hurt. The
original piece of hurling advice, that you can't get hurt if you get
stuck in close to the action, had struck me as daft until I saw how true
it was.

Abie would have been fully entitled to take me off in plenty of games, but he stuck with me. When he moved me from forward to half-back, it got better because I had some understanding of how to play facing the ball. I didn't have the skills to play up front – to win the ball, take someone on and finish. In defence I could win the ball, come upfield and either handpass it off or kick it upfield.

There were other issues: blocking and hooking are hard skills to pick up from scratch, and they're necessary if you're not going to get hurt, but I was miles behind the other lads and what they could do, even at twelve and thirteen. All I was contributing for a long time was charging into opponents and bowling them over.

But I was improving. Bit by bit. Inch by inch. It was taking a lot of work, but I could see the benefits, small as they were. I understood that that work had to continue if I was to make those small gains: I couldn't give hurling a good week now and leave it for a month, expecting to maintain that standard. I'd have to keep at it if I wanted to maintain that improvement.

And I did. Eventually I became fanatical about hurling. But at that age, if I'd had a choice, I'd have left it.

In 1989 we won a trophy, an under-thirteen C-grade championship. That was encouraging, and the following year there was another boost: Cork won the double and the cups came up to the school, the Liam MacCarthy and the Sam Maguire.

That brought it home: this is the goal. This is what you're aiming for.

Finding my age group initially presented an unexpected speed bump.

The two Sheehans, Barry and Gary, were a year older than me. Because I knew the two of them I was keen to play on their team, so I let on I was a year older than I actually was in order to play on with my two buddies instead of having to make friends with kids I didn't know.

Abie found me out eventually, though. He needed a birth certificate for something – probably to register me as a player – so he called down to the house to get one from Mum.

When he looked at it he said, 'This must be wrong, sure Seán Óg is twelve.'

'He's not,' said Mum. 'He's eleven.'

'Nah, he's twelve,' said Abie, before he realized my mother was hardly going to get my age wrong.

That meant I dropped down age-wise, but before I did I'd had a year or two playing against older, stronger players: the likes of Tadhgie Murphy, Mick Ahern and Mick Corbett from the Glen, who were very strong at that age. The Barrs had stars like Brian Hurley, Kevin Kelleher, Greg O'Halloran, Martin Desmond and Ian Keeler, while the Rockies had John Brown, Johnny Flynn and Eddie Gosell. Some of those lads wouldn't have gone on to long senior careers either with their clubs or Cork, but at underage they created a competitive environment which drove me and a lot of others on.

I got some recognition early on. I captained a Cork primary schools Gaelic football side when I was in fifth class, alongside Jimmy Barry-Murphy's son Brian, who went on to have a long career as a soccer pro in England.

I saw a photograph recently, taken before we played a Dublin schools side in Páirc Uí Chaoimh: myself, the Dublin captain and the referee, one Frank Murphy. Little did I know what the future held for Frank and me.

We had a very, very good team at my age group in Na Piarsaigh. Damien O'Sullivan, Brian Kidney, Dónal Murphy, David Forde, Gearóid Fitzgerald and Liam Hutchinson were outstanding underage players on that team. We'd clash with the likes of Douglas, Blackrock, Glen Rovers, St Finbarrs and Bishopstown, strong clubs all in Cork city. Outside the city, teams like Midleton and Ballincollig were very strong in our age group, but we were the best. Midleton had this tiny kid called Mickey O'Connell, so small the jersey was like a dress on him, hanging down past his shorts, but he was a magical hurler.

We had super battles against Midleton, collecting county titles against them in U-12 and in minor; they beat us in the U-16 decider.

Most of the underage club finals were played in Ballinlough, in Cork city. Ballinlough wouldn't be mistaken for the Camp Nou, but it was an adventure for us to file on to the bus for the trip to the southside. There was a scoreboard – a scoreboard! – and your studs made a distinctive clattering noise on the tarmac walkway coming down on to the field. If you win a game there, or a trophy, as you come off the field you walk up the same walkway, with the supporters high above you on the bank applauding you as you go back to the dressing-room.

The timber in those dressing-rooms might have been splintering, but it was a great hunting ground for us. Special. People say it's too tight as a pitch and the facilities need to be improved, but I'm very fond of it.

At the North Mon primary school, Denis Burns and Mr O'Leary played a blinder. They progressed me beyond the *ubh* and the *bainne* to the point where I managed to get into the Gaelscoil part of the North Mon secondary school, the AG. It's a separate school within the North Mon, though in my time you played on the all-school teams in sport and you had access to all the facilities of the main school, too. From the moment you walked into the school you were talking in Irish all day long, picking up words that you'd never come across otherwise. Total immersion.

That brought my Irish on a ton. Going into first year, my comprehension of Irish was fine but my confidence in speaking wasn't that high. That all changed after five years of total immersion. It was an environment where you heard Irish from 9 a.m. to 4 p.m. You had to improve.

I was a C student, frankly. Hard work got me through school, the way it improved my hurling and refined my Irish. We lived in a strict house. You were only allowed some slack through being involved in sport. Mum and Dad put a big emphasis on education, and we didn't watch much TV. After the news, if there was a documentary you might be allowed to watch it, but movies were a rare treat.

Dad was a labourer all his life, and one thing he said to me which stayed with me was, 'Look, you don't want to be in your fifties on the building sites.' He wasn't emphasizing the importance of third-level education as much as stressing that we should at least try to get through second-level education. It was a message that stuck with all of us.

With hurling the lessons stuck too, though in reality I was at least fourteen before I was in any way comfortable playing the game. I was captain of the Féile team and centre-back, and we went to the All-Ireland series, but I missed out on that with a broken index finger.

Which killed me. Fourteen years old and missing out on an All-Ireland final. No idea if you'd ever see another one.

Later in that year, 1991, there were trials for the Cork Under-14 team and I made it. That was the first time I met the likes of Dónal Óg Cusack, Joe Deane, Derek Barrett, and Austin Walsh – lads I'd go on to play with at minor and senior level.

Looking back, I was still a work in progress. Nicky Barry, a teacher from the North Mon, was over that team and he picked me – maybe the Mon bias was a factor – but it gave me a lift. If I was on the Cork team for my age group I had to be improving.

A good pal of mine, John Anderson from the Glen, was trialling on that U-14 team too. He was my first friend, really, in Cork, and the reason is simple. He beat me in a run we used to do in PE class in primary school: up to the Brothers' house, down the other side, back up the lodge to where we'd started.

It was a kilometre or two, easy, and no one beat me in that run, for the simple reason that I had an incentive: the winner got a Cool Crocker strawberry milkshake as a prize, and every time as we set off for the run I could almost taste it as I went around. I won it most of the time, but Anderson could beat me, and sometimes I had to go without the strawberry milkshake.

That sense of competition drove us on, but we were good mates as well. John and his mum, Betty, were very good to me as a kid. They didn't have to be, and I don't know if they just had a particular understanding, for some reason, of how we felt so far from home, but they were first class.

John and I are good mates to this day. We played together on primary, secondary and Cork teams, though he'd take your head off in a club game: the Glen and Piarsaigh would be Montague and Capulet in terms of Cork's northside. He'd drop up to Na Piarsaigh for a chat and fellas would be looking at him, and vice versa when I went to see him in the Glen.

Apart from the huge work Abie and Paddy put in, there were other aspects to my improvement as a hurler which people mightn't be aware of.

Teu was a massive help. He was learning to play the game at the same time as me, which meant I always had someone to practise with, someone who was almost my own age, at my own level.

If I'd been on my own – or if I'd been pucking around with someone who was far more skilled than me – then it would have been that much harder to improve. Teu helped me to improve and I helped him.

I think my competitive drive, the sense that I wouldn't let this game get the better of me, had something to do with my Australian background.

I'd brought that with me from school in Sydney – and it was true with the other members of the family as well. There's great love and respect among us all, but give us a game and we're competitive with each other. None of us likes to lose.

Abie had another trump card which drove me to excel at hurling: Tony O'Sullivan.

When I finally got Australia out of my head and realized we were going to be staying in Ireland, Tony became my sporting hero. Dermot Brereton and Robert DiPierdomenico of the AFL and Stevie Mortimer of the Bulldogs were gone: Tony was the man.

He was a legend in the Mon, one of the greatest players to ever wear the blue and white hoops. Long before I'd heard of him, he played in a senior All-Ireland final in 1982, when he was just out of minor.

Abie had coached Tony underage and had a good relationship with him. He said to me one evening, 'Look, Tony might be able to come up some evening and show you a few bits and pieces.'

And he did: that Friday evening Tony parked up and joined me and Abie out on the field. He gave me some advice – 'Shorten your grip when you're under pressure,' a few basic pointers like that – but it was mainly the fact that he was there that made such an impression.

It was a good move by Abie – he might have noticed that I was getting disillusioned with my lack of progress with hurling. That visit was a huge boost.

They say if you want to be a champion then imitate a champion, and Tony would have been my champion growing up. And you got a lump in your throat when he did well with Cork; you were up in the crowd and you'd want to say to the people around you, 'Hey, we know him, he's from our club.' What every GAA member dreams of.

Tony's Dad, Dinny, made hurleys, so that was another part of it: Abie would bring you up to Dinny's shed for a hurley, in there with the sawdust and the smell of varnish, and the photograph of Tony up on the wall in action for Cork . . . you were part of the whole thing. You were getting your hurleys from the man who made them for an All-Ireland medal-winner. You were part of that.

One evening Tony gave me something for myself to take home: a pair of his Cork shorts and socks. Even for a tall kid like myself they were far too big, but I wore them until they fell to pieces.

Tony's generosity was something I tried to bring into my own intercounty career later on. I often gave gear to kids myself when I played for Cork, because I remembered how much Tony's generosity had meant to me up in Na Piarsaigh all those years ago.

If you want to be a champion, imitate a champion.

Dad was the other major factor. Even if there had been a Rugby League team somewhere in Cork, I doubt he'd have let me play. The idea of falling in with a Rugby Union team would have just been 'notions'. It was Gaelic games for us. End of.

The one thing we all struggled to cope with was Dad's assessment of our performances. After a game he'd say, 'If you don't wake up soon I'll drag you off myself. You were useless here. You were a disgrace there. Why do I bother going to your matches? After all I've done and you serve me this.'

What made that kind of criticism hard to take was the fact that the game itself wasn't a labour of love for me. If it had been, that criticism might have been easier to accept but, certainly in the early years, the bad days outnumbered the good, and you knew that afterwards you were facing into his assessment of your performance.

Much as I wanted to say, 'You know what, I don't want to play this sport,' you couldn't say that to Dad. He was trying to live his sporting dreams through us. That's why he took it so badly when we didn't play well – it was like an indictment of him.

Deep down, I was playing hurling and football only to please him. He was pushing me – and the others – to the limit. He set high standards, and if you didn't measure up to them he'd tell you.

It was old school. In the car on the way home from a game, if he was silent you knew he wasn't happy with how you'd played. At home he'd say, 'How did you think it went?' and you'd say, 'I didn't do great' just to cover yourself.

If he was all chat afterwards you'd know you'd done well. I don't know if the others on the team got the same treatment from their fathers; maybe they did, but it seemed to me that his attitude was different from other parents'. More severe. More critical.

Years afterwards I read Andre Agassi's autobiography. He wrote about not liking tennis because of how hard his father drove him to excel at the game. I knew what he was talking about.

The games weren't for *us* at all, they were for *him*. It's that simple. A lot of people don't know that part of the equation. Dad is a quiet man most of the time, but he was very different when it came to assessing your game. He could be cruel when he did so, but that was what we were used to.

There were lads I played with, and you wouldn't see either of their parents on the sideline at a game from one end of the year to the next. I'd have to say this for Dad: he was always there. Every game we played, he was there.

And after every game he was there. And in the car you'd have that question, 'How do you think it went?'

3

No sooner were we in Ireland than Dad said, 'There are going to be people here who don't like the look of ye, so expect some remarks.'

That was our preparation for getting integrated into what was one of the whitest societies in Europe.

I don't recall there being anything racial in Australia. That's not to say there's no racism there, but the neighbourhood we grew up in was a melting pot of various ethnic groups. I'd never experienced racial abuse in Sydney.

When Dad said that, it surprised me. It's hard enough to settle into a new place anyway, and it doesn't help when you're wondering if you'll be hearing racial abuse. We didn't have to wonder for too long.

I'm talking about twenty-five years ago, so it wasn't yesterday or the day before; but in fairness I don't remember anything bad from the neighbours in Parklands. They were grand: for instance, Jim McAllister and Maureen O'Brien were the first people to invite us into their house, very nice people, and we have a great relationship to this day.

And most people were like that in the neighbourhood, we knew them and they knew us. There wasn't a problem.

It was only when we got into Cork city that there was anything said.

Early on we didn't have a car so we'd stroll in to town with Mum, a couple of miles, to help her with the shopping. We might be at the stop for the No. 3 bus in front of Eason's in Patrick Street and we'd hear it.

'Black fucking cunt.'

'Nigger.'

'Go home and wash yourself.'

We were raw, new to the country. We kept our heads down and

didn't engage. Mum and Dad would have told us not to get involved, and we didn't.

I didn't go into town on my own that often, and that certainly wasn't an incentive to head in there.

Sarote, Setanta and Aisake, who took the bus into the Modh Scoil in the middle of town, got abuse from the same kids over and over, and it got physical the odd time. Eventually it got so bad that they took a stand and confronted the kids who were abusing them, and that put a stop to it.

It was usually kids our own age, rather than grown-ups, who were dishing it out. It was ignorance, pure and simple. Cork was an over-whelmingly white society at that time; the only dark-skinned people you'd see might be African doctors in the hospital.

I didn't feel disappointed or hurt when I heard it. I felt like I didn't belong anyway and I wanted to get out of the place – away from the bus stop, away from the bus, away from Ireland full stop. I'd think, 'I wish I was back in Sydney,' and I'd look at Dad and blame him for it. I'd think, 'You put us here.'

We'd never say anything to Dad. Sometimes we'd tell Mum, but not every time. We just got on with it.

What could we have done, anyway? Complain to the gardaí? I'm sure they would have added that to their list of things to do: 'I must head off to wag the finger at a ten-year-old calling someone names.'

We went along with it. We didn't want confrontation.

You had to use your head. If, for example, there were three or four fellas taunting you, then you knew well what was going to happen if you got physical. You got yourself out of the situation as fast as you could.

I don't remember ever getting into a fight, because I never replied to the abuse. I knew well that there were fellas waiting to say, 'What did you say there?' and happy to carry on from there with a fight. You're talking about bored teenagers, young fellas that would take the chance to throw a few digs into you and feel that as a result it was a good trip to town.

I put the head down and pretended they weren't talking to me. They'd walk on, laughing, and that would be it.

I'm delighted that there are now anti-racism programmes in Ireland, but at times it can be uncomfortable for me to be involved with them. The first thing these programmes always advocate is reporting incidents of racial abuse, and that's something we never did. That goes against the message these groups emphasize all the time, and, while I'm happy to row in with them, because obviously there are a lot more kids now in the situation that we were in all those years ago, there's an obvious contradiction between what I'm encouraging people to do and what we did ourselves back then.

I hope the country's moved on and that kids today don't have it as bad as we did, but I've never been asked if I reported those incidents. We didn't.

We weren't prepared for Ireland and Ireland wasn't prepared for us. The racism is still around, too. If everyone in the country was happy with the different races here, there wouldn't be a need for these anti-racism campaigns, obviously. I'm lucky that I had sport, and that eventually I had a high profile through it, because people knew who you were and would – possibly – be slower to abuse you.

Though it wasn't always easy on the playing field, either.

It didn't happen every time I played a game. Not as often as it happened on the street in Cork when I was eleven or twelve.

Obviously, though, when you have aggressive kids playing a contact sport, clashing with each other in a physical game, then the easiest thing for some of them is to throw out 'go 'way, you black cunt' if there is a confrontation, however brief.

Reflecting on it later, I was convinced it was just something they heard at home. That they didn't know what they were saying and were just lashing out. Thinking about it at the time, though, I saw it as a sure sign they were cooked. They had no answers to my on-field dominance and their last resort was to attack me verbally. I drew strength from this and used the abuse to my advantage.

Obviously that's not how you should deal with it – accepting racial abuse as evidence you're doing well in a sporting situation isn't a workable solution – but it was the best I could do for myself at twelve, thirteen, fourteen years of age.

I was on my own, after all. A referee might be on the other side of the field when it occurred; what was he going to do, run back over and take some fella's name?

Even now, high-profile intercounty players like Lee Chin in Wexford are finding that racism still exists on Ireland's sports fields, and a lot of the action is retrospective. If a referee's attention is called to racial abuse in a game, he'd probably be wondering what action to take – black card, booking, what?

Now go back twenty-five years to the Ireland of the late eighties and ask what a referee would do. Or what an eleven-year-old child was supposed to do when another kid called him a nigger in the middle of a game.

Then there was the way I played. Once I settled into the backline with Na Piarsaigh, I was told to mark tight, not allow daylight between us, and I did that; I was athletic, I was quick enough and I was hard to get away from. And if a player couldn't get any freedom they'd get frustrated, and sometimes they lashed out verbally.

I kept the head down on the street when it happened, but I responded verbally in games now and again: 'Look at you, you fucking white ass,' or something along those lines. I'm not proud of that either, but it was either sink or swim and sometimes it was a matter of standing up for yourself. It was like boxing, where you're told to protect yourself at all times. I'd have responded only when it was particularly bad.

A lot of the lads I played with stuck up for me. There were plenty of occasions when I'd get abused and one of the Na Piarsaigh players chipped in with, 'What the fuck did you call him?' and they'd get stuck into the guy on the other team.

It's natural for sportspeople to be aggressive. I understand that people reach for the most obvious stick to beat an opponent with. It's unfortunate that there was racism on the field of play but, as I say, there was less of it than was on offer on the street.

I certainly wouldn't have heard anything from opposition coaches and managers. You might think that not being abused by adults on the sideline would be little consolation, but in the context of the times it was something to be grateful for.

4

I hate to disappoint those people who see us as the two revolutionaries trying to bring down the entire structure of the GAA in Cork, or the entire structure of the GAA, but Dónal Óg Cusack and I didn't start off wanting to storm the barricades.

He first came across my radar when we both made the Cork Tony Forrestal team. The Tony Forrestal tournament is held every summer for U-14 county teams in Waterford during the last week of August, so you train as a county side once or twice a week for the couple of months before it. It's the big time for a fourteen-year-old.

The first thing I noticed about Cusack was his runners, to be honest – he had LA Gear basketball boots, spanking new, top of the line, with fins on the side. 'This guy must be loaded,' I thought.

We didn't have deep conversations or anything, just in case anybody thinks we were unhappy about the standards of preparation. He was the keeper, a quiet chap I didn't really know. We didn't have a great run in the tournament anyway: a narrow defeat by Tipperary and we were gone by the group stages.

I met guys from around the county on that team, top players, and it was a wake-up call. Until then I'd have come up against the city teams, but some of these guys were extraordinary. They made me think, 'Hang on, I thought I was getting good.'

The watershed game for me as a young hurler came at the tail-end of my underage career.

It was February 1994. I was seventeen and playing Harty Cup, the Munster senior colleges competition, for the North Mon, and we had a challenge game against St Kieran's College, Kilkenny. St Kieran's was then, and always has been, a breeding ground for Kilkenny minors, and their senior colleges team is always sprinkled with a few stars of the future. That team had a few Kilkenny minors from the year before. I played on one of them and I did extremely well.

I'd always been able to mark tight and spoil an opponent, but I contributed more that day. I won puck-outs, I carried the ball, I delivered it to the forwards. By that stage I'd come to understand that being a stopper was all well and good, but I had to offer something more than that in order to progress. That day proved to me that I might be able to do more.

On the way back home on the bus, the two teachers, Gerry Kelly and Nicky Barry, were delighted with me. I was delighted myself. I knew I'd had a good game and it made me think big: I was going to be eighteen, the full age for minor, the following year, and I thought I'd have a shot at the Cork minor team in 1995. But that day made me think that the minor team in 1994 mightn't be out of reach.

There was a lot to consider on the journey home from James Stephens' GAA pitch that day in February. I'd turned a corner in my career, and I knew it.

Playing for the school was a great advantage in that regard. The club was the foundation stone, but playing for the Mon added finesse and broadened the horizons. I ended up playing against teams in Clare and Tipperary, different styles of play, different opponents.

Different stars, too. In my time Johnny Enright of Thurles CBS was the stand-out player in Tipperary. Rory Gantley of Galway was boarding in St Flannan's and was playing Harty when he was fifteen. Timmy McCarthy was the main man for St Colman's and I always dreaded marking him. Joe Deane was the star in Midleton CBS, a talented side backboned by most of the Cork U-14 side I'd played on, and now they were that bit older. Midleton had our number at U-15½ level. They beat us in the Munster final up in Fermoy, and were far better than us on the day. We put that defeat in the memory bank for another day.

Playing Harty improved your standards all round. Commitment, fitness, discipline: everything had to be better. We trained before school, lunchtime – and then after school. You got to know what sacrifice was; you went in over Christmas for training when everyone else was on holidays, though the alternative for me – heading up to Fermanagh – meant it was less of a Calvary than it was for the others. Christmas was spent in Fermanagh, at Dad's place. A long, long car journey to the middle of nowhere was how we saw it, and spending the school break training was, to me, far preferable.

Training involved going up the bank – a steep hill at one side of the field – over and over until you were crawling up the last few yards on the last ascent. After that you barely had the energy to stand under the shower.

It gave us a certain status. 'He's on the Harty team,' you'd hear the small kids say in the corridor; teachers were aware of it too and they tailored their disciplinary approach accordingly.

The tradition was all around us. The corridors of the school were lined with photographs of Harty Cup teams, young men with their arms folded in front of the old science room in the AG. Jack Lynch. Connie Buckley. Con Murphy. Dónal O'Grady. Teddy McCarthy. Tomas Mulcahy. Tony O'Sullivan.

The games were played on Wednesdays until it got to the semi-finals and final, which were played on Sunday, and we drew good crowds up on the banks in places like Fermoy, Buttevant and Charleville. Cork players, past and present, came down after the game to the dressing-room to say hello and to encourage you.

We had to learn to deal with new challenges: expectations, recognition, media attention. It was a first taste of what was to come if you make it to the intercounty level. But it was also distinct and self-contained, important in itself.

Think of *Friday Night Lights* with a Cork accent.

*

It stood to me, and to all of us. I look back with huge pride on my schooldays and I enjoyed the training. Gerry Kelly, Nicky Barry and Dónal O'Grady (who wasn't teaching in the school any more but came back to help with match days) brought sophistication to it, but we also worked on the basics. Hooking, blocking, striking.

I played Harty first when I was fifteen, against Limerick CBS up in Buttevant. They were good – they won it that year – and I felt way out of my depth, both physically and in hurling terms. Fifteen is young at that level – I was big enough in my age grade but against eighteen-year-olds it felt like I was up against grown men. I was barely shaving and some of them had moustaches. Intimidating stuff.

By 1994 I was bigger and stronger, and we had a decent team who scrapped our way to a Harty final in Fermoy.

It was played on your typical February day: wet, windy, miserable. We were huge underdogs against that Midleton CBS side who'd beaten us in other age grades; they'd blazed their way through their side of the competition, while we'd battled our way through our games.

There was a bit of an edge to it, too. Midleton had accused us of poaching players, for instance, which didn't improve relations between the schools. They were well fancied; when we beat Thurles CBS in Mitchelstown in the semi-final it was viewed as our final. Making the final was seen as a bonus for us, a day out to reward us for our efforts during the season.

But we had strong men in the dressing-room. Gerry Kelly and Nicky Barry brought in the likes of Dónal O'Grady, as well as Murt Murphy, who'd trained teams to Harty success in the eighties. The four of them didn't leave you in any doubt about what was at stake.

The tradition was stressed. The Mon was a school that went out and won and didn't give a damn about the odds. We weren't going to lie down to anyone, Midleton least of all. 'We mightn't have the money, but we have the heart, and not all the money in the world can buy heart' – that was the line you heard, going out the door of the dressing-room.

I was wing-back, marking Mickey O'Connell. Early in the game we went for a ball and he threw the shoulder and cut me across the lip. I knew him from Cork U-14s, but when that happened I thought, 'Fuck that!' and I drove on. No pals today, kid.

We had a strong breeze behind us in the first half and built up a good lead, but they came back at us and it was level at the break. Then, coming off the field at half-time there was an incident. One of their fellas hit Liam O'Keeffe.

There wasn't much made of it outside the dressing-room, but behind the door Murt Murphy went crazy: 'Are you going to let them do that? Are you going to let people walk all over ye?'

Classic motivational stuff, but we ate it up, and went out for the second half, mad for road. The crucial score of the second half came when John Anderson pulled on a loose ball and buried a goal past Dónal Óg Cusack. It was one of those days when a goal against the wind felt as though it was worth more than three points.

Their forward line – including Joe Deane, Mickey and Pat Mullaney, who went on to play minor for Cork – was pretty good, but we held them. Sean O'Farrell – another man who would play senior for Cork – came on as a sub and had a chance to win the game. One on one, odds-on to score – but Brian Hurley, our keeper, made an unbelievable save to win the game for us.

That summed up our year – we had a dedicated bunch and worked hard, and we got the rewards. Some of the lads never went on to play adult hurling for their clubs afterwards, in marked contrast to the Midleton side, many of whom played senior for Cork, not to mind their own clubs. The conditions were bad, which suited us, but our spirit was the difference.

At the final whistle people poured on to the field – classmates, family, former pupils. I'd been named man of the match – luckily – Jerry Buttimer, now a TD, who was doing GAA reports for local radio at the time, came into the dressing-room with a mike and interviewed me in the toilets. I didn't set the world on fire with my insights – 'Delighted to win' was about the sum total of my on-air contribution.

I remember Cliona Foley, another journalist, asking me about my background as well. I didn't think then those were the first of what would be a good few sessions facing a microphone or tape-recorder.

We went back to the school with the cup, and there were more people there waiting for us. On to Morrison's Hotel for food, and from there to The Keg, a nightclub down by the Mardyke. We were underage, but all bets were off: my parents wouldn't normally have let me out at night, but this was an exception. What else were they going to do? We had the teachers with us.

The following year most of the lads had moved on. We weren't as strong but we made it to the quarter-final. Lismore CBS beat us well. They had a couple of very good players: the likes of Dave Bennett was an excellent free-taker, and they had a big lanky guy, Dan Shanahan, who was very dangerous near goal.

I learned a lot from the Harty. It showed me the importance of having a dedicated bunch, that you had to go above and beyond the call of duty if you wanted to succeed, that you had to deal with media exposure and with playing in front of crowds. Above all, perhaps, you had to deal with representing a school with a long tradition. That was a huge driving force for me, to get my picture as part of a winning team up on the walls of those corridors in the Mon. The Harty was an All-Ireland to the likes of us. The actual schools All-Ireland, the Croke Cup, would have been a bonus. Winning the Harty was the be-all and end-all.

Winning a Harty medal in 1994 put players in the shop window for the Cork minor team. Deep down I'd have said to myself that it was a year early for me. But when you're in the mix you might as well go for it. That was my attitude.

I remember a phone call to the house, calling me to trials in Midleton CBS, then in Ballyphehane. The Harty and All-Ireland campaign took us out of the final trials, but I was named on the panel and told to go to Páirc Uí Rinn for training.

Unbelievable. Páirc Uí Rinn to train for a Cork team! It was my first encounter with Tommy Lynch, the groundsman who works at Páirc Uí Chaoimh and Páirc Uí Rinn. Tommy was always a bit cranky, but he ended up being one of the few good reasons why I liked going to Páirc Uí Chaoimh. He'd do anything for you, and god only knows the number of times I kept him to 10.30 p.m. to lock up the Páirc after a gym session there. We also had something in common. He has a daughter living in Sydney and would visit her every year, so our conversations often steered in that direction.

And I met the Cork minor coach. Jimmy Barry-Murphy. I'd come across Jimmy before. He'd trained the Barrs' minors teams of the early nineties and had a very good record with them, and Na Piarsaigh had played them in a City final in 1993.

We certainly noticed Jimmy. Even though he'd finished playing in the middle of the previous decade, his name still had power. If you were playing an underage game out in the Barrs, even as kids, someone might say, 'Look, that's Jimmy Barry-Murphy over there.'

And you had to look, to see if he was watching your game. He was an icon. A legend. No one had a bad word to say about him. Now I was sitting in the dressing-room and Jimmy was there in front of me. In the flesh. Talking, too, though I was probably too shy to answer him.

Over time he became the trainer, not the legend. You meet someone every day, or every couple of days, and they become more normal. That legendary status doesn't hold when they're knocking the mud off the studs of their boots next to you outside the dressing-room.

The sessions were short and snappy. Anything over an hour was exceptional, and there wasn't much physical stuff. It was nearly the same session all year: pucking in twos across the pitch, then some drills, then two teams playing against each other.

Jimmy always emphasized getting the ball in quick: on the ground, out of your hand, by whatever means necessary. There wasn't a lot of tactical sophistication, but that's what hurling was like at the time. You wouldn't have had fellas funnelling back; players held their positions, relatively speaking. With the Mon you had players who hadn't the same level of technique, so you had more structure; with Cork you didn't need that. That was the assumption.

To a seventeen-year-old, whatever Jimmy Barry-Murphy told you to do, you did, full stop. My assumption was that he was dealing with the crème de la crème of the talent in the county, and there was no need to do a lot of skill work.

Though I changed my views on some of these things later, at the time I was happy out, going along with the ride. Playing minor for Cork felt like a first footstep towards the big time.

We didn't pay much attention to the opposition. In the Mon we always did; Gerry Kelly would say to us, 'I was talking to a good guy up in north Cork who saw Charleville the last time, and Dom Foley hits the ball off his left all the time . . .'

Analysis on the opposition wasn't the done thing, really, an approach Jimmy repeated a couple of years later with the seniors. His philosophy would have been, 'I'm not interested in the opposition, I'm just interested in getting our own team right.' That's the sort of thing every manager says, but every manager worth his salt does his research on the opposition.

The one time Jimmy broke his own rule was against Clare. Jimmy was a very good speaker, passionate and articulate. Our first game was against Clare, who were trained by Justin McCarthy. I was only seventeen and I had only a vague notion who Justin was, but Jimmy had strong views on the matter: 'It's a disgrace, a Cork man training against a Cork team.'

We beat them, made it to the Munster final and beat Waterford in Thurles. Revenge on Shanahan and Bennett for the Lismore game. It was over before half-time, really, and the match was a disappointment for me. I hardly touched the ball.

Our game started at half one, with the senior game following at half three, and the crowds were coming in right up to the throw-in for the senior game, so by the end of our match the crowd was bigger by far than any I'd played in front of. We did a lap of honour with the cup. Happy days.

I made the Cork minor football team that year as well, which was where I encountered another Leeside icon.

Frank Murphy wasn't a minor selector, but before we played Kerry I remember he was invited by the management to say a few words. Frank told us to play with passion and abandon, with panache . . . he talked for ages, and then the selectors all clapped him.

His reputation as secretary of the Cork County Board – the all-powerful *rúnaí* – preceded him, so you listened, but players must have been wondering what was going on. I sure was, because we never saw this man from one training session to another. I rarely had any inter-action with him. If I saw him, I'd say, 'Hello, Frank,' and he'd say, 'Hello, Seán Óg.' That was it. I'd have known from the club that he was a significant person.

On the field, Kerry beat us handily. I was marking Jack Ferriter, who was a huge talent; he had me chasing shadows all day long. Mike Frank Russell and Barry O'Shea were also on that team.

The next year we had a decent team, but a little fella from Tipper-ary beat us on his own, almost, down in Killarney. Before the game we thought they'd sent out a fourteen-year-old, but we knew who Declan Browne was by full-time. He was sensational.

Alan O'Regan from Castletownbere was the big talent on our minor team – he played three years as an intercounty minor, which was some going. The only other guys from the minor team who went on to have a great senior career were Anthony Lynch and Nicholas Murphy, both of whom won All-Ireland and All Stars.

I'd worked harder on hurling all the way up, and people associ-ated me with hurling because our minor teams made it to Croke Park and the football teams didn't. But I found football easier, in that I was fit and strong, and marking an opponent was a more straightforward assignment than with the small ball.

We beat Down easily in the All-Ireland minor hurling semi-final, which was played before Cork played Down in the senior football semi-final. We travelled home with the footballers, and they were in the next carriage to us. Legends – Tompkins, O'Brien, Cahalane, Culloty, Davis. Brian Corcoran was still playing football at that stage, and he came in to chat to us about hurling. He'd probably had enough of the football talk in the other carriage, and he stayed with us for most of the trip. It was my first ever conversation with him, and it disproved the notion that you should never meet your heroes. The man was a class act in every sense.

Before the All-Ireland final against Galway we were in the dressing-room and I remember Micheál Ó Muircheartaigh coming in to check for changes and so forth.

He came over to me: '*Conas ta tu, Seán Óg, an bhfuil to reidh?*'

'*Oh ta me,*' I said.

Micheál Ó Muircheartaigh asking if you were ready. The big time.

We lost to Galway, a game we could have won. One of the things I remember was being told over and over not to be distracted by looking up into the stands for people, something I stuck to. I knew Mum, Dad, Teu and Setanta were there. Sarote would have stayed home, minding Aisake and Étaoin.

Another memory was being caught for an interview *as Gaeilge* by Seán Bán Breathnach – again in the toilets. For some reason I always seemed to be talking to journalists near the urinals.

In 1995 I was on the Na Piarsaigh senior team. Club hurling was very competitive in Cork in those years, and though I was big my body wasn't mature.

It was a big step up. In training I'd pick up someone like Mark Mullins, a seasoned guy, and he was far stronger than me, as I soon found out. In my age group I'd have knocked guys over no problem, but my challenges weren't even registering on these guys. That was intimidating.

And I got to play with my hero, Tony O'Sullivan. Only when I was on the same field as him was I able to appreciate just how gifted he was. One evening at training I managed to block him down, which was a huge thrill for me. He said he let me block him down for my own confidence, but I'd contest that assertion strongly!

There were other club legends like Christy Connery, Paul O'Connor, God rest him, Mark Mullins, Micky Mullins, Leonard Forde, Seán Guiheen, and the late Christy Coughlan who would have played for Cork at minors, U-21 or senior level. They gave me an insight into what was needed at the top.

I'd seen Na Piarsaigh win their first senior title. I'd seen the emotion that win sparked in people, and Dad and Teu and I had gone all over Cork to see them play. Now I was in the dressing-room with them.

Running in parallel with all of that was Dad's analysis. I was progressing as a hurler and footballer, scaling the ladder, but his critiques only became harsher. Fanatical. The only explanation he'd ever give for his criticism was, 'It might seem harsh, but it's for your own good.'

I never challenged him. I was a teenager in his house. There were times I felt like saying 'Look, you never played hurling, leave the criticism out.' But I never did.

When you played well, everything was hunky-dory, but you saw the bad side if you didn't perform, and it's only human nature that you won't put in a man-of-the-match performance every time you play. Even Muhammad Ali was beaten five times, after all.

It would start with the silent treatment on the way home. When we pulled in at the house, he'd scrutinize every mistake that you'd made. He wasn't the best at remembering other things, like birthdays, but boy was he sharp on remembering everything that you did wrong on the pitch. You might have done something positive in the game but this rarely got recognition. If he got riled up, you'd get the line, 'I was ashamed of the way you played. They were laughing at you.'

You'd get out of the car and head into the house with the head down, and Mum would immediately know what had happened. She'd say, 'Come on, I've dinner ready here for you.' She was the only person who showed you any love and affection, no matter how you played. Teu always says that it doesn't matter what we achieved, or didn't achieve: Mum would love us no matter what. He's dead right. Any true love we got as kids came from Mum.

Sometimes she'd have been at the match herself. After Dad said his piece, he might go upstairs, and she'd say, 'For what it's worth I thought you did well today, well done and don't mind him.'

That's just the way it was. Our normality.

In the early years, to be honest, it was a relief if he was working when you had a game. He'd work half a day on Saturday so he'd catch your afternoon games, but if you were playing in the morning you'd be delighted.

I understand that if someone has a bad game, then you don't tell him he played well. But I didn't understand the necessity to say, 'I wanted to crawl out of the place because of the way you played.'

What caused that in him? I don't know. I do know that if I have kids myself or if I were coaching kids, I'd do things differently.

Tom Walsh, who gave me my first football boots when I came to Cork, often went to games with Dad. When we'd drop him off at his home in Farranferris Avenue afterwards, he'd have read Dad's body language, and he'd lean back into the car: 'Seán, don't be hard on them now, they did all right today.'

But Dad was a very hard man to please. Myself and Teu definitely experienced the worst of him, being the eldest and second eldest in the family. You'd be going to games shitless from the previous talking he had given you, and this created enormous pressure to deliver. When you did deliver, it was some relief. When you didn't, you just braced yourself for that lonely car journey home. We always tried our best – for ourselves, for the team, for the family and for him –

but I'd often wonder if this ever registered with him. If it did, he had a funny way of showing his appreciation.

It wasn't so bad for Setanta and Aisake. As they came up through the underage ranks Dad was getting a bit older, a bit mellower – and Setanta himself would say to you that Dad seemed to favour him. Maybe because out of all of us he resembled Dad most. I don't know.

I didn't have a problem with that, it was just the way it was. When it came to the criticism, Setanta knew the drill because he'd been in the car when myself and Teu got it, and Dad was getting a bit older then anyway, getting into his fifties, and probably didn't have the appetite to be as harsh with Setanta and Aisake. That's not to say they weren't criticized, because they were.

He had no interest in going to parent–teacher meetings; Mum – fresh in the country – had to cover all of that. When they'd go to games, he wouldn't even stand next to her – he'd always go to the other side of the ground. 'I don't want to be annoyed,' was his line. We went along with it, but I just couldn't get my head around that one. Setanta and Aisake tried to go with her to matches so that at least she'd have some company. Wherever they were, he'd be well away from them. That meant at Cork games, for instance, no one would have a clue who he was, while Mum they'd pick out in a heartbeat, obviously.

For me, Dad's criticism lasted well into my intercounty career. Before I had a car, he'd be dropping me off to play for Cork and I'd say, 'Thanks for the lift, I'll see you later,' and he'd say: 'Stop, I want to talk to you for five minutes. The last day you didn't do such-and-such well, you have to improve on that, I'm blue in the face telling you to stop ball-watching . . .'

I didn't want to say 'I know' because he hated you doing that – it was as if you were trying to stop him from making his point.

When I eventually got a car myself, he wouldn't let me leave the house until he had said his few words. Sad to say, the best thing that ever happened to me was buying my own place and moving out of the family home. The independence was a breath of fresh air. I was in my peak years as a player. After years of receiving hard criticism, I ended up being my own worst critic.

5

One day, Tony Duggan, our Irish teacher and career guidance man, had an announcement: '*Ta cuarteoir againn inniu sa rang.*'

It was Finbarr Bradley, a past pupil from the AG who had started teaching a course in DCU: *Fiontar*, which was a business degree through Irish.

Finbarr gave a presentation about the course and all its advantages, and afterwards Tony asked if anyone was interested. A few hands went up, mine included. Politeness as much as anything: a guy comes all the way from Dublin, you don't want him to think you're drumming your fingers until he's finished his chat.

The interest in business was genuine, though, and came from accounting, a subject I was pretty good at. I didn't do science subjects for the leaving certificate, which would have limited my options, but I was honest enough with myself academically anyway. I'd have regarded myself as a C-plus student, and I knew medicine or electrical engineering wouldn't have been an option for me.

That doesn't mean I coasted through secondary school. The AG is a very good school with stellar past pupils, and the standards are maintained rigorously. Just as you walked along the corridors in the main school and saw famous hurlers and footballers in pictures on the wall, in the AG there were plenty of photographs hanging in the corridors as well. Those pictures showed lads who'd graduated from colleges and universities and gone on to success in academia, in business, in other walks of life.

It wasn't just a hurling factory; you were reminded that the main objective was education, and fellas were often reminded of what their older brothers or cousins had achieved. If you wanted to slack off, you could try it, but you were reminded pretty quickly that the AG wasn't where that was done.

I couldn't give you much of an account of how third-year geography went compared to our exploits in the U-15½ Munster colleges hurling championship, but I know for definite that we worked very hard.

That didn't bother me. I had that approach to sport and to training, and I knew that any time I did well in a game it was down to the hard work I put in at training. I applied that to schoolwork as well, so when the teachers worked you hard, I responded; I doubt that I'd have gotten the results I did if they hadn't worked us all so hard.

I thought I had my college years well mapped out: UCC just up the road, studying Business Information Systems, and hurling in the Fitzgibbon Cup, right where the Cork senior selectors could see me. But after Finbarr Bradley's talk, the idea of going to DCU started to grow. Finbarr had landed two lads from the previous year's class, Mick Aherne and Liam O'Keeffe. I knew them well from playing with them on the Harty team.

I went up to the open day in DCU and was impressed by the place. Tony Duggan took my expression of polite interest in the course as a declaration of intent, and practically furnished me with train time-tables from Kent to Heuston and bus times from the train station out to Glasnevin.

I put it down as my number-two choice on the CAO form. When the results came out I didn't have enough for BIS in UCC, so I took *Fiontar* at DCU.

I left the decision to the last minute. Part of that was hurling-related; I felt I'd have to be closer to home to figure in the shop window for the Cork seniors, and UCC would have been a far more attractive option in that respect – if I'd had the points, of course.

There was also a financial consideration. If I stayed in Cork, Mum and Dad wouldn't have to fork out for accommodation, obviously.

I mulled over staying in Cork and trying for UCC again, but

eventually we decided – my parents and I – that that would be a waste of a year. We figured that the worst thing that could happen would be I'd give it a year, and if I didn't like it I could always come back, no harm done.

So off I went, like a lot of Corkmen before and after, and got the train to the capital.

Early on I wasn't away for more than five days at a time. Na Piarsaigh won the senior county championship in 1995 and the week after that I was gone to Dublin. I was playing on minor and senior teams in the club, so every weekend between then and Christmas I went back to Cork to play a game.

There was no shortage of activity; the club was involved in minor and U-21 championships, and the senior side was in the Munster club championship as well. Come Friday evening in Heuston I was on the half-five train, waiting for it to pull out and head south.

I was homesick nonetheless. I stayed in digs with an elderly lady, May Cullen, in Glasnevin, whose family had grown up and moved out. She wasn't big into sport, which was no harm as far as I was concerned. The same went for most of my classmates. Some of them might have been aware at some level that I was playing intercounty but, given their backgrounds, they wouldn't have understood what that entailed.

Thursday night was then and is now the big college night out, and in fairness to them they'd often say, 'We're heading out there tonight, see you in such-and-such,' and I'd say, 'Yeah, see ye later.'

But I wouldn't be out. I wouldn't have had a notion of heading out.

'Oh, where were you?' would be the first question the following morning, and I'd say, 'Ah, I slept it out, would you believe that?'

I was busy enough with college work and sport, and I was also conscious that Mum and Dad were forking out for accommodation, food, travel – all of that. I didn't want it on my conscience that their money was being wasted. So while I relished living away from home,

I didn't really live it up. In fairness to Mum and Dad, every Sunday evening they would have said, 'Don't be short, shout if you need money.'

I wouldn't have been a huge spender anyway, but I certainly learned the value of a few bob while I was a student. Whatever I had in my pocket I made last.

I went to every lecture I could make – the only ones I missed were the ones which clashed with games I played for DCU. I'd have felt guilty if I'd missed any others. That was one time in my life when the regimented atmosphere I'd grown used to at home came in handy. I had a lot of freedom, but I'd plan out the week with military precision and discipline: be up at this time, be in for the lectures, train in college and go home to bed.

A boring life, really. In my first two years the only parts of Dublin I got to see were Belfield, if we were playing UCD, or Santry, if we were playing Trinity.

DCU played in the Ryan Cup, a level down in hurling from the Fitzgibbon Cup. There had been intercounty hurlers there before me, mostly minors and U-21s, but Ryan Cup is not at the same level as the Fitzgibbon. If you're a stand-out player that's fine, and for me it was more about keeping your eye in. I was home every weekend anyway, and in sports terms my aim was to get through the college season with a reasonable level of fitness and touch; I could improve on those when I went home for the summer.

I hurled with some decent players in DCU – Johnny Sheehan of St Catherine's was there and he was floating around with Cork until 2000, though his cruciates let him down. Dermot Byrne from Dicksboro in Kilkenny; Colin Herity from Dunnamaggin, an older brother of David, the Kilkenny keeper; George Jacob, a nephew of Mick Jacob, who would have had a few runs with Wexford around that time; and Shane Ryan, who played a lot of football for Dublin before joining the Dublin hurlers late in his career.

We were big fish in a small pond in terms of the Ryan Cup. When we qualified for the Fitzgibbon itself we came up against the big guns. UCC. WIT. Superpowers.

We were totally out of our depth. There was a link to Cork in the management team – Danny McGovern, our coach, was from Rathdowney in Laois, but had attended Cork IT when it was a Regional Technical College and had a bit of a *grá* for Cork. He drove it on when nobody wanted to manage the team, and some nights you'd only have six or seven players.

We made the Fitzgibbon weekend itself in 1998, and we played UCC in the semi-final, but reality struck then. It was over after ten minutes. Richard Woods from Clare was playing for them, as were Joe Deane, John Browne, Sean McGrath, Dan Murphy and Kieran Morrison, who were all on the Cork senior team, and Johnny and Eddie Enright from Tipperary. Plus some very strong senior club players. It was like Cork City taking on Barcelona, and we suffered in their Camp Nou, the Mardyke.

From my perspective it was enough to be tipping along and keeping my eye in. I couldn't afford to leave Kent Station for Dublin on a Sunday night and not touch a hurley again until I got off the train in Cork the following Friday evening. I needed to be playing the whole time.

Football was different in DCU. It's a football college, really; there's no comparison between the two.

The team had a lot of Dublin players, including Ian Robertson, who had a red-hot reputation at underage level, and Paddy Christie, who had less attention on him as a young player but did very well with the Dublin seniors.

The Dublin lads were a great bunch, and playing for DCU changed my mind about Dublin people in general, to be honest. I came to the capital with a Corkonian's view of the Dubs – the notion that you'd meet all the evils of the world between the Royal and Grand Canals – but they were the soundest you could meet.

Because DCU is so close to Ballymun, there's a strong Ballymun

Kickhams influence there. Gerry Hargan, who starred on Dublin teams in the eighties, came in and coached us. There was never a problem attracting high-powered coaches to DCU: Paul Bealin, who played for Dublin and later managed Wexford, was also involved.

I was the only Corkman in the group – the only player from Munster, I'd say. You had Dubs, lads from Meath, Louth, Cavan, Westmeath, all the Meehans of Galway. Great banter, great crack with them all. They wouldn't have had much interest in hurling but they knew I was playing hurling for Cork and they tried to accommodate me.

The Leinster Council put Tom O'Donnell, a full-time GAA development officer, into the college in my time and he was very helpful to me in ways that mightn't have figured in his contract of employment. For instance, if I was playing for DCU on a Friday afternoon, he'd make sure I made the train down to Cork that evening. Traffic lights that went red were more of a challenge than a prohibition when Tom was at the wheel, zooming us through the Friday rush-hour to get to Heuston Station. I think DCU viewed my presence as a handy recruiting tool for them in the south, where traditionally they wouldn't have attracted many students. They were happy to facilitate me.

Not that things were easy in the classroom. The *Fiontar* course was hard work – some parts of it were enjoyable, certainly, but hints I'd received about the demanding course schedule were certainly borne out. The financial subjects I enjoyed and was good at, and the same went for the accounting modules; the enterprise element was good as well, practical and applicable. The marketing was also enjoyable, and relevant to work.

The computer element of the course was less fun – computer languages such as C++ and Java didn't come naturally to me, and the same for SQL. I didn't see the relevance of the computer stuff to the business and enterprise focus of the course.

There was also a language element to the degree – French, in my case – and that was often hard going too: I'd done French for my

Leaving Cert and did OK in it, but French in DCU was another level altogether.

In many ways the real value of the course was the training in hard work and application as much as the raw material being studied. That suited me, too – the AG had worked me hard for five years, and keeping the head down to study was something I was well used to.

I moved out in second year and into a house with two Cork lads, Mick Ahern and Liam O'Keeffe. Finbarr Bradley checked in on me and the other Cork lads in *Fiontar* to see how we were getting on. He also helped me get a summer job in B. G. Turnkey, a company across the road from Apple in Cork. I was supposed to be in technical maintenance, but in reality I shadowed another guy who knew what he was doing. Most of the problems tended to recur, so I got the hang of it fairly quickly. I don't think they ever shut down because of the shortcomings of the junior maintenance man, anyway.

Jimmy Barry-Murphy rang in late 1995 to say he had the senior job and that he wanted to start blooding some of the newer lads, that he needed to rebuild the team, basically.

Myself, Dónal Óg, Joe Deane and Mickey O'Connell were brought in. He didn't say we were formally on the panel, more that he was just bringing us along to get to know the ropes.

Tom Cashman was a selector, and he'd ring the house in Dublin, and Mrs Cullen would be calling up the stairs, 'The guys from Cork are ringing.' Tom would tell me to be out in the Farm for a match that weekend: sound out.

Lots of players were trialled during that period. You'd be down for a trial match and there'd be two teams, but half of those players mightn't be around for the next trial game. This was all before Christmas – there'd be two or three games in the league just before the holidays, and Joe made his senior debut that year (1995) while he was still a minor, technically.

I made my debut against Tipperary down in Páirc Uí Rinn in 1996, the first game back after Christmas. Christy Connery from my own club was the other corner-back.

How did it go? Put it this way: it was a long, lonely train ride back up to Dublin after that.

Michael Cleary gave me an absolute lesson. I was chasing shadows: he wasn't a big imposing player, but his reading of the game was years ahead of mine. Literally. The ball would be pinging around midfield and it wouldn't have occurred to me that it might be on its way in to us – and then *bang*, he'd be gone, five yards away, ball in hand.

You can talk about senior intercounty, you can get the best advice from the best players, but it doesn't count for anything until you experience it yourself. You may think you're ready, you've been going well at minor level, but your first couple of senior games bring you down to earth. Hard.

I also played against Clare in Páirc Uí Chaoimh. They gave us a right trimming – but in fairness they were All-Ireland champions and close to their peak. I was corner-back on Colin Lynch. I couldn't get over the fact that he didn't have tops on his thumbs and had his hair long, in a rat's-tail. Intimidating enough, but I did OK. The next time I saw Colin Lynch he was one of the dominant midfielders in the game, not a corner-forward with a funny haircut.

The Cork senior panel started to firm up around Easter 1996, and we trained in Páirc Uí Rinn. Towards the end of the college year I'd have come down on Wednesday night, trained Thursday and stayed on for the weekend for challenge games leading into the championship.

But I missed a lot of the early stuff. I knew from Joe Deane that some of the older lads had been doing the heavy physical stuff before Christmas, but they'd dropped out – the only ones left were Jim Cashman, Teddy McCarthy, Sean McCarthy, Kieran McGuckian, Ger Cunningham and Ger Manley.

The preparation of senior Cork teams evolved dramatically over the course of my career. In those early days, hydration was an alien concept. Laps of the field were still the currency. Before games, we would be munching coleslaw sandwiches. The post-training meal in 1996? You could have chips with your chicken if you wanted to.

Tactics? The approach was, 'You're playing for Cork, and when other counties see that jersey their knees wobble.' Often enough there was a conflict between what you were told and what actually happened.

The only interaction the younger lads had was among ourselves, really. There was no 'How are ye doing?' from the older lads; it was more a case of earning your stripes, 'Come back when you've won an All-Ireland.' I don't recall having any kind of relationship with the elder statesmen on the team. Certainly at pre-match meals and having grub after training, we didn't mix that much. Teddy McCarthy ate on his own at those meals, which didn't strike me as a promising sign in terms of team spirit and togetherness. The only guy who made an effort was Brian Corcoran, who was a bit older than me and the other youngest fellas.

The atmosphere wasn't helped by the fact that we had a disastrous league campaign and got relegated. With the typical Cork outlook, we all convinced ourselves it'd be fine once the championship came around. The sun would be out, the ground would be hard and the ball would be hopping – sure we'd be four points ahead before the ball was thrown in.

Then we played Limerick down the Páirc and the shit hit the fan. Destroyed. Beaten by sixteen points.

I came on in the second half. Championship debut. I picked up Mossy Carroll, who welcomed me to the Munster championship with the butt of the hurley into the ribs. He winded me: I wanted to turn around but I couldn't, physically, and I didn't want to show any weakness. So Mossy came around to have a good look at me. Big smile on his face, the white gumshield gleaming. His expression said, 'Now, boyeen, how's that suit you?'

The game was over at that stage. Limerick were hard and seasoned.

They'd been improving for years, and they'd beaten Cork in 1994; they were approaching their peak, years ahead of us. Strong, mature men.

For us, the likes of Jim Cashman, Teddy McCarthy, Kieran McGuickan and Seánie McCarthy were at the end of their careers, and Brian Corcoran, Fergal Ryan, Alan Browne, Kevin Murray and Fergal McCormack were just a few years short of their peak. The bench was pretty inexperienced and so were the management team at that level . . . but we didn't expect that hammering, and there was no sparing us in the media criticism afterwards.

The funny thing was that I was insulated from all of that in Dublin. I was away from the heat that came on the lads in Cork. I didn't feel part of the team – not the way you'd feel part of other teams you played on, teams you'd trained with all year long, teams you'd bonded with over months.

I felt more part of the Cork U-21 team that year because I was back with the lads I'd played minor with, I was back in Cork working for the summer – it was more of a team unit.

Dad dropped me to Kent Station after the game for the trip back to DCU – the game was in May and the exams were kicking in soon afterwards.

An early championship exit with Cork and exams in Dublin soon afterwards. That was the pattern for a few years.

6.

I'd come on against Limerick in 1996, replacing a clubmate, Mark Mullins, but the Clare match in 1997 was my first start.

Clare were on a mission to redeem themselves in 1997, as they'd lost to Limerick in a thriller of a Munster final the year before. We were at a different level, literally: we came into that game on the back of a season in Division 2 of the league, playing the likes of Meath, which wasn't ideal preparation for a machine like Clare (who went on to win the All-Ireland that year). Some of us had a year to go at U-21 level, and Ger Cunningham in goal was the only guy left from the glory days of the eighties. We headed up to play them in Limerick as lambs to the slaughter.

The family were delighted for me, thrilled I was getting the start, but they were good about not pressurizing me in the lead-up to the game. They wouldn't have discussed hurling in the few days beforehand, in case the occasion was playing on my mind.

I started off marking Jamesie O'Connor – an absolute gentleman and an unbelievable operator on the pitch. It was an experience to mark him: he was the main man for that Clare team and a lot of their forward play went through him.

My brief from management was to stick with him, which was fine with me: I wouldn't have had the hurling for him, but I'd have had the fitness to stay alongside him and try to negate him, without necessarily contributing a lot of creativity to our cause. I was conscious going into the game that it didn't matter if I hit no ball as long as I could keep on top of him and deny him possession.

He caught me with a couple of things. For instance, he'd read the breaking ball slightly quicker than me and was away with the ball a couple of times as a result. Also, he took advantage of ball-watching – my big failing over the years – once or twice as well.

He was moved off me in the second half and I picked up different players after that. I coped. That was as much as you could ask for: the speed with which things happened was incredible. You had almost no time to strike the ball, and my hurling wasn't as refined then as it became. If you didn't get the ball in your hand with your first touch you could forget it, because you wouldn't get a second bite: the ball was gone.

Someone like Brian Corcoran could get rid of the ball in the tightest spaces, but I couldn't: I had to rely on my physical strength and power to break out of those tight spaces, and at twenty I wasn't always strong enough to do so. Your skills had to be perfect.

We gave them a better game than anyone expected. Even if we'd won that day, though, we didn't have the material with which to win the All-Ireland. They did, and it was no surprise when they did win the All-Ireland that year, because they were at a different stage of development from us altogether.

Diarmuid O'Sullivan made his debut that day, while it was only the second year for me and Joe Deane. We had youngsters on the bench as well. We were coming.

I've mentioned experiencing racism on the pitch, but until that match against Clare I'd never been racially abused in a senior intercounty match.

There was a switch in the second half, and one of the other Clare guys came over on me, and I continued with what I'd been doing all day – staying tight to my man. He didn't like it and turned around and gave me the butt of the hurley, and I gave him the butt back, the usual, and then he came out with, 'Look at you, Ó hAilpín, you're nothing but a black cunt.'

I said nothing. In my head I'd have said, 'Speak for yourself,' because the player in question always had a great colour, but I didn't respond and we got on with the game.

They won. I can't remember if I shook hands with him at the final whistle. I wouldn't have sought him out to shake hands, but if he'd stuck his hand out I probably would have shaken it and walked on.

I said nothing to anyone in the dressing-room afterwards. Nobody had a clue.

Early in 1998 we were in pre-season training down in Páirc Uí Chaoimh and I was talking to Brian Corcoran after one session.

By that stage Clare were champions again and there was an unbelievable air of arrogance about them. Myself and Corcoran were talking about how ruthless they had become.

It was then that I mentioned to him what had happened to me the year before. Corcoran was disgusted.

And there was no more said about it.

As it happened, we played Clare in the championship again in 1998, and they were even better than they'd been against us in 1997. There was a rope across the entrance to the pitch in Semple Stadium that day, waist-high, which was meant to divert you to one side of the field or the other.

When Clare came out they went out over the rope, literally, hurdling it and bouncing out across the grass. When Jimmy Barry-Murphy saw that, he supposedly said to Dr Con, 'We're in trouble here, Con.'

He was right. They were much better than us on the day and the game was over as a contest before the break. For some reason, we were flat, and we couldn't get going at all. At half-time we were looking for something or someone to spark us.

The usual thing to get fellas going in the dressing-room is to throw out the old 'Do you know what they're saying about us?' line. Everyone's heard that, or something similar.

We were gathered around, standing in a group with our arms around each other, before going out for the second half, and Corcoran spoke. He finished up by saying, 'One of them called

Seán Óg a black cunt' – but he didn't add that it was the previous year.

That was the parting shot. Out we went. And lost.

You couldn't keep something like that quiet, even if you tried. There would have been about thirty people in the dressing-room at half-time; if they each told one person what had been said, even in confidence, it wouldn't be long going around Cork, and further.

I was working in AIB on Patrick Street at the time, and Jimmy Barry-Murphy came in to see me the Tuesday after the game. He said that Frank Murphy had been rung about this and he wanted to know what the story was.

To be honest, I played it down. My memory is that the message from Frank was that, if we wanted to, we could go further about it, but I told Jimmy to let it go.

We'd lost the match, and I'd had a stinker – and the episode was a year old. It would have come across as sour grapes and I'd have gotten zero sympathy if I'd pursued it. Unfortunately, at the time there was no mechanism within the GAA to pursue a racism complaint.

Anything that can be used against you on the field, to get into your head, is fair game for most hurlers and footballers. I know a Kerry footballer who once mentioned his love of French movies, for instance, and for years afterwards he heard about French movies from every player that marked him. If I'd proceeded with a racism com-plaint in 1998 – a full year after the event – then, no matter what the outcome, I have absolutely no doubt I'd have heard about my 'whingeing' from every player who came near me. It would have been open season.

My attitude was that I had enough to do without taking on that cause, and that it hadn't happened that often anyway. I moved on.

Looking back now, even though I was four or five years in the Cork system by 1999 I was still learning my trade. I started in the 1997 and

1998 championships, but that had been a total of three games. I didn't feel I'd really established myself as a player.

We weren't making it to high-profile games like All-Ireland finals, so we weren't as well known, certainly to the general public. I'd always differentiate between GAA fame, if you like, and general fame. As 1998 turned into 1999, only hurling anoraks would have known us.

On top of that I was still in Dublin. There was one huge positive in that: I was spared some of the misery that the others went through in training.

Up in DCU I was training away on my own, doing two decent sessions a week without being overloaded. If I'd been in Cork, I'd have ended up doing two sessions each with the hurlers and foot-ballers, and it would have destroyed me.

Even without all the training, it was tricky at times. I'd have had one or two weekends which involved football on the Saturday and hurling on the Sunday. You'd feel it. After an intercounty Gaelic match you'd feel it in the shoulders and upper body; in hurling, the pain's all in the hands and the wrists where you've been flicked and flaked.

But you're young and fit, you'll take it. You know it's not going to last for ever, but you'll go as long as you can.

Training sessions for the Cork footballers, in particular, were fairly punishing. That was one feature of the landscape that became notori-ous all over Cork as a place where lads suffered.

If you went to the Macroom GAA field, you had a bank on one side for supporters, but the supporters stood at the bottom. They didn't go too far up the bank itself because it was about 150 metres high at a desperately sharp gradient.

If you go up, you'll start off fine but by the time you get to the top it's as though you had a guy squatting on your shoulders. Hard going. I only did the whole session there once and I nearly collapsed.

You'd sprint up once, jog back, and Larry Tompkins, the manager, would be waiting at the bottom to send you sprinting back up to the top again. How often? A set of ten, take a break, and maybe five sets in total.

In fairness to Larry, he set his stall out early: he wanted his players in peak physical condition. Given his own attitude to preparation and fitness when he played, that was hardly surprising. I got on well with him and he was very good to me. He understood my situation and he'd played with dual players like Teddy McCarthy and Denis Walsh, so he was good to let me off to play hurling, even though I'm sure he'd have preferred me focusing on football.

What helped was that I was a good athlete and could survive those runs, so he probably trusted me not to do the dog on it fitness-wise when I was on my own in Dublin. He played me at full-back in 1999. I'd have preferred to be out the field somewhere, but I was twenty-two and I wasn't going to throw the rattle out of the pram over the jersey I got.

You needed that fitness for Gaelic football, too; you needed extra conditioning, maybe. Part of that comes from the nature of the game: there's more physical contact, it's a hitting and possession game – to get the ball off a guy you've got to be strong, and to retain it under that kind of pressure you've got to be strong. Even going back to Larry's own time as a player in the eighties, there was a gym culture with Gaelic football that didn't exist in hurling, and which still didn't exist to any great degree early on in my playing days.

At a time when the notion of sports science barely existed there was also a focus on getting good sports science, that extended to taking ideas from other sports. Larry would have gone over to the F. A. training centre in Lilleshall in England to get ideas on preparation and training techniques.

It wasn't just Larry. Brian Corcoran often points out that when he was playing football for Billy Morgan in the early nineties, Morgan was using match analysis in a way that wouldn't have been out of place twenty years later.

In all honesty, I struggled with football. I wanted to play both codes, but even then, when preparation wasn't at the level it is now, I was having problems balancing the two, and it was invariably football that suffered. I certainly had more bad games of football than of hurling, and the knives would have been out for me after those because I was a dual player.

Sometimes the critics were right, though it wasn't always down to the time I was devoting to hurling. On occasion I just came across a footballer who was operating on a different level. In 1997 we played in the National Football League semi-final against Kildare, a doubleheader in Croke Park, and I got my game. Early on I got the ball, looked upfield for someone to pass it off to and said to myself, 'I'll just whizz past this lad here' – and I ran straight into Glen Ryan.

It was the first time I felt completely out of my depth physically. The impact made me think, 'Oh shit, what the fuck did I run into there?'

Glen was a big unit of a man, but it was the fact that he just stood there and body-checked me without exerting any real force that scared the shit out of me. I was left thinking, 'Welcome to senior football, son!' You're young, you think you're big and strong, and then you find out what strength really is.

More than once against Kerry I felt totally inept in terms of skill. Aodhán Mac Gearailt got two goals off me in a Munster final. Dara Ó Cinnéide gave me a tough hour on a couple of occasions as well. But the man who gave me a real lesson was Dessie Farrell of Dublin. He was coming towards the end of his career when I marked him and he was carrying the huge Pat Spillane-type knee-bandage, so the day I marked Dessie I was thinking, 'I'll handle this guy no bother.'

Not a chance. Physically he was far too strong for me – most of the time I was tackling his hand as he held me off and looked around the place to consider his options. His reading of the game was first class, and that showed in his runs for the ball, and the timing of his runs in particular.

A lot of forwards would see the ball in their midfielder's hands and make the run just a fraction too early. If the ball wasn't in to them fast enough the forward had some distance to travel for it, and if you were quick enough you'd make up the ground on them and arrive with a shoulder or a hand just as they were collecting the ball.

Dessie was different: he'd hold and hold and make his run as late as possible for the ball, and at that stage you wouldn't have a chance to make up the ground because he'd only be travelling a short distance to take the pass. As well as that, he rarely ran in a straight line; he'd cut left or right, so even if you got in front of him he was gone off on an angle behind you.

That's one thing you don't get from watching a game on television – you don't see the runs being made off the ball. Dessie's runs were always top quality.

The game was a little different, then. There wasn't the tactical approach you see now, with massed defences and players roaming forward in packs. In the full-back line, we held our positions much more than players would nowadays. I enjoyed being involved in both the football and the hurling camps, and there was no shortage of wit when it came to my dual exploits. If I'd been off with the hurlers for a few weeks, the footballers would jokingly say, 'Oh by god look who's turned up today, lads. It's very good of you to turn up! This man deserves a round of applause.' When I'd be off with the footballers for a stint and return back to the hurling dressing-room, remarks such as 'A championship game must be coming up, lads' would be tossed in my direction.

Something people used to raise with me was why we didn't go on strike in 1999, say, rather than 2002, if things were as bad as we said.

My answer to that is simple. We were winning, and when you're winning why would you be cribbing?

Looking back, there were a few issues. Annoyances more than anything else.

You didn't get as many All-Ireland final tickets as we got in later years, for instance. That might sound petty to a supporter scrambling for one or two tickets himself, or very petty to a county board officer who's being tormented by people for All-Ireland tickets in the run-up to the big day, but it's a bigger problem than you might think.

When you play for your county in an All-Ireland you're represent-ing your own family, your employer, your club — a whole raft of people. If you're married or have a partner, there's her family as well. At that time you got four complimentary tickets, but that wouldn't cover what you needed in a million years. We felt that it was a bit mean, given the efforts we'd been putting in since January. And we ended up spending the week of the All-Ireland final phoning this fella and that fella for tickets, running around meeting people to collect tickets, swapping hurling tickets for football ones with lads up the country . . . all of that messing drains you the week of the biggest game of your life.

And every time you'd say never again. As in, 'Never again am I driving halfway out the county to drop tickets off the Friday night before an All-Ireland final.' Or 'Never again am I making a rake of calls from the Burlington Hotel the night before the game to make sure everyone has their tickets.'

Food was an issue, or it had been. Before Ted Owens came in as physical trainer, in 1997, we were served chicken and chips and a bot-tle of fizzy orange after training, which defeated the purpose of training in the first place. Ted changed all of that. We ate properly after training and before games, and hydration became a huge prior-ity. He couldn't stress that enough, getting the water into you. Ted was telling us to take two litres on board a day. Two litres? We were only having a glass of water, maybe, with lunch.

In terms of gym access, the footballers had access to the facilities in the Silver Springs Hotel, and you could go to the gym in the Páirc, but those options weren't ideal if you lived an hour's drive away. The obvious solution would have been to provide players with member-ship of gyms near them, but that was unheard of.

Those things did bother us, but when we were winning games, then the games were the focus. The question of conditions and stan-dards was something for when you didn't have the distraction of concentrating on the championship.

We'd grumble about the other stuff in the dressing-room without ever dreaming you could actually change it. The culture was very much that when you won a couple of All-Irelands you could start to dictate how things were to be run. Of course, there was a circular aspect to that argument: you had a better chance of winning those couple of All-Irelands in the first place if things were being run properly.

The realistic target for me in 1999 would have been a Munster medal in both codes. I certainly wouldn't have seen myself as being busy in September.

But we rode our luck at times that year, particularly in the hurling. What it took us longer to realize was that the luck couldn't last for ever. To compensate for that you need to invest in your preparation and all the things you can control.

But it was an unbelievable summer, the way it took off. Everywhere you went you were talking hurling and football. And I'd finished college, which made it more special in a way. I didn't have a job, but I'd a few bob saved up so I was able to enjoy the ride without dragging myself out of bed for work the morning after all those training sessions.

Things didn't go well in the lead-up to the Waterford game in the hurling championship. There was a notorious challenge game against Tipperary which had to be blown up early because we were being destroyed, a game I missed because I was still in Dublin.

A crisis meeting was held after that game, and there were suggestions that Jimmy considered walking away, but the meeting cleared the air. Still, there were more questions than confirmations facing into the Waterford match — and they'd been to the All-Ireland semifinal the previous year, remember.

It was a huge gamble for him to give six players their debuts — Wayne Sherlock, Dónal Óg, Mickey O'Connell, Timmy McCarthy, Ben O'Connor and Neil Ronan — but those players had All-Ireland medals at colleges, minor and U-21 level. The pedigree was good and the talent was there, and the bonus was that everyone clicked. That was one of the breaks we got in 1999.

The main thing I remember from the Waterford game was Jimmy's speech beforehand. Gerald McCarthy was manager of Waterford. Jimmy tends to get very animated when a Corkonian is coaching another county against Cork. He asked us to win the game no matter what.

I remember the first time I met Mickey O'Connell, a tiny chap in a white helmet playing in an U-12 county final, so small you were half-laughing at the prospect of flattening him; it wasn't long before he showed us all his class, and the laughing on our side stopped. Against Waterford that day in 1999 he hit eight points off Tony Browne, the 1998 player of the year. To be fair to Tony, he played injured that day, but we didn't know that – and even if we had known, it wouldn't have contaminated our celebrations.

It was a break, one we ran with. Winning a high-pressure Munster championship game in front of a big crowd, qualifying for a Munster final, the new lads coming in and succeeding so well: it was all good for the confidence.

That year was the start of understanding what it was to represent Cork. Or, to be precise, what it was to win with Cork. The fanaticism that accompanies winning games – the energy, the passion people have: it was an eye-opener. There was a sense of 'Holy shit, this is serious' when we saw the reaction of the supporters.

It was a different time in the country, in fairness. The economy was booming, people had a few bob in their pocket and they put their ears back and celebrated after games. It was as if everyone who'd been bouncing up and down on the Town End in Thurles had just gone straight to the nightclub in Cork afterwards. No going home to put on a good shirt or new jeans: carry on with the Cork top you were wearing, and rock on into the small hours. It was fantastic. I was only 22, innocent enough, and loving every minute of it.

I have mixed feelings about the Munster final in 1999, though. The evening before we played Clare I got a phone call from the chairman of Na Piarsaigh. He told me that one of my clubmates had died, suddenly and unexpectedly.

This knocked me for six. I immediately relayed the news to Teu, who was equally stunned. This was a guy we had played with for a number of years and we had become good mates. The news made the notion of death very real, which it isn't for most people in their early twenties.

I wasn't sure whether I should play or not. I had a good chat with Teu and I decided that I was going to go out tomorrow and play in our friend's honour. That was the least I could do for him, and I'm sure he would have wanted it that way, too.

The following morning, I joined the lads on the bus. You switch into that pre-game mode, your ritual, as well as feeding off the nervous energy on a bus going to a big game. Everything is directed towards the battle, and there's no room for anything else.

Our supporters were not overly confident. Clare had won two of the last four All-Irelands. They'd beaten us in the championship the previous year. But we believed they were a year older, a year slower, while we had a young, fast team with good athletes in key positions who could attack them and damage them. And that's how it worked out.

Afterwards I was in no mood to celebrate. My feeling was clear: not today. The passing away of my clubmate was the main thing on my mind.

I headed straight into the dressing-room and sat down there alone, but Tony O'Sullivan had followed me in.

'I know we're suffering as club people today,' he said, 'but go out and do the team thing.'

I'd have done anything Tony said, so I followed him back out to the rest of the players. Most of them were probably unaware of what had happened – Seanie McGrath might have heard because he's from the northside too – but they wouldn't have picked up any vibes like that from me anyway. I'm good at hiding that kind of stuff; I can bottle it up and not let people see it.

The following day I helped carry the coffin from O'Connor's Funeral Home up to the church in Farranree.

We played Bishopstown the day after the funeral in the hurling championship. That game had to be played.

It was a strange week. Beating a powerhouse in the Munster final with Cork, then the funeral of a clubmate, and then playing with the club after that funeral.

7

Winning the Munster championship meant something to us. Not just because of the drought in Cork – we hadn't even reached a Munster final since 1992 – but because the Munster championship had real meaning then (much more than it does in the age of the back-door system), and because it was a medal in your back pocket – and because it delivered us to Croke Park for an All-Ireland semi-final.

That sank in a few days after the Clare match. Obviously we'd have played in Croke Park as minors, but for us to go in as the main event rather than in the curtain-raiser . . . the feeling wasn't 'Holy shit, this is too much for us,' but rather a pleasant sense that we were hitting the big time.

First, though, I had a Munster football final. The fact that I don't drink helped me because it meant I didn't head in to face Larry and the boys with a fuzzy tongue and a headache from the beer.

Believe me, there were plenty of hangovers going around. Celebrations went on for a few days after the Sunday night and deserverdly so. Apart from Brian Corcoran, this was the team's first major trophy at senior championship level and we weren't going to let the moment pass. Guys took days off work to let their hair down and savour the victory.

One thing I noticed was that even if everyone was out for the night, you wouldn't see much of the other lads. You'd hook up with members of your own family, with other lads from the club or school – and that probably suited everyone, too. The last thing you wanted to talk about was hurling, or the game; and, to be honest, we were so young that a lot of us wouldn't have had a lot of conversation. What was I going to talk to team-mates about, my business studies up in DCU?

Come the end of the night you might have a chat but it wouldn't be any more in-depth than 'Hey, you did well today, fair play' or 'That was some score you got there in the second half'; it wasn't some detailed discussion of tactics. If you had to sit down with a team-mate for the night and talk hurling for the night, you'd go off your head.

When I got a bit older I had good chats after games with the likes of Cusack, but it would have been directed at how we could improve the performance, or a statistic that John Allen or Dónal O'Grady called out at half-time. That was in the future, though; in 1999 we played hard and partied hard. That was how it was done.

The increase in interest among people was noticeable. I had no car, so I often thumbed it from Blarney into town for training. With the hurley and bag, and the success we were having, people would recognize you and stop and be very encouraging. We all fed off that kind of recognition. Not in an arrogant sense, but we were young fellas, we were being recognized – who wouldn't love that?

It was funny enough, dealing with it. I'm naturally shy, so listening to people say 'You did well today' was something I'd play down, but naturally enough I enjoyed it too. Who doesn't like to hear praise? But the longer it went on, the less I enjoyed it and the less time I spent in that sort of environment – I'd head home after games, particularly late on in my career when I was in a solid relationship with Siobhán and neither of us had any interest in heading into town the night of a game. But I'd still head in and meet up with the lads on a Monday because it was less busy and you could talk.

When the wins didn't come, you got the other side of it. A bit of alcohol on board and people weren't inclined to sugar-coat the criticism.

'Ye were fucking terrible today, what's wrong with ye?'

'What's the story with those puck-outs, what's Cusack at?'

'Timmy was shocking today again, fuck sake.'

My approach was just to agree. The one thing you didn't want was confrontation, to get drawn into a scuffle or something. By agreeing with people you took the heat out of all those discussions because it was the last thing they expected. I'd say, 'Do you know what, you're right, I'll say that to the manager and see if he'll take that on board, thanks.'

That was my approach. Some of the other lads would take a different tack, and I'm not saying mine was the right way, but it was the strategy that worked for me. If I heard someone say one of the lads was cat I'd just say, 'Thanks for that, great point, I'll pass that on to the boss man.'

There was one huge drawback to my engaging with the public. I became known as the nice guy you could talk to. I got to hear a lot of drunk people's views on games over the years.

Looking back, it was no big deal. The supporters are part of the whole thing. Players are locked into the bubble, they're trying everything to prepare well and so forth, and there's no time to take a step back to see the thing in its entirety, but all of these people – the supporters, the county board, the media – they're all stakeholders in the thing and you've got to engage with them.

Eddie O'Donnell, who's a great friend of mine, would have pointed out to me that there's always a dividend. You should be decent with people anyway because everyone's entitled to be treated with respect.

After we beat Clare, I was back with the footballers on the Thursday evening, to prepare for the Munster final against Kerry the Sunday week after that.

As the year rolled on there was more and more attention being paid to the fact that I was a dual player and might have a chance of emulating Teddy McCarthy, who'd won hurling and football All-Ireland medals in 1990. That year was still very fresh in my mind, and Teddy had been a boyhood hero of mine, and now I was closing in on a similar season.

That was a good Kerry side. A lot of them had All-Ireland medals from 1997, and most of them would figure early in the 2000s when

Kerry were a dominant force. In 1999 Maurice Fitzgerald was still on the scene – just pure elegance with the ball in his hands – while Darragh Ó Sé and Dara Ó Cinnéide were becoming seasoned campaigners, and Tomás Ó Sé and Mike Frank Russell were coming through.

And Seamus Moynihan. What a champion he was for Kerry. I remember going to a Corn Uí Mhuiri game between the Mon and St Brendan's of Killarney when I was fifteen and seeing him solo the length of the field before burying a goal. That was my first memory of the freak in action.

So there was quality in that Kerry team, but we were up for it in 1999 and managed to get a rare victory. Once we got our momentum in the second half, in a wet Páirc Uí Chaoimh, they couldn't stay with us. The benefit of training on the hill in Macroom and on the dunes in Inchydoney showed that day. The longer the game went on, the better we got. Kerry stayed in touch, thanks to a couple of goals from Aodhán Mac Gearailt (marked by S. Óg Ó hAilpín), but the winter work told towards the end and Cork got a grip on proceedings. In that respect it was a game that offered a template for the season.

The celebrations were far crazier than the hurlers'. It made sense: there was a tradition of winning with hurling, an expectation that you'd be collecting silverware, even though they hadn't actually done so for a number of years. Traditionally the footballers wouldn't have had as much success . . . and it showed.

The celebrations were crazy, but in a good way.

Fellas became sex symbols overnight. After big games we'd be out and girls would be saying, 'Oh, I was at the game there today.' If lads had their wits about them they'd pursue that line of questioning to good effect, and some of them did, but other players would assume the girl would actually want to talk about the game, and the conversation wouldn't last very long before they heard 'See you later, bye.'

What can I say? We were an inexperienced team. I wouldn't have been to underage discos; I attended an all-boys school; and I didn't have a lively social life in DCU to sharpen my skills either. The likes of Ronan Dwane and Neil Ronan were far more accomplished when it came to the patter. I'd be bringing politics or whatever into play conversationally when the girls just wanted to chat.

It's great that women are interested in the games and go to matches. There was a time when it was ninety per cent men at matches, and it's fantastic that there's a mix now in the stadiums. And it also showed how the whole county rows in behind a team that's winning – you'd be out after a game and meet girls from the locality, everyone out together having the crack. Or having the crack as they listened to yours truly talk about current affairs.

Then it was back to the hurling. Offaly in the All-Ireland semi-final, a team we had no first-hand knowledge of. None of us had played against them at underage level, let alone at senior championship level.

They were the reigning All-Ireland champions, but we were confident. We had a young, athletic team and we felt our speed would trouble them. A lot of the Offaly players were coming towards the end of their glittering careers. The experts went with Offaly because they were the tried and tested team. I understand that better now than I did at the time: if a team has a track record of achievement, you'll naturally back them against unproven opponents, particularly when you're talking about Croke Park, because it's the biggest stage, and nerves come into the equation.

They did for me, certainly. No matter what any player says, if the game is of any consequence, he's nervous.

The lads had different ways of coping with the tension. Some would read a programme. Some would go into the warm-up area to hit the ball around. Others would crack jokes with Dr Con.

The attitude in the dressing-room before we played Offaly was that they were All-Ireland champions, fair enough, but we were more concerned about what we were going to do. That was Jimmy's outlook: we can think about the opposition all we want, but at the end of the day we have to look after our own game and get ourselves right.

There was no in-depth analysis of what Offaly would bring to the table, but unless you were living on the moon you knew that Brian Whelehan was an outstanding hurler and someone who could hurt you from anywhere on the field; the same for Johnny Dooley. We knew that, obviously, but there were no specific orders from management, say, to keep Whelehan out of the play on our puck-out by hitting our man on the opposite wing.

That was a big difference to the football team: Larry would have spoken about the opposition a lot more, targeted their weaknesses and drawn on the knowledge of contacts he had around the country.

For all that, we were ready for Offaly. Training had moved to another level because we were out of Munster at last. It became more focused. The forwards would work with Jimmy and Seanie O'Leary, and Tom Cashman and Johnny Crowley took the backs.

To their credit, management got us to Croke Park on the Saturday before we played Offaly. The renovations had been going on and we hadn't been there since playing as minors in 1995, so they wanted us to get a feel for the place. We got to walk around the dressing-room and take in our surroundings. Offaly were far more familiar with the stadium, but at least it wouldn't be a complete shock to us.

And we needed all the help we could get. I've had manners put on me by Kilkenny plenty of times; I've come home and thought, 'These guys are on a different level.' But that Offaly team was right up there. We won the game by the skin of our teeth, but it was a seventy-minute education in hurling style.

They were very economical in their play, and the skill, the touch, the understanding between them was unbelievable. They were hurling together for years, they knew all the time what each other was doing and what kind of ball they wanted.

We had to work much, much harder for our scores in that game than was usually the case. We weren't yet playing the support-and-move game that Dónal O'Grady would bring in, but we relied on speed and athleticism a lot. We were getting the ball in to the forwards and then sending players running in to support them.

Offaly didn't play that way. They'd just get the ball to a guy in a good position. He wasn't waiting to flick a pass out to someone flying by him; he'd just pop over a point himself.

Their cuteness was evident all the time – if you were slightly ahead of one of them going for a ball, for instance, they wouldn't kill themselves trying to beat you there, they'd let you have the ball and then bottle you up with a hook or a block.

There's a lesson there: the classic trap in that situation for a young player who's slightly behind his man is to go all out to win the ball – and concede a free. Their game was based on moving the ball forward, forward, forward, moving it all the time until it got to the man who could do something with it. Experience versus exuberance, and experience often won.

I was on Paudie Mulhare early on, and ended up on Michael Duignan in the second half, but my main memory is of Brian Corcoran and Brian Whelehan playing ping-pong the length of the field in Croke Park. Offaly looked to have a grip on the game in the second half, but we came into it late on, our athleticism began to tell and we came on to more breaking ball to win it in the end.

Even as the clock ticked down, we were nervous. They were the Houdini of all Houdinis and hurled to the maximum of their potential. When I think of Offaly, I always think of the stand their supporters took in Croke Park in 1998 after their game against Clare was blown up a couple of minutes early; they wouldn't move until they got their replay, which sums up that never-say-die Offaly spirit. You'd have to have good time for people like that.

The dressing-room was a great place to be after that one. An All-Ireland final was no longer the dream but a game we'd play in.

Jimmy said, 'There's a lot of work to do, let's not get carried away – but well done.' And that set the tone, it struck the note of confidence. After the Munster final there was an air of 'Sure we'll give it a go,' but after the Offaly game it was more a sense of 'We might as well finish the job.'

For me, though, it was back to football: Mayo in the All-Ireland semi-final. I had a rough day at the office against them. I was marking James Horan, the current Mayo manager, and he was one player I never got to grips with. He had me on toast that day.

I wasn't tight enough, and the few times I got close to him he was far too strong for me: he'd palm me off, take a look and pop the ball over the bar. He was a mature player, in his mid-twenties, and I saw the difference myself when I got to that stage of my career.

At twenty-two I wasn't doing weight training religiously – just a few odd sessions. There was still a school of thought that strength training would slow you down. I wasn't physically mature enough, and it showed against Horan.

I had to be taken off him and, if that switch hadn't been made, I'm convinced Mayo would have won that game. I knew it myself. Ronan McCarthy came in on Horan and curtailed his influence somewhat, I went to corner-back and Philip Clifford got a good goal before half-time, against the run of play, which set them back.

Again our conditioning kicked in during the second half and we got on top. My man drifted outfield looking for the ball, which suited me.

The knives were out for me after that game – 'It's very hard to be a dual player' and so on. My big problem was that I wasn't tight enough to my man. As a full-back you need to get within touching distance of your opponent.

A few things came against me in the dual role. One was that I didn't get enough high-tempo football. The games rolled on two weeks apart for the summer, hurling and football, but there'd usually be three or four weeks between the games in each code. So with football, say, I'd miss out on the hard graft, the high-tempo sessions, in the first two weeks of that three- or four-week cycle – the A versus B games and executing your skills at that top speed. While the others were doing that I was getting ready for a hurling game. Then I'd come in for the last two weeks of the cycle, when the drills and routines were being wound down in terms of pace. I wasn't at the required speed starting off each championship game as a result.

Secondly, you were marking fellas who weren't trying to play hurling. They were concentrating solely on football. Not only was I slightly behind where I should have been, they were operating at the peak of their powers, they'd concentrated everything on that game. Me? Two weeks after trying to handle them I could be in on top of DJ Carey or someone at that level: a hurler at his peak.

I wasn't working that summer, but between training sessions for both codes and club games and so on . . . it took its toll. Young and fit as I was, the body and mind were working overtime.

And it wasn't just me. I'm not putting this forward as an excuse, but in Cork even intercounty hurlers would play football for their clubs, and the number of games fellas ended up playing was huge compared to other counties.

At that stage I felt I couldn't say no to training, but there were probably times when I should have sat out the odd session. I'd have been fresher in the long run for the games. But at twenty-two you think you're Superman and you can go for ever, and with the euphoria in the county you just wanted to ride the wave, along with everyone else.

And there was plenty of euphoria to go around. With a double on the horizon Cork was bubbling, and I got plenty of attention.

When the hurlers had a press night ahead of the final we had a training session, the media came out on the field after we finished, and two hours later I was still answering questions, standing around after the session in my gear, talking to everyone. It was a time the *Gaeilge* didn't help, as I got roped in by Raidio na Gaeltachta for interviews as well.

I had to be pulled off the field by Teddy Owens in the end – 'Sorry there, lads, that's enough.'

I had a busy enough summer, media-wise. Mobile phones were around but not everybody had one. Though Esat Digifone were sponsoring us, and there were phones available at a discount, I didn't bother getting one – and I didn't get a mobile until I absolutely needed one for work when I started work with Ulster Bank in 2004. So, if someone needed me, they could try the landline at home.

Of course, once reporters figured out I had a landline they made the phone hum, and Mum was far too honest when she'd pick it up.

'Oh yes, he's here, I'll get Seán Óg there now for you.'

'Who's that, Mum?'

'I don't know.'

I'd pick up the phone: reporter. Good going, Mum!

The weekend of the All-Ireland you head up on the train to Dublin and land into the Burlington around five o'clock. You're left to your own devices, just warned to stay out of the lobby because obviously there'd be a Cork crowd down there, and many of them looking for tickets.

Diarmuid would always bring a crew to the movies on the Saturday night, a taxi load of them heading to the Savoy on O'Connell Street. I'd head to the bedroom, though on the floor you'd have a team room as well, and you could go down to watch a DVD, or have a chat, get a rub from one of the masseurs. Tea and sandwiches at ten, and bed.

The 1999 hurling final was probably the last time I had a decent sleep before an All-Ireland final.

Mass for the team the next morning, Bishop John Buckley doing the honours, but it wouldn't be exclusive. You'd have Cork people in there for mass, supporters staying in the hotel kneeling next to you.

The All-Ireland is different. That sounds like the most obvious statement in the world, but I'm not talking about the game. There are a lot of distractions. Having to get out on the pitch for the TV schedule, the Artane Boys' Band, shaking hands with Uachtarán na hÉireann before the game. It can be hard to keep your focus.

That morning there might have been lads having a full fry-up for breakfast. I know Diarmuid says he had the full Irish the morning of the final, and that wouldn't have raised any eyebrows. I had what I'd always have at home before going out for a game: a bowl of muesli with a banana chopped into it, and scrambled eggs on toast afterwards. Orange juice. Nothing unusual in that for me, but there certainly wouldn't have been anyone going around the breakfast tables checking up on lads. Diet is monitored more strictly these days. The environment then was one of 'Whatever the players are comfortable with, let them have.'

After breakfast you had an hour or two free, and some lads would puck around, or head up to their rooms and come back for a pre-match meal at half twelve. That's hard going, trying to get a full meal down not long after breakfast. You're not hungry, really, but I remember learning one serious lesson that year: stuff it down into you, because you'll need it.

Credit goes to Teddy Owens there, because he would have ensured we were properly fuelled up and hydrated.

It's all fun and games in the hotel, there's no shortage of wisecracks, but when you get on the bus the realization sinks in. It's real. It's serious. The thought of losing, of what that would mean . . . You can get hung up on that. The fear of losing can be greater than the will to win, and it can paralyse you. In later years you were encouraged to imagine positively, to focus on fielding a ball, sending a free over the bar or making a game-breaking tackle.

We'd have had music on the bus. When the gates opened to let you into Croke Park, the last song on the CD deck, which was the Wolfe Tones song 'Celtic Symphony', would be blaring. Fellas would stamp along with it. Then, as soon as the driver hit the brakes, fellas got up out of their seats and started roaring – 'Here we go now, lads' – to relieve the tension. Once you got into the dressing-room the silence settled down upon the team all over again. An hour till the throw-in.

There were no televisions in the dressing-rooms at that time, so if you wanted to see the minor game you had to stroll out the tunnel and watch it live. Not me: my ritual was to stay away from people as much as I could, just as I'd done in the hotel the night before.

I stayed in the dressing-room. I would never read the programme there; I like collecting them but I wouldn't look at it until we were on the way home after the game. I togged off straight away and got to the warm-up area to limber up, and made sure to get my stretching done.

At ten to three everyone was back in the dressing-room, wishing each other well, fully togged out. Landers said a few words, Jimmy said a few words, but at that stage . . . managers probably feel they have to say something, but how much do you take in? At five past three the knock on the door, you're going up the tunnel, flying out at a million miles an hour towards the sunlight. (It must be a GAA tradition, because Setanta and Aisake would have been reared with that, and out in Australia they stroll out on to the field before the game. You could pull something if you weren't well warmed up before sprinting out the way we do here.)

Deafening sound, light, you're focused, you work up a sweat – and then you have the President, and the parade.

The heart rate goes down and you're standing around in your sweat, which probably isn't ideal, but for all that I wouldn't get rid of the pre-match ceremonies, and the parade in particular. It's the last time you get to talk to yourself before the game begins.

I wouldn't spend the stroll around picking out people in the crowd. I'd look straight ahead, talking to myself in my head, reinforcing the three goals I set myself before the game.

It wasn't a matter of reminding myself of specific management instructions. We wouldn't have focused on their players that much – the only person who'd picked out their key man was Larry Tompkins, ironically enough. Jimmy had him talk to us before the final, and Larry stressed the importance of getting stuck into DJ Carey because he was so important to Kilkenny. I was used to Larry with the foot-ballers, and he was a good motivator, but the other hurlers were saying 'What's going on here?' The hurlers had overheard Larry's team talk to us before the Munster football final, and afterwards they said to me, 'Thank Christ we don't play football.' Larry lifted the roof of Páirc Uí Rinn that night.

Kilkenny had a very seasoned team – Pat O'Neill, John Power, DJ, Willie O'Connor, Andy Comerford, Canice Brennan, Philly Larkin, Charlie Carter and Brian McEvoy – and they probably had a point to prove after losing the previous year's All-Ireland final. But that can have an adverse effect on a team, too: the fear of losing another final can overwhelm the will to win.

That was the only year I was confident of beating Kilkenny. In other seasons we'd have been conscious of the players they had and what we needed to do to counteract them. But not in 1999. We didn't have much of a history with them – the only time we'd played them was in an All-Ireland minor final which we'd won well – and we were confident as a team.

Now, looking at the teams on paper, and the fact that Kilkenny had been in the previous year's final – there's no way we should have won. But I'll take it because we had games since then that we lost but maybe should have won.

It was bone dry when we came out, but when we went over to meet the President it started to pour out of the heavens and never stopped. That probably had an impact on the game, which was very scrappy.

We did well enough at the back, holding Kilkenny at bay and not conceding a single goal, but the forwards were finding it hard to make any headway.

I picked up DJ, but he alternated with Henry Shefflin, who was in the corner. I'd seen Henry before – he came in as a Kilkenny sub in our league game that year – but he'd really made his name with Waterford IT in the Fitzgibbon Cup. There was a touch of the trick card from Brian Cody, maybe, in playing him in that All-Ireland final, because an unknown often comes up trumps in that game –

look at Aidan Fogarty and Walter Walsh of Kilkenny in later finals – but certainly at that stage Henry wasn't King Henry, if you like. He was still a prince at that stage. That season he might have been their fourth- or fifth-best forward.

DJ was the man. For a long time during Henry's career I'd have thought, 'He's good but he'll have to do more to measure up to DJ.' In Aussie Rules the best forward is always matched up with the best back on the opposing team, second-best forward with second-best back and so on, because they're always trying to avoid a mismatch. In GAA it's a bit different, but in 1999 if you'd been following the Aussie model, you wouldn't have put your top defender on Henry; you'd have focused on DJ.

And anyway, Jimmy's approach wasn't to worry about that, but to line out how we lined out. The best man we had for DJ was probably Fergal Ryan, probably the quickest back and an established player, but he was in the corner.

At half-time we were positive. We knew we hadn't played up to scratch – we seemed to be reacting to them rather than playing our own game. But there was no panic. They hadn't scored a goal. The feeling was that we weren't flying but we were in touch, and could catch them on the counter late on.

Jimmy brought on Alan Browne and he got a good point, but Kilkenny got on top midway through the second half. There were a couple of signs that it was their day, maybe: Brian McEvoy cut a sideline over the bar, for instance, which was a hell of a score to get in those conditions: that put them three up and it wasn't a game in which you were going to get many goals.

We had a kick in us, though. Timmy McCarthy was moved to midfield and came into his own after Landers was substituted. Timmy started running at their defence and caused havoc. Kevin Murray came on as a sub and chipped in with a point, and Seanie McGrath was brilliant towards the end, having been held for most of the day.

We had the momentum late on and they couldn't come back at us. It's always good for a team, if their opponents have the upper hand, to get a score or two just to stay in touch, but we were on top in defence – and there just seemed to be far more Cork people there as well in the last quarter. The roar when we equalized was like something from an entirely different stadium.

In the second half, though, I felt physically sapped. Very low. And afterwards I went through what I'd done wrong by a process of elimination, and I realized I hadn't fuelled sufficiently at the pre-match meal. I'd had only a chicken breast and a slice of bread because I was too full from breakfast.

In later years I either forced it down or cut back on my breakfast to build up hunger for the pre-match meal, but that's the benefit of experience for you. In 1999 in the second half there was no gas left in the tank. At one stage I went for a drink during a break in play, and even though I was parched I found it hard to force the water down.

As the time ran out we were still ahead. The final whistle went and it seemed strange: I thought there was a free, but some of our subs started running onto the field, and Pat O'Connor took the ball and waved his arms.

All over.

Initially I thought, 'Is that it? Is that what 1990 was like, is this all there is?' It was almost an anticlimax. I thought, 'Fuck it, we've won it.'

I shook hands with DJ and some of the other Kilkenny players, and I remember thinking, 'That's it. That's what it's like to win an All-Ireland.'

When the others landed on top of me there was more of a sense of what it meant; the same when we went to Hill 16, where the Cork crowd were.

I remember Brian Cody coming into the dressing-room after the game. He took off his cap and he was very good, in fairness.

'Look, if there's any crowd we don't mind going down to, it's Cork,' he said. 'Ye deserved it on the day, we're disappointed after last year as well, but I know Jimmy for years, best of luck.'

No excuses, no complaints. Whatever you might say about the

Cats, if you beat them there's no cribbing: they take it and move on.

We went to a reception in the stadium afterwards. We were high as a kite after winning, and the Kilkenny lads didn't want to be there, so it was a strange room: one half jubilant, the other half depressed.

Back to the Burlington, where it was . . . crazy. After the TV formalities ended it was fall of Saigon stuff. The place was mobbed with Cork people, obviously; I met up with my family, people from my club and old faces from the Mon. There's a banquet for the winners but after that people are wandering in and out of the lobby, the carpark, the rooms.

I made it to bed at four, and I wasn't too bad because I wasn't drinking. But I got a call in the hotel room from local radio before eight the next morning and I'd say I sounded like the most hungover man in Ireland. I'd lost my voice from shouting and talking to people the night before, and I sounded like I'd been on the beer for the previous ten hours. A complete injustice.

Most of the players were together in the train carriage again, and you were able to catch up properly. Picking up the papers and seeing what was written about you. Any player that got a good write-up was torn to shreds, of course. 'Are you paying this fella to write this?' – that kind of crack. The atmosphere was electric.

We stopped in Mallow for a reception, and a few lads had to be helped on and off the train. But at least they were aboard.

One of the lads slept it out: he didn't get to sleep till about 10 a.m. and told the others to wake him when we were ready to leave, but they forgot. He came down to the lobby: no players, no bus. (He ended up getting a lift with someone and met up with us down in Cork, at least.)

When the train pulled in to Cork, it was the best homecoming I was ever at. The other homecomings took a different route, but in 1999 we came around Paddy Barry's corner and down over Patrick's Bridge. The traditional winners' journey in Cork. Huge crowds, people looking like they'd get squashed under the bus.

It made the whole thing real, to see fifty thousand people in the city welcoming us home.

On the Wednesday, though, I was down in Páirc Uí Chaoimh, training with the footballers.

Páirc Uí Rinn isn't that far away, and I could hear the P.A. working above there: Micheál Ó Muircheartaigh was up there commentating on the GOAL charity match between Cork and Limerick. The hurlers went out that night again but I didn't hook up with them. I was in football mode.

The footballers were outstanding to me on my first night back. They congratulated me individually and before we started training Larry spoke: 'Lads, before we start there, a round of applause for Seán Óg and congratulations on winning last Sunday; hopefully we can keep that going.'

He would have been good that way, in fairness, and the lads were very welcoming, genuine in their applause. But it was a miserable, wet evening and once we got out on the field Larry was barking the instructions. Back to business.

I hadn't been drinking but I'd had little enough sleep, simply put, since the previous Sunday. The hurlers' intercounty season was over but we had Meath that Sunday week.

I knew I'd be under pressure to hold my place after the semi-final disaster, but Larry reassured me.

'Look, you'll be playing,' he told me on the quiet during that same session. 'Get the other game out of your head. You'll be starting against Meath. The team isn't finalized, but you'll be full-back. Get your focus right for that.'

His reassurance helped. I'd been thinking about the semi-final – worrying about my performance – but the final was one of my best football performances of the year, which was a huge relief.

Winning the hurling helped as well. My attitude was, 'Well, I've won one anyway,' so I felt I had less to lose and I could have a right cut. And I'd been through the All-Ireland final routine already that year.

He also helped in one other way: he let me slip away when the footballers had press duties, so I didn't have another two hours on the field taking questions.

I prepared for the football final the same way I'd done for the hurling. I relaxed, well away from the public, on the Saturday night and the lead-in to the game, then ran along the same lines as the hurling final.

That helps hugely. If you're in a highly charged environment – and an All-Ireland final dressing-room qualifies comfortably on that score – then routine and regularity are a huge help. Tog on at this time; warm up at this time; out the door at this time. Break away from that and anxiety slips in.

Graham Geraghty had been playing full-forward all year for Meath, so I expected to pick him up. There were no specialist instructions from Larry or the selectors. I was told to tighten up compared to the semi-final, but they didn't harp on that game too much either.

Larry would have been quoted about me in later years, saying that I could coach myself, and I was mature enough at twenty-two. I didn't need to be told too much; I knew Geraghty would be a handful.

He was a player a lot of people had strong opinions about, but in my experience he played the ball, full stop. If it was there, he went for it hard; if it wasn't, there wasn't a word out of him.

Later that year he got into trouble for racially abusing an opponent when he was on the Compromise Rules trip in Australia, so people said, 'Oh, Seán Óg must have gotten that off him as well.' Not a bit of it. He said nothing to me.

I'd put him on the shortlist of top opponents I marked, certainly. Great athlete: few players can manage playing back and forward at intercounty level, but he could, easily.

Meath's game wasn't a matter of rocket science – they pumped the ball in long to a couple of good finishers up front. Ollie Murphy was one, and one of those balls broke to him, and he got a crucial goal.

We were well in the hunt even into the second half, but they had the wind behind them, and Trevor Giles started to use it, pointing long-range frees and 45s. They were probably that bit more experienced than us in terms of big games – a lot of them had All-Ireland medals from 1996, whereas most of our lads had never played a football final.

As the game wore on they had the belief they were going to win. Harsh as it sounds, when we didn't get our rhythm going in the second half, the way we had in previous games, I'd say the mentality clicked in: 'Look, we've had a good year, we've given a good account of ourselves and we'll be back again' – though that's not how it worked out for most of the lads.

At the full-time whistle I was disappointed to lose, but also relieved that I hadn't had a stinker, frankly. It wasn't that I did exceptionally well, but I was happy I'd done enough, given I was marking Graham Geraghty.

It certainly brought me down to earth after the joy of a couple of weeks before. I had an All-Ireland hurling medal, but the other lads on the football panel were coming away with nothing.

Afterwards, I experienced the truth that people just want to be associated with winners. After the hurling final, every Cork person in Dublin was trying to get in the windows and down the chimneys of the Burlington. The Cork crowd was much smaller at the football banquet. There were people waiting when we got off the train in Cork, but it was a fraction of the crowd a fortnight earlier.

At the end of that summer I was sick of it, to be honest. Na Piarsaigh were out of the hurling championship, but though we were still in the football I was keen enough for some time to myself. I'd spent the summer at everyone's beck and call.

There were consolations. I had finished my university studies and took some time off, during which I visited a lot of schools with the cup. Nine years after I'd seen Tony and Tomas and the lads rock up at the Mon with Liam MacCarthy, I was able to do the same myself. It was great. I enjoyed reminiscing with Nicky Barry and Gerry Kelly about playing for the Mon – 'Remember that day up in Effin' – that kind of thing. Priceless.

I saw some old friends in the primary school, too. Denis Burns, the man who taught me about *ubh* and *bainne*, and my old primary school teacher, Mícheál Ó Laoghaire. They were generous when we brought up the cup: 'You've come a long way,' and I thanked them. They were some of the people who'd helped me along the way.

There were plenty of other trips, and end-of-year socials. By Christmas I was cooked. So much for taking time off for myself!

But it was time to settle down. I sent out a few CVs as the year wore down, and I got a job with AIB finance and leasing. In Sandyford.

All the college years in Dublin, and here I was heading north again.

8

It'd be easy to say I knew we were in trouble early on in 2000, that I could see the warning signs, but that'd be wrong.

When we flipped to January on the calendar we were still living the dream. You're still going to gigs and events with the cup, you're getting your back slapped and hearing you're fantastic, you're not thinking of the fall from grace.

We were young. We weren't thinking about being the hunted in the new season. It was our first taste of success and we milked every minute of it as soon as the final whistle had gone in Croke Park.

I certainly wouldn't have seen warning signs in terms of lads over-doing the drink or anything like that. The culture of the time was that you trained hard, you played hard, and you partied hard, and our group was no different.

Early in the new year I was staying with John Hunt and his lovely wife Ber out in Knocklyon, which is at the foot of the Dublin mountains. I first came across them back in 1995 at the Anner Hotel in Thurles, before we played Galway in the All-Ireland minor hurling semi-final. They were going to see the game and I couldn't figure out how a Clare man living in Dublin would barrack for the Rebels.

My next encounter with John was after a league game in 1996. Jimmy came into the dressing-room in Páirc Uí Rinn and asked how I was going back to Dublin.

'By train,' I said.

'There's a guy outside driving back to Dublin, if you want a lift back for company,' Jimmy said. 'I've come across him before after Cork games and he is a decent man.'

So John and I headed off up the road together, and the rest is history, as they say. We are very good friends to this day. John is native of Tulla,

Co. Clare, but his father hailed from Doneraile in north Cork and brought him to all the Cork games, so he kept that tradition on himself. Good news for me: when I was in DCU and going to Cork for games, I'd get the train down and come back with John in the car.

We had some memorable trips over the four years I was studying in Dublin. This was before the motorway, when you rolled through every town from Watergrasshill to Naas, before hitting Dublin, and the speed limit wasn't under threat. As a driver, John only had one fault: his choice of music. He was infatuated with Engelbert Humperdinck. It was the only music he played on those car journeys. I didn't like his music, but I didn't want to disappoint John, so I let on for four years that I liked him. One day I asked his wife what the go was with Engelbert, and asked if she liked his music. She said she didn't, which was a relief to me. Years later, when I had moved back to Cork, John and Ber were heading on a road trip somewhere and Ber told him not to put Engelbert on. John didn't take this too well, and Ber replied by saying, 'Even Seán Óg never liked him.' Poor Ber had hung me out to dry.

Being in Dublin was a liberation. I'd get the bus from Knocklyon to Sandyford for work. Nobody ever said, 'Aren't you . . .' or came over to me for a chat about GAA. Happy days. After winning the All-Ireland, if I'd stayed in Cork I'd have been slaughtered everywhere I went, so the anonymity of being back in Dublin was terrific.

I worked in Dublin from January to June. During the week I fell in with St Vincent's for training. A mate of mine from college days, Ciarán MacCriostail, was playing for Vincent's and he organized for me to join in. The former Dublin footballer, Gay O'Driscoll, was training the team and Pat Gilroy was still kicking ball for them. I then headed home for the weekend for games. Working life in Dublin wasn't a whole lot different from my student life in Dublin.

Early in the year – end of February, March – Mark Landers was in Dublin for a work course for a couple of days, and he rang me. He wanted to do a bit of training.

Grand job: I had a run mapped out for myself out past Knocklyon, which looped up into the Dublin mountains and back down. I did it once a week on top of field sessions with St Vincent's to keep my endurance up. I told Landers to come out and do it with me, and he said, 'Sound, put me down for that with you Monday night.'

He came out and collected me after work, and off we went. Now in fairness I'd been doing it for a good while – I was well conditioned to the uphill climb at that stage and I'd do the whole circuit in thirty minutes.

But that night it took twice as long. Poor Landers struggled and had to stop a few times, blowing hard. This was with the National League practically on top of us, and I was thinking, 'He's only getting fit now?' The general attitude at that time – not just Landers – was, 'I'll be all right, come the championship.'

That mindset always worried me. In later years Dónal O'Grady summed it up perfectly by saying that 'Ah sure, championship, it's all on the day' was a load of rubbish. Another thing that irked me was the perception that I did training for fun – 'Well, Seán Óg does that because it comes natural to him, he's always training.' I hate to disappoint people, but I don't find training natural and at times I don't enjoy training at the top level. It's bloody hard work. The reason why I forced myself to do it was because there was no other way to achieve results and fulfil my potential. One of the reasons I had a long career is the effort I put in, but it was always an effort. I wasn't blessed with great skills, so I had to fanatically make up for it with sheer graft and commitment.

That was all in the future. Back in early 2000 the outlook was very different. If it had been a few years later, I'd have had a clear-the-air conversation with Landers: 'Look, you need to shape up, because this is serious shit.'

But I was twenty-two and he'd been the captain the previous year. I said nothing. At that point, though, it was a worry.

I had a hamstring injury early on in the league so I missed the

Kilkenny game in Nowlan Park. That game was over in ten minutes – obviously they wanted to put down a marker after losing the All-Ireland final. We lost some of the other games too, but there wasn't any panic.

The attitude to the league was different then. Nowadays if the reigning All-Ireland champions lost a couple of league games there'd be talk of a crisis in the camp. Back then, it was seen as a warm-up for the real stuff in the championship. The thinking was: you tried a few fellas, you rested others – and, as Landers was probably thinking, some fellas used the league to play their way into full match fitness.

And the way the championship turned out, the lack of panic seemed justified. We beat Limerick, thanks largely to Joe Deane's great goal, an overhead pull; we were well over Tipperary in the Munster final until Tommy Dunne got a couple of goals in the second half to make the closing stages of the game very exciting.

Tipp had hammered us in those challenge games early in 1999, remember, so they probably felt we'd lucked into a soft All-Ireland that year. I'm sure they felt they had every chance of turning us over.

What people probably remember from that game is Paul Shelly of Tipperary carrying Cusack around his back in the first half and winning a penalty, but Diarmuid O'Sullivan was well on top that day. It had been billed as the clash of the heavyweights, Sully versus Shelly, but Sully gave a best-on-ground performance that day. One of the best big-game players I've ever shared a dressing-room with.

That's the day the authorities decided to bring in the blood substitution rule, according to Doctor Con. At one stage Alan Browne took a big wide swing and connected with Fergal McCormack, splitting his head open; Fergal had to go off for a while, which left us down a man, and that, according to the Doc, spurred the authorities to allow temporary substitutions in case of blood injuries.

That was administration. We were Munster champions again: that meant celebration.

Once we'd beaten Tipperary we had an All-Ireland semi-final to prepare for, against either Offaly or Derry. I was sitting at home watching that one on television. Offaly were hot favourites, but Derry gave them a good rattle.

For us, that was a disaster. The best outcome for us would have been Offaly strolling past Derry at their ease, knocking over a huge score. The fact that Derry had given them a game, that we'd beaten them the year before, that they were all now a year older . . . those all became factors in our minds, eating away at the focus. The mindset wasn't right for that game.

To give management their due, it wasn't as though anyone said in the dressing-room beforehand that it was going to be a cakewalk. But unconsciously it was in my mind, and if it was in my mind I'd say it was in other players' minds. Nobody said, 'We'll handle this crowd easily.' The decay was more insidious than that.

For instance, that was a hot summer, and there were times down the Páirc for training that fellas would wear runners for training instead of their boots. Jimmy had to crack down on that.

It seems a small thing, right? Wrong. That's not on: it's only a step from that to lads wearing shades as they go training. You might think it's common sense, lads saying the ground's too hard to wear studs and that runners would be better for their feet, but that kind of slip in standards spreads like a disease within the group.

Jimmy warned us that Offaly were not a side to be underestimated – 'The time you expect to beat them they'll do a job on you.' He stressed that last year was last year and the shoe was on the other foot now. We were champions.

The night before the game there were warning signs as well. We broke with tradition and stayed out in City West on the Saturday night, rather than the Burlington. Cork were in the minor semi-final and Setanta was on the panel, so I had dinner with him and a couple of his team-mates before heading off to bed.

The story's gone around since then that some of the lads would have been up until all hours playing cards that night. I didn't see it. Like nearly all teams we would have had a card school among us – Alan Browne, Landers, Joe, Pat Ryan, Fergal Ryan, Ronan Dwane all played cards on the bus to and from games, but I wouldn't have seen that card game at first hand myself on that Saturday night.

The game itself went according to the script in the first half – Joe had a great first thirty-five minutes in particular – but as well as we were playing, we weren't finishing them off. We dominated the play but we didn't show that on the scoreboard, and in the second half the whole thing unravelled.

What happened to me was typical. I picked up a lot of ball myself, but Johnny Pilkington was my man and he got three points from play. If every forward gets three points from play in a game you'd be delighted with them. Gary Hannify started to dominate Brian Corcoran, our linchpin, and I ended up moving to centre-back for a while in the second half to try to rein Hannify in.

The longer the game went on, the better they got – they tightened up at the back and were able to cut out the lovely low ball that was flying into Joe in the first half. And any ball they got into our half they made count – economical, as usual – while we showed our immaturity.

We were only four or five points down, which isn't a huge deficit, but we started going for goals far too early: the classic sign of a team that's panicking.

The differences between 1999 and 2000 were twofold. We were probably playing as well, generally speaking, as we did in 1999, but that isn't good enough the following year. It never is. You only have to look at the Olympics, where a guy comes fourth in one Games with a time that would have guaranteed a gold medal in the previous Games.

The other difference was luck. Not that Offaly were lucky to beat us, but it was clear we'd had the breaks that were going in 1999. Everything had fallen our way. In the Munster final David Forde missed a free from twenty-one metres out at a vital stage, and Joe's goal in that game had come from Seanie McGrath swinging a hurley at a ball going wide. That ball could have gone anywhere. In the final, we'd got a let-off when Charlie Carter sent a goal chance flying over the bar in the second half.

In the euphoria of an All-Ireland win you don't sit down to analyse coldly how lucky you were, and rightly so. An All-Ireland's there to be celebrated, and we did so. Add in the fact that it's hard for lads who've never won an All-Ireland to recapture the hunger that enabled them to win that first medal, and it was always going to be a challenge to retain the title. We just didn't know that.

The Offaly game didn't go to the wire. It was gone long before the final whistle. Whatever we tried, it wasn't happening.

The dressing-room was shell-shocked afterwards. The game had been a rehearsal for the All-Ireland final, really, in our minds. We were recalling the previous year, and the month before the All-Ireland final, which is the best of times – the pay-off for the hard slog earlier in the year.

Training for those few weeks is great – your body is in peak shape and you only have to keep things ticking over. There's a carnival atmosphere, you're being fitted for your final suits, and there's the ultimate sign that you're having a good year: the evenings are closing in. You start the season, training in the dark of winter and, if you make the All-Ireland, you end your training sessions in the dark as autumn comes in.

That was in our minds before Offaly, there's no denying that. We'd had it the previous year, we were seventy minutes from the same thing all over again, then it was gone.

Jimmy made a speech in the dressing-room and we got the impression that he was gone, though he didn't announce it formally. Frank Murphy spoke immediately afterwards to say the team was still young and that he, Jimmy, was the man to take us forward.

From where I was sitting, though, I had a good view of Jimmy behind him, and he was shaking his head even as Frank spoke. He was finished. In fairness, as Jimmy has pointed out himself since, someone like Seanie McGrath would have been listening to him as manager for seven or eight years at that point.

The embarrassment afterwards is fresh in my mind. People threw it at us – 'Ah, ye were listening to the pundits, ye were cocky, ye fell into the trap.' You can't defend yourself when you've lost. It was a huge anticlimax.

The middle of the week after the Offaly game I got a call from New York: would I come and play hurling for the Limerick club out there? I'd left the AIB job in July because the travel up and down to Cork for training was taking its toll.

New York. Why not?

I'd been to the States briefly. At the end of 1999 there was a GAA trip there, to Canton near Boston, with the 1998 hurling All-Stars playing the All-Ireland champions, and the 1999 All-Ireland football finalists playing a game – I ended up playing one half in each game. The GAA there was relocating its playing fields and the matches were to mark that, but it was a short trip.

New York was different: I stayed there for three months. Myself and John Browne headed over and were put up by the club – both our own clubs back in Cork had been knocked out of the county championship. We weren't the only intercounty players playing in New York. We got to play alongside the Moran brothers, Ollie and James, Mark Foley and James Butler of Limerick. Browner's brother, Alan, came out later and played for Westmeath. Mark O'Leary, Liam Cahill, Eoin Kelly and John O'Brien of Tipperary all hurled for Tipperary New York, while James Ryall, Charlie Carter and Henry Shefflin of Kilkenny togged out for Kilkenny New York. I marked Henry Shefflin in one of the games; he was very good, but not the Karl-Heinz Rummenigge he became later.

I played football for Kerry out there as well – so there are probably pictures of me somewhere, in the green and gold – and they were a great bunch. There was one other Corkman with them, Louis Holland of Bantry, but they were mostly lads from Annascaul and Castlegregory, a right west Kerry mafia, but great lads, very decent. They always had a priest in to bless the team before a game; sometimes, however, the help was a bit more earth-bound: they brought over the likes of Johnny Crowley and Dara Ó Cinnéide to help in big games.

They were mostly living in Queens, and the Limerick hurlers were based up in the Bronx, so I did a fair number of hours on the subway, heading to training at the different venues.

I was the quintessential tourist when I got there first: I had a crick in the neck looking at the buildings and wandering around, thinking to myself, 'Oh, that place there was in such-and-such a film.'

Visiting Manhattan for the first time was an unbelievable experience. I did all the things you're supposed to do: went to the top of the Empire State Building, and the Twin Towers, which at that time were still standing at the tip of the island. Of course, you can't get away from the GAA, no matter where you go on earth. When I got to the top of the World Trade Centre, who did I bump into? Tommy Dunne from Tipperary, the man who got the goals against us in the Munster hurling final a couple of months beforehand.

Of course you get used to it. After a couple of weeks the skyscrapers don't register at all. What I remember particularly was the nightlife: going to clubs late at night and leaving at 9 a.m. with the party still going strong behind you as you stepped out into the daylight. Inside it was dark, and it could have been any time of the day or night, but you came outside and ended up going for scrambled eggs for breakfast.

Boxing was another highlight of the Big Apple. From an early age I'd had an interest in boxing, and Dad would have gotten us up out of bed in Australia for heavyweight world championship fights involving Mike Tyson, Tim Witherspoon and Larry Holmes. During the nineties, cable TV got a grip on the American boxing world. We could watch fighters like Frank Bruno, Lennox Lewis, Chris Eubank, Michael Watson, Nigel Benn, Steve Collins and Richard Woodhall, but not the big US bouts. A good mate of mine from college, Ciarán Ó Méalóid, had gone to the States on work experience in 1997 and he told me to check up on a boxer by the name of Roy Jones Junior. He had seen him fight in the States that year. While in the States I started to get fascinated by other tremendous fighters like Oscar de la Hoya, Bernard Hopkins and Felix Trinidad.

You have to remember that the Internet wouldn't have been at the level it's at now, with YouTube and so on; these were guys you'd heard of vaguely, but there was little enough footage of them available. So that was the life: you could stay in and watch the boxing and then head out to one of those all-night clubs afterwards. They only warmed up around 4 a.m. Usually we'd go to Nevada Smith's first, because a Cork guy owned it, and head on to a club around Webster Hall. If we wanted to mix it up, there were other places on the West Side, old industrial warehouses that had become hip dance venues.

The lads from the team showed us the ropes. One of them, Tadhg O'Callaghan, was from Charleville and had been on the Cork minors with me. He looked after us that way: telling us where to go, where to avoid.

And how to dress. Back in Cork, lads would tuck the nice smart shirt into the chinos when heading out to a nightclub, but that wouldn't do in New York when we were there; if you tried that look, lads would think you were dressing for an entrance interview in Harvard. Tadhgie showed us that T-shirts and jeans, the casual look, was what was required. He made sure we didn't look like Carlton from *The Fresh Prince of Bel-Air*.

I became friendlier with John Browne over there, too. We'd been on the same Cork teams for about five years, but we got to know each other much better when we shared a house in the Bronx.

The Cork minors made the All-Ireland final that summer, and we wanted to see that because Setanta was on the team. We played a game in Manhattan the day before, went out for the night – the whole night – and fell into a pub that was showing the game. We had our breakfast, saw the minor game – Galway beat Cork – and were home before the final whistle went in the senior game. We didn't bother waiting for the end.

I was never tempted to stay in New York. After 2000 I felt we had unfinished business.

9.

Tom Cashman took over from Jimmy. He'd been a selector, so he knew us all well. He was a living legend as a player, but an unassuming man. Even as a selector, when Jimmy asked him if he wanted to speak before games, Tom might say a few words but would rarely hog the mike; and he didn't change too much when he took over. He'd say the last few words before we went out to play, but it was left to Ted Owens, in large measure, to drive it on. That's not to say Ted overstepped the mark, or took over, but it wasn't Tom's form to be the centre of attention. That was just his personality.

The training bordered on torturous at times over the winter. We were in Páirc Uí Chaoimh, but not on the pitch.

What would happen was that the tunnel under the stands and terraces of the Páirc would be opened up all the way around to create a complete circuit – all the dividing gates would be pulled back fully – and you'd do laps of the stadium in that tunnel. There was great endeavour in that, but it was hard to sustain. You were going to a dreary environment, dark, damp and unwelcoming, on miserable nights, and it got monotonous for everyone. It served its purpose, to get fellas somewhat conditioned, but it wouldn't be acceptable according to the sports science that's now available.

It's surprising we didn't pick up more injuries, pounding away on a concrete surface with dips and hollows and puddles of water and dampness in places that the sun never reached. Fellas slipped and fell sometimes, and it's surprising no one got seriously hurt.

We did a couple of laps to warm up, and then there were competitive laps to finish up with, before we headed into the gym room for weight training. For the competitive laps you'd have the *maillot jaune* group, consisting of the two O'Connors, Pat Mulcahy, Brian Corcoran, Mickey O'Connell and myself. In the peloton you'd have the majority of the lads. Then there was the Teletubby group, who would be looking for petrol tickets in the back. It wasn't unusual to see Cusack with the Teletubbies, not because of weight issues but because initially he wasn't a great runner. Being the competitor he was, he improved as the years went on and worked himself up to the head of the peloton. The likes of Diarmuid O'Sullivan, Kevin Murray, Fergal McCormack, Mark Landers and Alan Browne would have featured in the rearguard. Jesus did they hate the tunnels, and running, full stop. Guys like Fergal Ryan and Joe Deane would also have started there, but moved into the middle of the pack as they got fitter. Those lads were fast-twitch athletes, with great explosive power. They weren't suited to middle- or long-distance running, but over twenty metres they were supreme and got their own back on the rest of us. No coincidence they were all in the inside line, full-back or full-forward, constantly racing for possession against their men.

The lads in the half lines and midfield needed endurance, of course, but speed was something we could have worked on more as we weren't naturally blessed with it. That was certainly true of me – I worked nowhere near as hard as I should have back then compared to later years. Even at that stage the game was gradually becoming more about speed and power.

In fairness to that group of players, the commitment was there. Some of them partied hard, but they did whatever was asked of them in training, and put themselves through whatever it took to get them right.

One of the most significant games for us – ever – was the league game against Wexford in the spring of 2001.

Wexford set out their stall early on. I picked up Darren Stamp, who was wing-forward and just out of minor ranks. He was a fiery competitor. When the ball was thrown in, I got the hurley into the ribs. It was the same all over the field: Wexford went the physical route.

Whether we weren't prepared for it mentally, or we weren't tuned in, the day turned into a disaster for us. They had a good home crowd roaring them on in Enniscorthy and they were well on top: every time a Cork guy was put down, there was a huge cheer. It was a long day at the office.

Mike Morrissey from Newtownshandrum was playing centre-forward for us and there was a knot of players around the ball at one stage. He went down after a pull and he stayed down. His ankle was broken. Destroyed.

Lads going over to see what was happening ducked away when they saw how bad the injury was, and he was carried off. Later, Brian Corcoran got the ball, and Paul Codd charged into him. Corcoran went off with an injured collarbone.

We weren't equipped for that kind of game, that level of aggression. Our training wasn't geared for it at all – at the time a lot of the skills sessions were high speed, but you weren't put under physical pressure from an opponent in them. There was nobody flicking your elbow with his hurley, or poking your back or legs as you tried to control the ball; there was no replicating what happens in a game, when you rarely get time and space to handle the ball on your own.

Nowadays, if you go to any intercounty training session you'll see there's plenty of contact in the skills sessions. We were picking the ball up on our own, no pressure, whereas now you'll see one player picking the ball in a drill and two others coming in to hit him as he does so, to replicate match conditions.

Wexford bullied us, and it was a lonely ride back to Cork. Nothing was said to address the fact that we'd been beaten, or how we'd been beaten, or the fact that we needed to step up the approach in training. We should have cleared the air ahead of the championship, but the soul-searching that was done on the way back was strictly a matter for individuals.

Limerick were confident ahead of our date with them in the championship. They had won their first of three U-21 All-Irelands in a row, we'd only just beaten them the year before, thanks to Joe's spectacular goal, and they had no doubt noticed what happened to us against Wexford's physical approach.

The Thursday before that game I was in Dublin for a Guinness promotion – they were sponsors of the hurling championship at the time. I headed back to Cork after lunch for training. A pal of Dad's, Enda McDonnell, was recovering from an accident, and he lives between Roscrea and Templemore, so I said I'd drop in on the way. I had time to spare.

As soon as I got in, his wife Olive rolled out some grub, and we chatted away until about half-four, when I had to head off for training.

I went through Templemore and made for the main road back to Thurles. I was panicking a little, because time was pushing on and you don't want to be late on to the field for training the week of the championship.

I was near Loughmore-Castleiney – close to the home place of Paul Ormond, the Tipperary hurler – and there was a car ambling along in front of me. I spent a while considering whether to overtake, and then I said to myself I'd go for it.

There was a bend up the road, and as soon as I swung out and tried to pass I knew I was in trouble. I should have just braked and come back in, but I was young and thought I was invincible, and I carried on.

I saw flashing lights as a car came towards me. Bang: a head-on collision.

After the noise, the impact, I realized the radio was still on in the car. The crash had turned my car around, and I was facing back the way I'd come, towards Templemore. The car that I'd collided with was jammed up against the ditch. When I got to my senses and realized what had happened I started shouting and roaring.

I looked down and saw a big lump in the middle of my thigh. At the time I thought it was just a swelling from a bruise on my leg; in fact it was my kneecap. There was no pain initially: I was in shock, the adrenalin was pumping.

After a few seconds the driver of the other car came over to me. (It turned out he'd been bringing four kids to a soccer game, and the only one who was hurt seemed to be the one sitting in the middle of the back seat, who got a bit of a scrape.) Now, I'd been on the wrong side of the road, and the other driver was well within his rights to lift me out of it. When he got close enough to see me, your man said: 'Don't tell me you are Seán Óg Ó hAilpín?'

The front of my car was like an accordion, all squashed in, so the door was crushed too tight for me to open it myself, but he was able to yank it free. I tried to get out, but I couldn't lift my leg off the floor of the car.

When I eventually worked my way out of the car, my leg buckled underneath me, and the pain started to kick in. The other driver helped me over to sit down on the ditch, and Garda cars, the fire brigade and ambulances started to arrive.

That's when I started thinking of the game that Sunday. It was 24 May, two days after my twenty-fourth birthday, and at that point I was thinking a couple of days' rest would sort me out.

I was taken by ambulance to Nenagh Hospital and X-rayed, and the pain was excruciating. They dosed me with morphine.

The doctor explained to me late that night that your kneecap floats on top of the joint, where it's held in place by tendons. I'd severed the tendon below the kneecap, which was like cutting an elastic band – nothing held the bone in place. My thigh muscles pulled the kneecap up my leg.

The doctor said I'd have to fast because they wanted to bring me to Limerick for an operation. I rang home to tell them I'd been in an accident but that I was OK, and then I rang Tom Cashman.

At first he thought I was putting him on – 'Tell me you're kidding me' – but when he realized I was serious, his only concern was about my health. The game didn't come into it.

I rang Dr Con and he thought I was pulling his leg as well until I convinced him I was in the hospital in Nenagh. And straight away he asked to speak to the doctor there and he told him to send me down to CUMH for an operation. That's the kind he is: as soon as he knew I was in trouble he made sure I was looked after properly.

I slept for a while, and when I woke up John Hunt was there beside the bed – he'd driven down from Dublin when he heard. Then I was taken to CUMH, where I met the family. They were cut up, but relieved that I'd survived a head-on crash.

The surgeon, Dr Kieran Barry, came along and explained the procedure to me. I asked if I'd be OK for Sunday. He was probably thinking, 'Is this guy for real?' He said no, that I'd be out for the rest of the year and that Dr Con would talk to me after the operation.

He said the fact that I was in good shape had helped me. If I hadn't been at a peak fitness, three days out from a championship game, I could have suffered other significant injuries, he said.

But all that stayed with me was the loss of a season. That's what I fixated on as he said goodbye and left.

The tears came down my face then.

After the operation the doc came in to have a good chat to me.

'The surgery was a success,' he said. 'In terms of rehab, though, not many people come back after an injury like that, not to the highest level. But I know you will.'

Whether he believed it or not, I don't know, but it was encouraging.

The family came in, and John Anderson came up to see me, and there was a bit of talk about getting me down to the Páirc for the game, but I was raw enough after the operation, and I didn't want the focus to be on me, sitting uncomfortably on the bench, when there was a championship game for the lads to win.

John Anderson came back up to the hospital to watch the game on TV with me that Sunday. I told him to head away down to the Páirc, but he stayed. As the game went on you could sense it wasn't going Cork's way. With Corcoran injured, Pat Mulcahy went in to centre-back, and there were other changes made because I was out, and the lads were probably a bit unsettled by all of that.

In the second half Sully came out with the ball, did a Jonah Lomu on Jack Foley and hit a point from a hundred yards. It was a great moment, but Cork couldn't press it home. You could see it wasn't going to be our day.

That year the backdoor system kicked in only after the Munster final, so that was the season over. In a strange way, being selfish, if there was a year to miss it was 2001, when the entire championship for Cork consisted of just seventy minutes.

I was in hospital until the following Wednesday. I remember visits from Jim Cronin, who was chairman of the Cork County Board at the time, and Ted Owens and Tom Cashman, and Graham Canty and Ronan McCarthy and Aidan Dorgan from the football team.

The tendon was stitched together with mesh and the kneecap reattached. I had had a stroke of luck in that the bone wasn't cracked or broken, which helped in the healing process. My whole leg was in a cast, hip to ankle, and that was on until early August.

While wearing the cast I had exercises to do – squeezing the quad for five seconds at a time, because it wasn't being worked, obviously. In the early weeks the leg was sore from the operation, but I tried hard with the squeezes – hundreds upon hundreds of them, over and over again.

It was awkward early on. Getting around was hard because I had to sit in the back seat of the car, manoeuvring in and out. Night-times were long, as you couldn't turn in the bed without pain.

But gradually the pain turned to itching, which encouraged me. I upped the exercise regime to tying bags of sugar around my ankle, and lifting the leg up and down, up and down, up and down. That was all I could manage with the plaster still on.

I did hundreds of sit-ups, chin-ups and push-ups, morning, noon and evening. We had a pole mounted in the shed at home, so I got Setanta and Aisake to lift me up to the pole for chin-ups. They'd hold me while I was doing them, but they were at it as well and we'd end up having competitions with each other. Aisake was and still is the king at chinnies.

Diet was something else I kept an eye on. My old failing, the ice cream, was always a temptation.

The doctors played down the chances that I'd ever get back to the level I'd been at, but I treated that as a challenge. I swore to myself I'd get back, that I'd play intercounty again.

As part of that I went to as many games and training sessions with the club as I could manage. I was determined not to be a hermit: there were times Mum would be gone to town and I'd be stuck in the house on my own, but any other time when I could get out I would.

When the time came for me to get the cast off, my leg was like a matchstick, all wasted away. I thought I'd been ticking over with thousands of sit-ups and so on, but seeing my leg like that was a huge knock. I'd read *Miracle in the Andes* while I was recovering, and there's a passage where two survivors of the plane crash leave camp and climb to the top of a mountain, thinking rescue will be on the other side, only to despair when they see mountains upon mountains ahead of them. That was how I felt when I saw my leg.

It was a disaster. I felt like looking in the cast for the muscles from my leg. It was unbelievably weak, and so stiff that if I bent it more than one degree I nearly had to bite my knuckles with the pain.

I was given a knee brace to support it for a few weeks; the aim was to get me back walking, to a decent standard of living. I had a different aim: to make it back playing with Cork.

I was going into the unknown with that aim, though, and that saved me. I didn't know what was ahead of me, so I was optimistic all the time. The aim to get the red jersey back seemed realistic to me – I didn't know any better. My attitude evolved from 'Why me, God?' to 'Thank you, God.' I started to see things differently. You realize gradually there are other people who are in a worse situation, and you latch on to the fact that there's hope. And because of that, you go for it.

By August I was in the middle of rehabilitation. I had physiotherapy up in the Orthopaedic Hospital in Cork – treadmill walking, exercises, all of that stuff, just to get the nerves stimulated because they'd been shut down for a couple of months.

The funny thing was the first thing every morning, waking up: I'd have forgotten about the car crash; it was a case of eyes open and ready for the day, then the memory of the crash would come back. After that I'd try the leg to see if there was even a millimetre of extra movement in it.

There were little victories along the way: the first time I was able to walk on my own, without crutches, for example. But progress was slow until a friend intervened.

Jimmy McEvoy was a masseur with Cork, a friend of mine from Blarney, and he'd fallen in working with Ger Hartmann, the physical therapist from Limerick, when Ger was helping Kenyan athletes in London.

I didn't know much about Ger Hartmann – I thought he was German with a name like that – but Jim said to me that if there was one guy who could help me to rehab, it was Ger. I was up for anything that would help, so I asked if he'd put in the word. Although he was up the walls with work, Ger said if I made it to Limerick he'd have a look at me at least.

Ger had a plastic skeleton in the room. He showed me what had happened and what would have to be done. When I hopped up on the examining table, he said, 'Oh, we have a bit of work to do here.'

He started digging into my muscles – calf, quad, poking around, paying little enough attention to the knee. It was savage sore – my leg was very soft because of the lack of physical activity, and I was sweating bullets. I was also thinking, 'Why's he digging into every part of my leg bar the knee? It's my knee that's the problem.'

Eventually he moved the knee, and there was a visible improvement in the range of movement. He'd loosened out the muscles completely.

The session lasted about an hour and a half. At the end, he said there was a lot of work to be done and he wasn't giving any guarantees, but he said we'd work away and see where it got us. He gave me a programme to follow for three weeks, building up strength in my wasted muscles – quad exercises, leg-raises, mini-squats and balancing on my injured leg, and then balancing blindfolded on the leg.

That was the winter. Every three weeks or so I'd go up to be assessed by him, and every time he'd improve the flexibility in the knee another bit. Another win. Another advance.

He said I'd never get the range of motion back to what it had been, to what it is in my left leg, owing to a range of factors, including scar tissue after the operation and permanent damage to the knee. But he added that I wasn't a gymnast. The deficit wouldn't affect my running and jumping.

That was positive, but sometimes in the three-week cycle the knee would react. I'd go through a heavy session and the next morning the knee would be swollen. I sometimes doubted that I was going to make it, but I continued with the programme. I always followed it religiously.

By November he had me running.

It wasn't a great return. There's a soccer pitch down the road from the family home in Blarney, and one morning in November Jim McEvoy drove me down to it.

'Do one lap,' he said.

I managed one, and Jim said to try another, and I did, but then I had to stop. I hadn't run in six months and I thought I was going to have a heart attack. It was great to be back running, but that first attempt only showed how far I had to go.

The next day I tried a third lap. A couple of days after that, a fourth lap. Building up all the time.

Ger gave me other exercises as well, quirky ones to work on my twisting and turning: hopping up and down stairs on one leg, for example. That one tormented my family as I bounced noisily while they were watching television.

I was in the pool, exercising. In the gym, lifting much heavier weights. Doing balancing exercises, again with the eyes closed to trigger the nerves to work.

The only downside, as I moved into 2002, was that I hadn't touched a hurley since the accident.

Bertie Óg Murphy had taken over from Tom Cashman as the Cork hurling manager, and he rang me to ask how I was going. At the end of January I went back with Cork.

The training had moved from Páirc Uí Chaoimh up to our place, Na Piarsaigh, where you could do the work indoors. I didn't mind where the training was, I was so thankful to be back.

My approach to training – to everything – changed. I appreciated my opportunities a lot more. I didn't let things off, to be taken care of the next day. I'd been in the habit, at the end of a session, of grabbing five balls and taking five sideline cuts in a row, but if the session had been heavy I might skip it. Not after the accident: I made sure I took them, no matter what. If there was a run to be done, I'd push it to five yards beyond the finishing line.

The intensity that I brought to training post-injury had its downsides in later years. If we were doing a run during winter training, I'd tell myself that if I didn't win it I'd have a terrible season: putting myself under huge pressure. Or I'd have to win the last sprint, or squeeze out another few chin-ups.

Those became benchmarks for me. They drove me on, but there's a thin line between using them to your advantage and leaving your best form on the training ground.

The accident put paid to my Cork football career.

I decided to concentrate on hurling. Ger Hartmann had advised me strongly to focus on one code, as this would give the knee a better chance to recover. Hurling was my first choice.

My right knee will never be as good as the left – I can bring the heel on my left leg up to touch my backside, but my right heel won't go all the way up because the knee won't bend that far. I feel any damp or cold in it, as it gets very stiff, and winter training in the couple of years after the accident was hard enough. But compared to the outlook when I was sitting on the side of the road in Loughmore-Castleiney on that May afternoon, I'll take it.

It was my worst year hurling-wise, and it got worse, not better, as the year and the games rolled on.

No matter what I wanted to do on the field of play, I was always playing catch-up: slightly off the pace, slightly behind the ball. Looking back now, it was as if my mind and body weren't in sync – which is hardly surprising, given the nature of the injury I'd had.

I survived. I did OK. But the only game I was satisfied with that year was the very last one, against Galway.

Given the effort I'd put in to get back, that made 2002 hugely frustrating for me. I'd been rehabbing the knee like a maniac in the belief that I'd be right as rain once I got back, but that was far from the case.

Experience comes in here again, though. I took the lessons I picked up coming back from that injury into the other knocks and recovery periods that I went through afterwards. Granted, I didn't have any other injuries as serious as the car crash, but I was better able to deal with the inevitable setbacks when rehabbing.

There's a misconception that once a guy gets himself physically fit after an injury or an accident he's ready to go, good as he ever was. That's not true at all; in my case, when I had the knee back to a level where I could train at intercounty level, there was still tightness, soreness, stiffness. I wasn't miles off the pace, but just that few percentage points away from the top level.

It was inevitable, having lost almost a year of hurling, but that was no consolation to me. I'd always been honest enough about my need to have the hurley in my hand constantly, to keep my touch sharp, but returning from the injury taught me I had to step up my hurling skills a level or two.

You can be fit – very fit – but hurling fitness is totally different – hurling fit. That can be hard to explain to people, but in a game like hurling, there's no time to think. That was my big problem when I came back: though I was physically fit according to the split times I was achieving in running drills, I was thinking about my hurling, and when you're hurling fit that doesn't happen because you act before the thought even forms. A ball breaks and you're on to it before the brain even sends the signal – that's what it feels like, anyway.

I realized I needed more hurling. Whether that was off the wall at home or in the ball alley up in Na Piarsaigh, I needed to do more.

The knee wasn't one hundred per cent that year. I'd be well aware of a heavy training session or a hard game the morning afterwards, thanks to the throbbing in my right leg. It never got to the point where I couldn't get out of bed, but it'd be raw and sore, and very swollen.

Because I was still trying to get myself right, I wouldn't have been fully cognizant of the growing unrest within the squad, or of the growing influence of the Gaelic Players Association. Now that the GPA is officially recognized by and is part of the GAA itself, it's hard to remember that there was a time when it was trying to establish itself as a player representative body. Back then, it was regarded as a nuisance by many within the Association, and nuisance is putting it mildly.

I didn't fully appreciate the importance of the GPA's work at first. I had other priorities, for starters getting back on the Cork senior hurling team. I eventually came to my senses, though, because here was a body that was airing grievances we had been afraid to talk about publicly.

Still, there were incidents you couldn't overlook. The bus journey from Cork to Derry and back, for one. Fellas had to get off work early on a Friday, head up on a bus to Monaghan, overnight in a hotel there, get on the bus again the next morning and drive on further to Swatragh, in Derry, play the game and get back on the bus for the trip all the way back to Cork.

In previous years there'd been flights for a trip like that. The County Board claimed they'd looked for flights, but there was a strong sense in the panel that everything was being done for the convenience of the Board rather than to facilitate the players. Niall McCarthy, one of the youngest players on the panel in 2002, picked up a serious facial injury. Although he received some attention at the game, it was clear on the long bus journey home that he needed more work done to the gash on his cheek. As bad as that journey was for the rest of us, it must have been horrendous for Niall, and to this day I don't know how he managed it. He was new to the panel so I didn't know him too well, but I was to find out in the coming years that Niall is one tough hombre. When we got back from Derry in the early hours of Monday morning, Niall's mum collected him and took him to the regional hospital to get properly patched up.

There would have been tension about the GPA, too. Frank Murphy was a selector that year, and he was not amused when there were Cork players photographed at the GPA conference. An atmosphere was building, and it came to a head for the league final that year.

What was the fuss about? We qualified for the league final and so did Kilkenny, and a protest was agreed to forward the cause of the GPA. Both teams – ourselves and Kilkenny – would roll their socks down and leave their shirts untucked for the pre-match parade. But word came down from Kilkenny a couple of days beforehand that the players were being pressurized not to go along with the protest. Andy Comerford rang us with that news, but he said he'd do it anyway, and he did.

As protests go, two teams with their jerseys out and socks down was hardly going to bring the GAA crashing down around everybody. The fact that Kilkenny didn't even do that pissed us off no end. That's the kind of thing that would annoy you more than anything that happens on the field of play – when you need people to stand by you, and particularly when they've committed to doing that and don't go through with it.

From a Cork perspective, our admiration for Andy skyrocketed, because what he did couldn't have been easy. He showed serious *liath-róidi*. What annoyed us was that, apart from that handful of guys, Kilkenny reaped the benefits without taking any of the brickbats. I know Peter Barry commented after the league final that he was only interested in wearing the jersey, which didn't go down well with us. I also know that he rang Dónal Óg years later to explain what had happened and to add that he was behind what we were doing; but by that stage, for me, the damage was done.

But the protest wasn't unanimous on our side either, it has to be said. Some of the players didn't go along with it, so you could say we weren't in the strongest position at the time to be criticizing Kilkenny for not rowing in with it.

We lost the league final as well, and when you lose you hear it: 'Concentrate on playing, that's what you're there for, and leave the administration to the administrators.'

Morale leaked away after the league final. The team was fractured. Nobody stood up and made a stirring speech along the lines of 'This GPA is a load of rubbish, ignore it,' but it was clear that there were mixed feelings. Not all of our guys had taken part in the protest before the league final, and I recall Alan Browne not being in favour of the GPA. The same Alan ended up being a tower of strength for the panel later on when it was needed.

Waterford beat us in the championship. We had a chance to progress through qualifiers, but in terms of the atmosphere it might as well have been ten years previously, departing after a defeat in the first round.

We beat Limerick in a qualifier; John Gardiner made his Cork senior debut as a nineteen-year-old that day. The next qualifier, against Galway, in Semple Stadium, had a farcical prelude. We were in the dressing-room, waiting to go out as Cork versus Tipperary wound down outside in the Munster football final, which ended in a draw. Diarmuid O'Sullivan had played in that game and he was barely in our dressing-room before the number 3 hurling jersey was thrown over to him and he was gone out again with us. No rehydration, probably gulped down a banana and out for another seventy minutes.

Galway tanked us. We had no foundation, no heart, no passion – no team. If fellas are unhappy off the field, it'll show on the field, and the first thing fellas do when the ship is sinking is they look after themselves. There's no unity. Fellas were just happy the season was over.

Journalists were allowed in the dressing-room at that time, and I was asked what had gone wrong. I said something along the lines of, 'If you don't pick the best team . . .' That was a reference to Setanta, who'd been on fire in some challenge games we'd played, but didn't make the squad – he'd been asked to come along and carry the hurleys. I was frustrated on his behalf.

That was reported, and Alan Cummins later backed that up in an interview of his own. But those were just a few comments after a disappointing loss, not a call to the barricades.

I hopped into the car with Siobhán and her uncle, and we headed out to her house. As far as I was concerned, I wouldn't see the rest of the lads until the pre-season for 2003.

The rumbling started when Dónal Óg called out the *rúnaí* in a radio interview. A lot of fellas had probably done that in private, but he did it in public. It made waves pretty quickly, and the likes of Landers rowed in behind him to back him up, but it wasn't an orchestrated, pre-choreographed campaign.

Cusack was standing up to the shit that was being thrown at players – he was making the point that what people saw was only the tip of the iceberg. He was trying to convey that the supporters had no idea what was going on and shouldn't pass judgement based on what they saw at games. There was a constant battle with the Board over player welfare. Training gear and boots were slow in coming, or nonexistent. We wanted membership of gyms convenient to players, not convenient for the Board. Tickets for players was an issue. Niall McCarthy's injury was an issue. It started to mount up. I'd been in hospital in 2001 for the Limerick game so I'd missed out on the pre-amble to that match — the Garda escort to Páirc Uí Chaoimh not turning up, the lads having to go in cars and getting caught in the crowd, getting in just in time for the game and then having to piss in buckets in the corner of the gym. Limerick won that game by a point.

By early October I was asked to go to a meeting in a solicitor's office in the South Mall. The solicitor was Diarmaid Falvey, a club-mate of Cusack's. I didn't know him before I walked into his office, but he became one of our strongest allies: a man you could trust with your life.

Not every panellist was there, but Fergal Ryan, Mark Landers, Joe Deane, Dónal Óg, Diarmuid O'Sullivan and Alan Browne were all present: elder statesmen and my generation, if you like.

We talked about incidents which had occurred over the previous year or so, but we didn't meet that night to go on and pick a fight. The theme of that meeting was more along the lines of 'The way we're going, what chance do we have, realistically, of seeing Croke Park?'

That was the bottom line for us, but people missed out on that point. We were trying to improve things in order to improve our chances of success. It wasn't as if we woke up one morning and decided to cause trouble with the Board. All of us had better things to be doing than meeting up like that, but we felt it was important. It was about Cork winning, pure and simple. Not money. Not the GPA. Not pay for play. It was a matter of concerned players, after a terrible season, looking to improve things.

We called a meeting with the Board to discuss our concerns, and we were invited down to the inner sanctum, Frank's office, to meet them.

It didn't go well.

For one thing, there were too many people there. It's hard enough to get anything decided if you have three or four people sitting around a table, but there must have been twenty to thirty people at that meeting. Too many players, too many Board representatives. It was a futile exercise.

Initially it was all lovey-dovey and plenty of jokes, but the longer the meeting went on, the more we felt the Board were using the meeting to show off their one-liners.

When we discussed gear, for instance, one of the Board reps asked if we were thinking of opening a sports shop. We mentioned the meals after training down in Páirc Uí Chaoimh – some people wanted to shower after a session and get home, while others, after a long day's work and a hard training session, took their time before heading in for the grub. If you did take your time, though, you got the message in the dressing-room from the catering staff to hurry up because they wanted to go home. That annoyed players, because we thought, in our innocence, that the meal was for the benefit of lads who were putting in a huge effort in training. When we mentioned it in that meeting, though, the Board's reaction was to ask what the difference was between your mother calling you in for dinner and the kitchen staff putting the hurry-up on you.

Frank said very little in the meeting, but he did react to a comment I had made about him. I said that as *rúnaí* Frank had too much influence over team affairs, and he didn't like that: he said that others were putting words in my mouth and that I didn't believe what I was saying.

Our relationship went to another level after that. A lower level, needless to mention.

I wasn't the only one who felt the lash. Kevin Murray would have backed me up, saying that he'd often seen Frank influence selectors on the sideline, regarding substitutions, and Frank's response was, in essence, that Kevin would know because he'd sat on every bench in Ireland.

Then it got heated. No more lovey-dovey.

The meeting fizzled out without coming to a conclusion. We'd brought in a list of points we wanted addressed, and the Board said they'd take it away and consider it, fair enough. We thought the

My brother Teu, my sister Sarote and me, at home in Greenacre, Sydney

In Na Piarsaigh gear, aged 12, holding the U-13C Bord na nÓg trophy, in 1989

With the Cork Primary Schools select football side that I captained against Dublin at Páirc Uí Chaoimh in 1989. I'm standing in the back row, fifth from the left

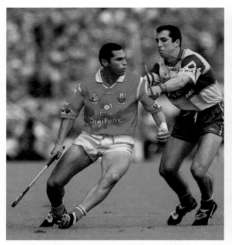

The 1999 Munster final against Clare: I'm being marked by Enda Flannery. Our victory ended a long drought for Cork in the Munster championship, and put us on the road to the All-Ireland title (*Brendan Moran/Sportsfile*)

We lost the 1999 All-Ireland football final to a fine Meath team. Graham Geraghty, marking me here, was one of the best footballers I ever came up against (*Ray McManus/Sportsfile*)

Arriving at the Imperial Hotel with Dónal Óg Cusack, Fergal Ryan and Diarmuid O'Sullivan for the press conference at which we announced we were going on strike in November 2002 (*Pat Murphy/Sportsfile*)

With Setanta after the final whistle of the 2003 All-Ireland final, which we lost to Kilkenny. I was disappointed with my own performance. That was Setanta's last match for Cork before he headed down under to play Australian Rules football (*Irish Examiner*)

Sprinting away from Tipperary's Paul Kelly in an All-Ireland qualifier in 2004. Both sides were terrified of losing; we won (*Brendan Moran/Sportsfile*)

Evading Henry Shefflin in the 2004 All-Ireland final. We beat
Kilkenny 0–17 to 0–9 in what might have been the sweetest win for
that group of players (*Ray McManus/Sportsfile*)

With Setanta and Aisake after another sweet win in the autumn of 2004:
for Na Piarsaigh over Cloyne in the county championship. That was the only
trophy the three of us ever won together (*Matt Browne/Sportsfile*)

With my Hurler of the Year trophy
at the GAA All-Star Awards, 2004
(*Brendan Moran/Sportsfile*)

Winning a high ball against Alan Kerins
of Galway in the 2005 All-Ireland final
(*David Maher/Sportsfile*)

Lifting the Liam MacCarthy Cup as captain after the 2005 final. My speech was in
Irish, but I regret not throwing in a bit of Rotuman! (*Brendan Moran/Sportsfile*)

The physical therapist Ger Hartmann helped me immensely after my serious knee injury in 2001, and later. Here I'm doing a conditioning session with Ger (*centre, waiting to catch the medicine ball*) during the summer of 2006

Contesting a dropping ball with Martin Comerford of Kilkenny in the 2006 All-Ireland final. The match was not a classic, but Kilkenny were clearly the better team that day, and this was the first of four All-Irelands in a row for them (*Brendan Moran/Sportsfile*)

In December 2006 my partner Siobhán Quirke and I spent a week in Rotuma
for the filming of the documentary *Tall, Dark and Ó hAilpín*. Left to right:
My cousins Anna Marfono, Emeli Flavia and Henry Marfono, Siobhán,
my aunt Sarote Jieni, myself, and my cousin Petero Tifare

Another strike, another press conference: at the Maryborough
House Hotel in Cork in January 2009

My partner, Siobhán Quirke, put up with a lot during the years
when I was a senior intercounty player. Going home to her is, for me,
the most pleasing part of the day

When I was awarded the Freedom of the City of Cork, in June 2011, I got
to share the day with some special people: (*sitting, left to right*) my mother, Emeli;
Cllr and Lord Mayor Michael O'Connell; myself; Siobhán; (*standing, left to right*)
Étaoin's partner Neil Waters, Étaoin, Teu (holding our niece Letiah
McSweeney), Sarote, and Sarote's husband Dónal McSweeney

meeting was over then, but it wasn't. Not quite. The Board had tea, sandwiches and barm brack brought in. There's a big table in Frank's office, with a green baize top, and in a few seconds that was covered with plates of food. I remember thinking, 'What the fuck is this?' We headed off, and left the barm brack after us.

When the Board gave us their response, there was no engagement on the issues, so we had to consider the next step. We met the team in the John Barleycorn pub in Glanmire; we gave them the play-by-play from the meeting and we threw it open to the floor.

The consensus was that it had all been a waste of time meeting the Board, and that our options were limited. We could accept the conditions and go back, or we could down tools.

Option number two was a serious matter. Some guys would have been mulling that over, but it was the first time many of the lads heard it as a possibility, and it was scary to contemplate. It certainly frightened me. We said, though, that if anyone didn't want to go that route they could opt out and there wouldn't be any recriminations.

It was tricky for a lot of lads. Kieran 'Hero' Murphy's dad was a selector. Diarmuid O'Sullivan's dad was on the executive of the County Board.

We didn't decide to strike that night. We met again soon afterwards in the Vienna Woods Hotel and there was one significant difference from the previous meeting: Dessie Farrell of the GPA came down to talk to us. He was by no means telling us to strike, far from it, but he said that whatever action we took, the GPA would be behind us. I think he was trying to get a sense of the frustration and hurt in the room, and he did say that we weren't the only county squad who were frustrated by these kinds of issues. He commended us on our unity – but he didn't stay in the room for the important decision. He left when we were mulling over the possibilities, so he wasn't in the room when we agreed to go on strike.

Diarmaid Falvey stayed in the room with us. He advised us on the ramifications of the decision. We needed him. We were only kids, and we didn't know what we should do next.

Diarmaid did: hence the famous Imperial Hotel press conference. I was working in AIB on the South Mall, and on the morning of the press conference, a Friday, I asked my boss if I could leave at 3 p.m.

There was a huge media presence at the Imperial. Joe read a statement and then we took questions. There were several player representatives at the top table, and each of us was prepped to answer questions in a particular area.

There was a perception that the team's representatives at the press conference were the ringleaders or were the only lads who wanted to go on strike. Not at all: for that press conference and others that followed in 2002 and later, the representatives were just the lads who were picked by the panel to represent them for that particular event; sometimes they were the only fellas available because of the others' work commitments.

There was huge sympathy from the journalists, which didn't surprise us. The only negative questions came from a couple of local journalists who were also County Board delegates, asking if we realized the damage we were doing.

After the press conference we went away up to Rearden's nightclub and reviewed what had happened. We *didn't* fully realize what we'd done, to be honest, but we were focused on what we might have to improve upon if we ever had to do another press conference.

At half three or so, as I was driving the lads home, we pulled into a garage down in Tivoli to see if we could get the *Examiner* and check out the coverage.

It wasn't in the sports section. It was across the front of the paper, a huge picture of the seven of us in the Imperial. Holy shit! It started to dawn on us that this was for real. No turning back.

There was a media frenzy after that. The feedback I got from people on the street was very positive, because they'd had the notion that you were looked after like royalty when you were with Cork and they were surprised to hear about what was really going on.

We were lucky to have Diarmaid Falvey in our corner. The only payback he wanted was success in September, not money. In preparing us for the meetings he played the bad cop, grilling us in character as a journalist or County Board official to the extent you'd break out of the scenario occasionally to say, 'Jesus, Diarmaid, they're not going to bring that out,' and he'd come back even harder. We'd be in his office late some nights and lads would be getting restless but he'd lay down the law: 'We're not going anywhere until we get this right; all it takes is one or two slip-ups and you'll come across as unprofessional and disjointed. You can't have that.'

He covered everything. He insisted on suits for the Imperial press conference, we had dummy runs for that presser, and he raised questions we'd never have expected.

The Board came to terms fairly quickly. They gave us practically everything we were looking for.

Those few weeks of the 2002 strike bonded the team unbelievably, and made us for the next four years.

II

Bertie Óg Murphy and his selection committee were collateral damage in the strike – they resigned en masse – and Dónal O'Grady came in as manager for 2003.

I knew Dónal from my time in school, so the minute he was announced I started getting phone calls about him – from Dónal Óg, Joe Deane, Mickey O'Connell – and I gave him a good reference.

During his time as manager, Jimmy Barry-Murphy had invited Dónal in to take a few sessions with the backs. That was the first time we'd have come across specialized training, and Dónal worked hard on organizational stuff which was simple and common sense a lot of the time, but very helpful.

People have a notion, if you're playing senior intercounty, that you're the finished product, that you're so sophisticated as a player that you need super-sophisticated drills and preparation. You don't. O'Grady brought in simple plans, simple options to take. For instance, if you were on your own wing and two or three opponents had you bottled up when you were trying to strike the ball, O'Grady would say, 'Hit it up the same wing, don't try the crossfield ball.' His logic was simple: get it up the same wing because players instinctively move towards that wing in anticipation of the ball ending up there. When it arrives, there should be enough bodies around to contest the dropping ball. If it's won by us, then goal achieved. If it's lost by us, then we should have bodies to press up on the man in possession and make a tackle. If the ball crumbs, we'll have bodies at the breakdown trying to win it. Simple but sensible.

I remember him telling me not to try to catch every ball that dropped in my vicinity. He stressed the importance of not letting the ball past; it was enough sometimes to just break the ball down. 'You've enough athleticism and speed to get on to a ball that you bat down in front of you,' he'd say.

There were other lessons. O'Grady was the first man to show us the importance of having your hurley up to cover your hand when you handpassed just in case an opponent threw out a flick and intercepted that handpass.

'You've got the hurley down by your side when you're handpassing?' he'd say. 'A Kilkenny fella will flick across just to see if he can get contact on the ball. Protect yourself. Keep the hurley up.'

If you were bottled up, he'd suggest dropping the ball and kicking it on. Common sense again.

Jimmy had played with him with the Barrs and Cork, of course, and had also worked with him in the underage section of their club. I remember Dónal telling me when we lost to Clare that year in the championship that I'd done well, and that meant a lot. But that was it. A few sessions in 1997 and that was that. The next time we crossed paths in training terms was 2003, when he came in as manager.

I'd have told the lads he had a track record making average players into winners, was highly organized and demanded a lot: he could be hard to please because he strove for perfection. I was delighted, because I knew how good he was.

Early in 2003 there were training sessions in Ballygarvan, outside Carrigaline, where we got to know the back of the cornflakes box. We'd spend two years looking at that cardboard rectangle. O'Grady would assemble us at seven o'clock on the dot, talk for a minute or two, with a speech that usually involved the words 'We've a lot of work to get through this evening, lads.' Then he'd hold up the piece of the cornflakes box: he'd have his training plan written out on the inside.

I've said I was delighted with Dónal's appointment, and I was, right up to the moment he lifted me out of it at an early training session. I was late up to the Old Mon Field for training and when I wandered in he took the head off me, pointing out that as a senior player I was under an obligation to set the tone and to give a good example.

I wasn't late again.

One of O'Grady's best decisions was the appointment of Sean McGrath (not the hurler) as physical trainer. He'd have consulted with Ted Owens in previous regimes without taking the sessions himself, and ran the fitness testing for us.

He was outstanding, but there were times, particularly in that first year, when he was a hard bastard. When he'd say, 'Lads, we've got a tough three-week block of training ahead of us,' everyone knew there was no time for joking. Sean's not an authoritarian, but because of what he was doing, players regarded him as hard. That's no surprise – nobody looks forward to the hard physical slog. Everybody wants a hurley and ball in their hand.

Seanie got to know players' bodies inside out. For instance: in 2004, his second year, he was weighing us regularly, and after one session he pulled me to one side: 'You'd tell me everything that's going on, right?'

'I would, Sean.'

'Well, your weight's gone up by five kilograms but you're posting the same running times as last year. What's going on?'

I told him I was taking protein supplements as I felt I needed more strength in my upper body. He said he wanted to see a sample of what I was taking, and then he got another sports scientist, Donal O'Gorman, to test it. It was fine, but Seanie warned me that some of the supplements on the market mightn't be what they claim to be.

He had us taking our resting heart rate when we woke up and he'd take that data to fit the training. If some guy's heart rate suggested he needed a break, Sean left him out: 'There's eight repetitions of this run but you fall out for numbers three, six and eight,' or he'd excuse a guy from the physical stuff after the ballwork.

Two or three weeks into the training, then, Sean was putting us through our drills and another guy was working with the heavier guys and the rehab group. That was Jerry Wallace, who came to the fore more and more as the year went on, and when Sean went off to compete in the Paralympics as a sailor, Jerry stood in for him.

The sessions were well structured. Typically Sean and Jerry would take the forwards, say, for a running session, while O'Grady worked with the backs on skills. After about twelve minutes the whistle went and the two groups swapped over. In the course of a session you'd have three or four switches like that. Just because you were doing some ball-orientated training with O'Grady didn't mean you got a break from the physical intensity: those could be torture. If you counted the metres you covered to hook, to block, it mounted up unbelievably.

The difference with previous regimes was marked. The solo skills drills I referred to before – the ones which didn't prepare us for Wexford in 2001 – weren't near that level of intensity. A guy might have three others around him in a circle, all of them peppering him with sliotars to improve his touch for two or three minutes at a time, but invariably your focus slackened after forty seconds, and the time remaining in the drill was seen out at a slack enough pace. With the O'Grady regime those kinds of drills didn't run more than forty seconds, so your intensity never waned: out you'd come after forty seconds, get your breather as you peppered the guy who'd gone in, and you were back in then yourself. No let-up. No slackening. Gut-busting work.

No matter how well the session went, O'Grady was never happy. Never totally satisfied with the outcome. He always said there was more in us, and whether he believed it or not, it seeped into us and strengthened our hunger. Because of all of that, our hurling was super-sharp. Fitness-wise we were humming. Running the tunnels in Páirc Uí Chaoimh was a distant memory.

Over the years we'd have been told what to do and we'd have followed it. The attitude would have been, 'Well, the trainer must know what he's talking about, if he says to do something we'll just do it.' But over the years, sitting down with Sean McGrath after training, say, you'd ask, 'Sean, why did you run that drill that way today?' and he'd go through the reasons, the science behind what happens to the body and relating that to your experience in the game, showing how it applied to a game-specific situation.

And you'd become interested in why you were doing certain things at training, obviously, when it was explained to you. In Sean's case he was able to explain everything, to give a reason for every drill – and at the base of that was Dónal O'Grady's interest in a particular type of game. As those months went on you could see fellas' body shapes change, but that was because diet became important too.

Sean's attention to detail was evidence that we'd been given everything we'd sought from the Board. That brought pressure. The spotlight was on us. Whether it was articulated out loud or not, the view was that if we got what we wanted, we should deliver the big one.

Nobody questioned Dónal's authority, or Sean's. The buy-in was complete from the panel. We were missing a few guys who'd soldiered with us – Fergal Ryan, Mark Landers, Kevin Murray, Fergal McCormack – and who trained with us in the first few weeks of 2003 before being told they were no longer required. That must have been tough to take, and I know some of them are still sore to this day.

There were replacements. Cork had won the 2001 minor All-Ireland and lost the 2000 minor All-Ireland, and the likes of Paul Tierney, Cian O'Connor, Brian Murphy and Martin Coleman from those teams came in. Kieran 'Fraggy' Murphy, John Gardiner and Setanta had been introduced from the year before.

Setanta got the sporting talent we all craved. As good as I got at underage, Setanta was the kiddy growing up. He was unbelievable. Winning games on his own, scoring goals at will.

He was a big kid, which obviously was a help, but he dominated games on his own. It was like he'd take a kick-out, be out at midfield to catch the ball and bury it to the back of the net, just like his namesake in ancient Ireland. Whatever Dad was at with the names, he certainly got Setanta's right.

Setanta was always hugely interested in watching games. If I had a match to play, he'd be the first out, perched on the back seat of the car. He never needed to be asked or coaxed, he always wanted to be going to games, even at five or six.

Eventually he became known, and he'd have a job to do. Back in the eighties and early nineties, a lot of clubs wouldn't have had those big nets they have now behind the goals, so Setanta would be assigned to the patch behind one of the goals, wherever we were playing, to get the ball. You'd see him bounce off down the fields after sliotars during the game, but there was always a pay-off: he'd have a few slio-tars of his own in the pocket when we got back to the car after the game.

By the time he was thirteen, fourteen, he was big enough to puck the ball back to the players from behind the goal. He'd hit the ball out to Brian Corcoran or Diarmuid O'Sullivan, and then he'd be at home or with his pals and it was 'Sure I was talking to Corcoran there the other night,' or 'I was pucking around there with Sully the other evening.'

Rubbing shoulders with the greats. Where he belonged.

He thought big and he had huge confidence in his own ability. 'That fella, I'd make mincemeat of him' – that kind of thing, which wouldn't be my way at all. I'd have a German kind of sports mental-ity – train hard, compete hard, don't pay too much attention to the compliments. He'd be more Brazilian in his thinking: flashy, confi-dent, not slow to slag you off: 'Jesus, all the training you do, all that running, and that's the best you can do? I'm doing none of that and I'm banging in the goals. Fuck sake.'

That was him at fifteen.

But it was done with a grin. He stood out. He made the underage Cork teams all the way up, made the Cork minors at seventeen and won an All-Ireland minor medal the following year, 2001. At sixteen, seventeen, he had a growth spurt and he hadn't grown into his body, so he struggled for a year or two. He started to fill out after that, and his game blossomed then. But even in 2003 he was like a foal, still not fully mature.

He was in WIT at the time, so during the week we didn't really see him, but he'd come with me at the weekend for games and so on. The senior lads knew him from the year before when he'd been on the fringes of the panel.

We played Clare in the league up in Ennis, and the night before we'd played O'Donovan Rossa Skibbereen in the football championship – I was still playing club football. My leg was sore after that game so I pulled out of the Clare game, and Setanta came on as a sub. He was marked by Frank Lohan, but as soon as he came on he got a point with an overhead pull like something out of the forties, and from then on he gave Lohan enough of it.

I knew he had the innate ability, but I'd have wondered how he'd do at the top level. That was a first glimpse. The second came against Kilkenny in the league down the Páirc, where he was outstanding. Setanta caught people's attention in that game. He wasn't the finished article – he hadn't filled out yet – but it was obvious that he was going to have to start in the championship. You couldn't ignore him. There are two games that people in Cork measure their hurlers by, and that's against Tipp and Kilkenny. O'Grady was bringing him along bit by bit, but that was the main audition, and he passed.

There were bumps along the way, though. After the Kilkenny game we played Galway in Salthill and Setanta was on Ollie Canning, as good a defender as you could find, and he was taken off. The form wasn't good on the bus back to Cork after that, and I'd say it didn't improve when he had to get on another bus from there down to Waterford.

People had the impression that I'd be coaching my brothers all the time in what to do, what to eat, how to exercise; and when Setanta broke through they probably thought I was in his ear the whole time.

I wasn't. I wouldn't be like that anyway; I'd be hoping the younger guys would emulate my training, but I wasn't telling them every-thing they should be doing. It was the same with Setanta. If we were heading to a match he'd ask me what I knew about his marker, and I'd tell him, but it wasn't a situation where I walked him through every possible scenario he'd face. When we got to the game it was a case of 'Good game now today.' 'Same to you.' And that was about it. You can't hold a guy's hand all the time. There comes a time when a new player has to trust in the work he has done himself.

I certainly wouldn't have been the one who told him to say, 'I don't do points.' That became a bit of a saying around that time, something of an urban legend around Cork, but I don't think Setanta ever actu-ally said it. In a game against Wexford, O'Grady advised him to take his point rather than getting battered by the defence trying to get through, and Setanta said something like 'Points, that's not what it's about.' Not as snappy as 'I don't do points,' but it could be where the story originated. Certainly at underage he had an uncanny ability to get a goal; if it was a possibility he went for it and usually he got it.

Training brought him on, too. Diarmuid O'Sullivan spent a lot of 2003 at corner-back, so they'd have marked each other at training, and whatever he faced in competitive games wouldn't be as difficult as Sully, who didn't believe in sparing guys just because it was a practice game.

Between the challenge of training, learning from competitive matches and his own self-confidence, Setanta came on in leaps and bounds that year.

I had a new colleague further back the field myself.

When Brian Corcoran retired after the 2001 season, Ronan Curran didn't appear to be the next great centre-back in waiting then. He was on the fringes of the panel in 2002, but he was carrying an injury and was only twenty-one.

What stood to him was the fact that he was fast becoming a stand-out player for the Barrs at senior level at just twenty-two years of age. He put in a particularly strong display on Alan Browne in the club championship of 2002. Curran was catching ball over Browne's

head, which was never an easy thing to do – ask anyone who has
marked Browne – and he had a long Fitzgibbon Cup campaign with
CIT in late 2002 and early 2003.

I remember we played Galway in a practice game in Cratloe around
February. Curran played on Cathal Moore, who was as good a player
as you'll find, but Curran dominated him completely. That's when I
started to notice his talent and potential. You can tell he had it.

He wasn't yet playing the quarter-back role that he developed
under O'Grady's famous running game. That approach, working the
ball to runners, was still in the future. At this point, O'Grady still
wasn't sure who his starting fifteen for the championship were.

The structured pre-game warm-up was something we were used to
from previous regimes, but by 2003 it had gone up a few more gears.
Ted Owens had first introduced the use of cones in the warm-up for
a league game versus Waterford back in 1998, but he was told to
ditch them fairly lively as Jimmy said he had spotted people he knew
laughing at us from the bank in Dungarvan. In 2003 the cones were
back and the intensity that we were working at made people believe
we were tiring ourselves before the main event. But there was science and good reasoning behind it. It involved each player handling
the sliotar, working on first touch, but more importantly getting
the muscles warmed up and joints loosened. The whole thing took
up to twenty minutes, starting off at a slow tempo and gradually
building up.

We'd have practised it in training. The last session before every
league and championship game we would do a pre-run, so come
match day it would be second nature to us. By the time it was finished, the heart rate was at max and the legs felt like jelly; you'd think
after doing it, 'I don't know if I'll get through this game.' But it
worked. Sean wanted the lactic acid building up and the heart rate up
so that you'd be operating off your second wind as soon as the game
started. You'd have heard from lads over the years that they were
humming in the second half. We wanted to start off at a hum.

You felt looser, much more flexible, moving freely as soon as the ball was thrown in, and it fed into O'Grady's belief in *tús maith leath na hoibre*. If you could get off to a flying start, get a couple of scores and put some doubt in the opposition, you were on the front foot all through.

It's evolved since then to the point where teams have mini-games with the squad in different-coloured bibs before matches, but we never had contact warm-ups. Management consulted us on what we wanted from the warm-up and took our suggestions on board. Sean's focus on getting the heart rate up was crucial – and we understood that and took it on board. It was a good example of the amount of hard work and planning that was being done behind the scenes by management, and a good example of the communication between players and management.

I think the warm-up we did for games didn't annoy people half as much as the cool-down afterwards. Cusack said to me one time that he'd had comments relayed back to him second-hand. Stuff along the lines of 'Who do they think they are? They're really rubbing it in, those Cork boys.' Traditionally when the final whistle sounded, teams headed back to the dressing-rooms right away. But again there was science to what we were doing. We were flushing out toxins and lactic acid from our systems in order to make a better recovery.

It seemed to put people's noses out of joint, but that didn't bother me, or any of the lads. Performance covers a multitude, and once we were winning it didn't matter what anyone had to say about how we prepared.

One day early in 2003, I was one of the first into the car park out in Ballygarvan for training, and I pulled in next to O'Grady. He beckoned me into his car's passenger seat.

Larry Tompkins had asked me to get involved in football again, and initially I said I would. O'Grady didn't beat around the bush.

'What are your plans for the football?'

'Well, I'd like to give it a try.'

'Is that advisable with your knee?'

'It's going fine so far.'

Then he pulled out a training schedule, a year planner, and showed me the various days marked on it. 'These are the sessions we need to do, and if we don't see you at those sessions it'll be hard to pick you. They're the sessions we need to do to get to this point.'

By 'this point' he didn't just mean the Clare game, our championship opener. He had days and sessions marked in going all the way to the All-Ireland final in September.

'I'm not telling you what to do,' he said. 'But if we don't see you at the hurling training sessions . . .'

That was the end of any potential return to intercounty football for me, though that wasn't the main point I took from the conversation. We'd been dumped out of the championship the previous year by Galway, remember, and here somebody was, planning for the All-Ireland final!

Club football was different. It never occurred to me not to play football for the club and I still do. But I preferred hurling. If there was a call to be made, that was always going to be my choice. I wanted to play both, but I also wanted to give myself the best chance of making the hurling team. Dónal O'Grady was a new manager and wasn't going on past reputations, so I felt I wasn't guaranteed my place on the team.

I rang Larry and said, 'Look, Larry, I'm just going to concentrate on hurling, I think it's the best option for me.' And give him his due, he couldn't have been better about it. He asked me to have a re-think, but when I told him my mind was made up he wished me the very best of luck for the year.

That made it easier for me, certainly.

As the year went on, what O'Grady planned started to come to pass, and the penny dropped for lads: the preparations, the atmosphere, the planning, all of it was first rate, and we were reaping the benefits. Even the famous hooking and blocking, drills you teach to ten-year-olds, began to make sense. When O'Grady started us hooking and blocking, the players were stunned to be doing such basic drills – lads with All-Star awards, All-Ireland medals. But eventually evenings came when he'd forget it, *mar dhea*, and the players would start saying, 'Hey, are we doing hooking and blocking tonight or what?'

Before 2003 there was often a Board presence in the dressing-room at training and matches, or on the team bus going to games, but that stopped after the strike. Mick Dolan, vice-chairman of the Board, was our liaison man and wasn't intrusive about it, while Jim Forbes, the chairman, dropped in every now and again.

Being left to our own devices helped, no doubt about that. We'd resolved our differences with the Board, but there was no need for them at training, and pre-game preparation. Maybe they didn't have any great desire to hang around looking at us either. Whatever the reason, we got on better with each other in our semi-detached state.

We went to Clonea in Waterford for a bonding weekend and we beat Offaly comfortably in a challenge match down there. John Allen was a selector and he organized a quiz in the hotel – he'd have been good that way – and the vibe was good. I can't remember if O'Grady won the quiz, but it wouldn't have been like him to lose.

First up for us in the championship was Clare. They'd been in the All-Ireland final the previous year, and they still had a number of their 1997 All-Ireland-winning team, but we had them beaten before half-time. The intensity in our play, the pressure we put them under – all of that related to what we'd been doing with Dónal O'Grady and Sean McGrath. Everything fitted together and worked like a well-oiled machine. We were on our way.

12

It was the summer of Setanta. In the Munster final we played Waterford, and by his standards he had a quiet game, but he still struck for the crucial goal. Stephen Brenner, the Waterford 'keeper, paused for a split second going for a ball that dropped short of the goal, but Setanta didn't – he stepped in and buried a goal from a narrow angle.

In the second half we kicked on and Joe got the goal that made it safe. We were Munster champions. O'Grady had been right after all, planning his training sessions deep into the summer.

Before that, some of the lads wouldn't have been convinced by O'Grady, though they mightn't have said it to me because they saw me as being close to Dónal, going all the way back to schooldays at the North Mon. We weren't that close, though – a lot of people can identify with the scenario where someone who's taught you as a kid remains *an mhúinteoir*. The pupil–teacher relationship can be hard to overcome. I knew Dónal better than most of the lads, but because of that I knew there was a line you didn't cross.

It was like 1999 all over again. The whole city and county seemed to have rowed in behind the team, you went to summer camps and the kids were all over you – and everybody wanted a piece of Setanta.

That's where Eddie O'Donnell came in. In March of 2003 we had a league game in Offaly and the team bus stopped for the north Cork lads in Mallow. Along with Timmy McCarthy, the selector Fred Sheehy and a couple more, this grey-haired fella came on, and every fella on the bus was saying, 'Who's that chap?' Dónal introduced him as our stats man for the year, and Eddie worked away on that side of things quietly. At matches he'd be in the stand and he wouldn't be an intrusive presence in the dressing-room.

The demands on Setanta's time were threatening to get out of hand. The Celtic Tiger was beginning to roll and businesses had some money for marketing, and Setanta was getting calls morning, noon and night. In 1999 there had been one or two gigs for us, but by 2003 it had gone to another level, and Setanta, being young, found it hard to say no.

Dónal was getting concerned because he wanted to protect his player. He said, 'Look, we'll take it out of your hands. If someone wants you for anything, say to them they'll have to talk to the guy who looks after your diary – Eddie.'

And that worked out well, because Eddie could filter out stuff that Setanta should stay away from so he could concentrate on playing. That could be difficult at times. He didn't have a mobile and was living at home, and sometimes the phone screening wasn't as efficient as it might have been.

'Seán Óg, you're wanted on the phone.'

'Who is it, Mum?'

'Some chap from a newspaper.'

'Tell him I'm not here.'

'Oh sorry, I said you were at home.'

That was the problem – Mum was too good-hearted to be cruel to the journalists. They didn't realize what an ally they had answering the landline at home.

Wexford was next. They had turned over Waterford in the qualifiers and got their season back on track, but we were confident. They were similar to Clare in that they still had a few old-stagers – Larry Murphy, Liam Dunne, Larry O'Gorman, Adrian Fenlon – and we felt we'd have too much toe for them.

O'Grady and the management team tried to knock that complacency out of us, but we were in trouble in that game. Wexford hit us for goals and we were hanging on until Setanta turned the game our way. Sully bombed in a long free, he caught it, turned and kicked it – miskicked it, really – and we had a goal.

We needed that. He started the comeback, we started to roll, and when Alan Browne hit a point from the sideline I thought it was game over. The prospect of a goal never occurred to me, but they worked their chance in the last second, Rory McCarthy had his shot: goal.

And they deserved it on the balance of play. They'd made the running early on, they'd led, and a draw was a fair result. We didn't make any mistakes in the replay and an extra game in Croke Park didn't do us any harm at all. Leinster teams have an advantage – in hurling and football – because they're in Croke Park all the time. It's a different environment, for one thing, but for Cork – and for other counties a long way from Dublin – you're overnight in Dublin, in a strange bed, a different routine, and it's not ideal compared to playing in Thurles, where you're just an hour and three-quarters away and you can sleep in your own place.

Of course, typical O'Grady, he tried to counteract that. He told us we could have our pillows from home brought up, which lads found hilarious at first ('Sully, did you bring your pillow?'). But it was common sense. Controlling anything he could control was O'Grady's mantra.

(Lads didn't see the reasoning behind one of his other diktats. Spray deodorants were banned in the dressing-room while he was there: all roll-ons after your shower. I don't know if it was in case lads were chesty and might react to the spray, or whether Dónal was unexpectedly leaning towards Greenpeace, but there were no hissing spray-cans in the Cork dressing-room on his watch.)

Ahead of the first Wexford game a PR firm approached me and Setanta to have Paddy Power stamped on our hurleys. We were offered a few bob and we said yes – if you got a few quid without harming anyone, what was the problem? It was gas: a courier called to the house and brought away the hurleys, and a couple of days later they came back stamped with the logo.

Soon enough, we started getting calls about it. We weren't the only ones involved – Brendan Cummins of Tipperary and Paul Codd from Wexford did it as well – and Croke Park weren't happy. There must have been calls to Páirc Uí Chaoimh because the County Board contacted O'Grady. In the end Setanta dropped out. I played with the logo but Setanta didn't because we felt he was too young to be getting that kind of focus. Because Setanta wasn't going to play with a logo on his hurley, he had to use a different stick from the one he'd been training with. Maybe that's why he kicked his goal against Wexford.

John Allen was a selector that year, and more than once during the season he facilitated discussions among the panel. We'd go to training for seven, say, and be told there'd be a discussion first for twenty minutes or half an hour.

John was very good in leading those talks – about goal-setting, for instance – he'd give us the model that corporations used to achieve those goals. And after the Wexford game he brought up the fact that guys' lives would change because they were playing in an All-Ireland final, and that it would help to embrace that change and to be comfortable with it – but that the various things that spun off the on-field success had their origin in that on-field success.

Kilkenny were waiting in the final. They were the reigning All-Ireland champions, and had a string of stars with great experience throughout the team.

Management ramped it up, telling us their sources in Kilkenny were telling them that the Cats saw the game as a foregone conclusion. The league final the previous year was brought up a few times as well. A few pundits rowed in, writing us off, though they had grounds for doing so. Kilkenny destroyed Tipp in their semi-final and were coming to a peak. They were deserving favourites.

You couldn't have convinced people in Cork of that, though. We had a day for the supporters one Sunday morning and we were mobbed. Or, more precisely, one of the players was mobbed.

The intentions were good and the planning was good, but there were thousands there. We were at tables around the field and there were lines for the queues set up with tape. People were supposed to come up one by one, but the whole thing broke down almost immediately. People got impatient, they came around the back, lads you knew jumped the queue and you couldn't say, 'Get back to the end,' and the people queueing honestly got pissed off as well.

It was chaos, and what was supposed to last one hour stretched to two hours, and with all the people slapping his back, standing in for photos and hugging him, Setanta took more punishment than he got in most of the games he played that summer.

I didn't room with Setanta for the final. He bunked in with Alan Browne, who was one of the best captains I ever worked with. A fantastic captain, and a great guy: what you saw was what you got. He suffered during the physical training but he put it in, and you have to give someone credit when they don't find the training easy. Any time that year that Setanta got grief off any of his markers, Alan was in straight away to back him up.

We were confident. Training had gone well – very well – and the feeling can seep into a team that's put in the work. The build-up was low key, and we'd given Kilkenny no ammunition. But Kilkenny did all the hurling in the first half. We didn't play at all. The cliché about playing the occasion rather than the game was never as true. In the first half the only constructive play I had was a shot after Joe Deane played a backpass to me in space: it went wide.

At half-time we were expecting O'Grady to blow a fuse. He can get heated about things, and one thing he'd said more than once to us during that season was, 'What gets me about ye is that ye have the ability.' So we were expecting a lambasting, but O'Grady turned it around totally. 'This is going to surprise ye,' he said, 'but ye're not doing too bad. The scoreboard is not a true reflection of what I'm seeing.' Maybe he felt he had to say it, the lads were so down. He went on to say that we'd had plenty of possession but our composure was letting us down. 'Cut out the needless frees, express ourselves the way we can, and we'll turn this around.'

That lifted a weight off. Walking into the dressing-room we'd have been thinking, 'Maybe we're a year too early,' but walking back out we'd have thought, 'We're not out of it.'

We took the game to them in the second half. Sully came out like a train and scattered three Kilkenny lads; that was inspirational. They couldn't find space easily, which was a big O'Grady focus. He often said, 'If I stand ten feet away from you, then you're going to look like Christy Ring; if I stand one foot away from you, it's going to change your mindset. Get in their faces and we'll see how good they are.'

We did that and chipped away at the lead, and then Setanta struck. Goal. The game was there to be won. They were rattled, and Brian Cody came on to the field, shouting at lads to move, which would be rare enough to see.

Niall McCarthy came close to getting us the lead, but he had a shot come back off the post. There was no blame attached to him afterwards, and when he gave a man-of-the-match display twelve months later, it felt like his just reward.

We were having all the play towards the end, but there was one final twist – Kilkenny came through and Martin Comerford had a shot. I got a block on it, but I should have jumped on him and thrown myself totally into the tackle. The ball took a wicked deflection and a false bounce, and it beat Cusack. He'd have beaten himself up over that, but it wasn't his fault. Not at all. But the goal finished the game for us.

It wasn't a great day for me. I was on Henry Shefflin for a lot of the game and I struggled badly against him. On those days you've got to keep up the front – to give no sign to the opponent that you're under pressure; if you do, he'll murder you. I try to murder them when the shoe is on the other foot: if, after a couple of plays in a row, or a couple of runs, you see your opponent bent over and blowing, you punish him even further.

In previous years Henry would win the ball and head for space to get his shot off; in 2003, he was much more aggressive, driving hard at me with the ball when he was in possession, testing me out. No verbals, but definitely test your appetite early on to see if you're up for it.

There are other questions Henry can ask his marker. Kilkenny didn't come with a complex puck-out strategy that time; they didn't need to with him, John Hoyne and Martin Comerford in the forward line, all of them savage warriors under the dropping ball. The key to their approach to the dropping ball is that they vary their play; they don't try to catch the ball all the time. Sometimes they pull, and keep it going; but one thing they're the experts at is they go up with the hurley at a slight angle and they deflect the ball past the ruck of players.

If you can do that – and Henry does that better than anyone else – then you're on the front foot, because you have half a second's advantage over everybody else. You know where the ball's going to go, and if you're any good at all you're gone after it while everyone else is wondering where it's gone. Sometimes from a puck-out when the ball was dropping, he would deliberately stand off you and not let you have body contact on him. Then, as soon as the ball landed in the drop zone he'd launch in from the side and take you, hurley and ball. Smash.

Their quality in the air is based on that variety. If a guy catches one or two balls I play his hand to make sure he can't catch it; that's what I'd do with Dan Shanahan, because he'd try to catch it all day. You'd put your hurley across his eye-line or catch his hand as though you were going for the ball. You just wanted the ball on the deck to get a chance to win it. But it was harder against Kilkenny's variety.

There's a great photograph of myself and Setanta at the final whistle. He's on the ground and I have my hand on his back trying to console him.

I hadn't had a good game and I was disgusted with myself. On top of losing an All-Ireland final, not to play to your potential . . . but I wouldn't be one to show emotion in those circumstances.

Setanta certainly did better than me – he'd rallied us with that goal, and he was well entitled to be emotional. I wanted to get off the field and go home, because I felt embarrassed. That might sound strange, but you've put in so much, everything's been directed towards performing, and then you don't produce . . . I was trying to convey to him that he'd done his bit, unlike big brother.

Cody came into the dressing-room and was gracious. Always starts his speech the same way, with the respect between Cork and Kilkenny. O'Grady thanked us for the effort all year – there was no blaming, no 'We should have done this or that' – and he said that we'd learned a lot from the year.

There was a lot of hope for 2004. Setanta was a big part of that, because people expected, reasonably, that he'd be even better in 2004 than he'd been in 2003. Nearly every era in Cork has had a marquee forward, and whether or not he'd have matched up to the names of the past we don't know, but the potential was there. The year ended on a downbeat note, but the optimism soon kicked in: the team was young. Why wouldn't you be upbeat?

The only downer was Alan Browne, for whom that All-Ireland was always going to be his last Cork game. I desperately wanted him to lift the Liam MacCarthy Cup as captain, as he had been a fantastic soldier for Cork over the years.

The big concern after the final was O'Grady, ironically. There was no mention of the following year in anything he said, and that frightened a lot of guys. Whatever about the start of the year, he'd certainly convinced the panel by the end of the season that he was the man to bring us forward, but he hadn't committed to 2004 and there was no sign of him doing so in the days following the game.

You'd wonder if he'd have committed to a second year if we'd won in 2003. If that was what convinced him – that there was unfinished business – then 2003 must have been the only example of a worthwhile defeat ever. He'd taken over a ship that wasn't so much sinking as holed and sitting on the ocean floor, and had gotten us back on track: he'd organized us, convinced us, and improved us. He'd made hard calls and dropped lads who'd soldiered with us for years, which had left them sour enough in cases, but he was totally focused on what would improve the team

In early October I got a call from Bernie Collins, from Castlehaven, who'd played Aussie Rules with Western Bulldogs for a couple of years. The previous October he'd been at a trial organized by AFL scouts in DCU. A call had gone out for tall, skinny, athletic lads, and I'd driven Setanta and John Gardiner to the trial. They were put through skills with an Australian Rules ball – indoors, because the weather was bad – and then they were given a Gaelic football to kick and handpass. Eventually they went outside for more drills, fielding and so forth in a one-versus-one scenario. There were about twelve lads at the trial that year, but none were signed up. Setanta certainly wasn't singled out and told, 'We'll be in touch.'

Now, Bernie asked if Setanta was still interested in Australia. I said I'd ask him. If Setanta had gotten a call in 2002, I'd say he'd have jumped at it because the hurling hadn't gone well for him. I said to Bernie that after the way 2003 had gone for him his feelings might be different.

Setanta was game ball, though, as usual. He'd try it. Why not? I relayed the message to Bernie and after a few days Bernie gave us the news: Carlton were interested, would he come over for a six-week trial?

That's when the whole thing kicked off. People might have thought that Setanta was mulling over the offer for the summer, even as we were advancing on the All-Ireland, but he wasn't. It all happened very quickly, in the couple of weeks before he actually flew out to Australia. While he was banging in goals in the hurling championship, the AFL was the furthest thing in his mind – the trial had been a bit of crack, heading up to Dublin for the day, and it seemed as though nothing had come of it.

Circumstances also helped to put the opportunity his way, stuff that was far beyond his control. Carlton had breached the salary cap in the AFL, trying to hold on to some ageing stars; there was a big investigation, the club president was sacked and they missed out on draft picks as a punishment. As a result, they were at a crossroads. The only way to get in new talent was to go international, so they contacted scouts who'd been at the 2002 trials to see if there were any prospects. Colin Corkery, the Gaelic footballer, had played with Carlton, so it wasn't an outlandish prospect to them to recruit from Ireland.

Bernie met Setanta for a chat about it, and a few days afterwards the Carlton recruitment officer, Shane O'Sullivan, rang and offered him the trial; there was a flight booked for him and Shane would meet him at the airport.

We tried to keep it quiet. Na Piarsaigh was to play in the Munster club hurling league final, against Kilmoyley of Kerry. The game was to be played on the day Setanta was to fly out.

I said good luck to him, watched the Rugby World Cup final, and then headed off after the rugby game to meet the lads up in Na Piarsaigh. Dad meanwhile drove Setanta to the airport and he set off on the first leg of his trip to Australia.

'Where's Setanta?'

'Ah, he went to New York and won't be back for a few days. The attention was getting too much for him and he had to get out for a while.'

The lads weren't too happy to be travelling for a final without the best young forward in the country, and we lost.

Then it started to seep out from Australia that there was an Irish guy on trial with Carlton, and Shane O'Sullivan ended up on Irish radio denying that he was poaching players.

As you start playing intercounty, people think they own you. I'm cool with that, and I loved every minute of playing with Cork, but an example of the downside was the reaction when that news got out. People saw Setanta as a son and a brother, and they weren't happy the Australians were taking him away.

For his part, it was an opportunity. What was the worst-case scenario? Six weeks in the sun down under. That was probably our view of it at the time, that he'd have the holiday of a lifetime and would be back before Christmas.

Setanta rang us on the weekends from Melbourne, and during one of those calls he told us he'd been offered a two-year contract. Carlton had advised him to go home and think about it – to enjoy Christmas and to discuss it with his family.

And he did. That was our last Christmas together as a family, the last of Cork, really, for Setanta. He didn't commit to signing that contract when he was out there for the six weeks, but we knew he'd go for it. In his own mind he'd committed to it. We had a chat about it and weighed up the pros and cons; and, much as the GAA had been good to us, we all felt that Australia might open up opportunities for him.

When I say 'we', it was mostly Mum and Dad. I'd have advised him but it was really between the three of them, and Mum and Dad gave him their blessing. It was an adventure and that intrigued him, and he always had a fall-back position. If he didn't make it, he could always come back to Cork and hurl again, and we would have stressed that point – no matter what happened, he always had a place back at base with us.

His flight out to Australia was on a Wednesday, and our team holiday for the 2003 season was on Sunday – we were going to Vietnam and Thailand – but I was working on the Wednesday morning, so, the night before, I said goodbye. I said, 'Look, I'll say 'bye now because I'm gone early in the morning and there's no point you getting up too early. Good luck in Australia and we'll be in touch soon.'

The next morning, then, I didn't bother knocking on his door as I went out, but when I was getting into the car to head off he appeared at the door in his boxer shorts.

'Look, I couldn't leave without saying goodbye again,' and he gave me a massive hug.

And that's when it hit me, that it would be the guts of a year before I saw him again. You're the big brother, you've got to hold it all together, but it sank in as I pointed the car towards Cork: he was gone.

Later, he told me he never stopped crying on the flight from Cork to London. Years later, when he was well settled in Australia, he came back after the playing season and was on the flight from London to Cork when a lady came up to him.

'You don't know me and you don't remember me,' she said, 'but I was on the flight the day you left Ireland for Australia'. She remembered him bawling on the journey to London. 'Five years on and look at you, I'm glad it worked out.'

13

There were probably ninety people on the team holiday to Vietnam and Thailand that year – players, management, Board, plus spouses, plus small kids if they had them.

Given the strike, you might imagine there would have been some tense journeys in lifts, but in truth on those trips you don't spend a huge amount of time all together. At the airport going out and if you're changing hotels you might see the entire group, but you're not thrown in with people all the time. Siobhán was with me and we'd have been hooking up with the others some nights and doing our own thing other nights.

Dónal O'Grady would have asked John Allen to make sure we did a couple of training sessions, and so after we landed in Ho Chi Minh City we strolled around, trying to find a spot. There weren't too many open, grassy spaces, and when we found one we got run off it by a groundsman or attendant.

After a week we went from there to a five-star hotel just outside Da Nang, right on China Beach: a stunning spot, the beach stretching off to the horizon on either side as far as the eye could see.

The lads cut loose on the holiday, and rightly so. That's why you go away: lads deny themselves a lot the whole year, and the holiday is the pay-off. For some guys, cutting loose meant drinking; for me, the pay-off was that I could bring Siobhán on a nice trip to make up for the nights I'd be off training or playing matches.

I wanted to get some individual training in as well, but I'd try to get that done early in the morning when there was nobody around. That way you've the rest of the day free for whatever you want to do – and you're not hanging around the hotel in your gear, getting in fellas' faces when they're on the lash around the pool. It wouldn't bother me to get up early – you'd be lying out on the lounger most of the day anyway – to go to the gym.

Dónal Óg was often my training partner. He was bitterly disappointed with the goal he'd let in against Kilkenny – it eats him to this day – and later that season he let in another soft goal for Cloyne in the club championship against Blackrock. Because of the strike the previous year there would have been no shortage of lads ready to stick the knife into him as a result, and I noticed the change in his attitude on that holiday. He'd have partied hard on previous holidays, but in Vietnam he said he needed to become ruthless with his training. He still enjoyed his nights out, but it wasn't every night. On the nights that he did go out, he told me that if he wasn't outside my bedroom door the following morning for training, I was to break his door down and drag him out of bed. Of course that wasn't necessary – he was there every morning without fail.

There was a daily soccer game between the country guys and the city guys. One morning we were playing and there was a commotion down at the water's edge. Two lifeguards were trying to save a man who was struggling in the water, but in the end the poor guy drowned. A few of our lads went in to help the lifeguard pull the body out, and that was the end of swimming for us.

One morning, training was called, a stamina run down to a stump on the beach – half a mile down, half a mile back. There were a few guys there who'd been partying hard, Ronan Curran among them. When we set out, the lads who'd had a late one were the back markers in the group with the exception of Curran, who kept up at the front with the fresh heads.

On the return leg, after we turned the stump, Curran was going strong with us still, and as fellas dropped out of the leading group, he kept going and was getting stronger, unbelievably. He produced a sensational late kick to win the run. Unbelievable. He finished, laughed and looked back before jogging off up to the hotel.

There was an excursion to the tunnels of Cu Chi, an underground Viet Cong complex during the Vietnam War. The tour guide was the size of a small jockey, i.e. the right size for the tunnel, which got smaller and smaller the further we went. There were a few panicky questions along the lines of 'How much further?' and some relieved men when we got out the other end: a lot of fellas bent over, getting their wind back. In later years there were a few pointed comments about opportunities lost: 'You know, we could have sent a few of them down a side tunnel in Vietnam and all our problems would have been solved . . .'

We rubbed along well with Frank on that trip. As soon as you leave Cork Airport he's like the greatest guy you could meet; he switches into holiday mode straight away. When you land back in Cork Airport after the holiday he might walk past you, but on the trip he's good enough crack. Siobhán would be saying to me, 'Is this the guy you were giving out about? He doesn't seem so bad,' and I'd be saying, 'Yeah, I'm kind of changing my own mind now.' I prefer a bit of consistency in my enemies.

O'Grady set the tone for 2004 early on. In his first address to the group he said, 'I'm sick of people bickering all winter, saying we should have won this, we should have won that. Someone told me many years ago that at the end of a game you look up at the scoreboard and if you haven't won, you didn't deserve to win. This is the last I want to hear of 2003 and what should have been. The scoreboard told us we didn't win, so we didn't deserve to win.'

It was important for him to get that out there – to get fellas to stop using excuses. If you're good enough you'll get back and prove it.

The training in 2004 wasn't as hard as it had been the previous year. Sean McGrath didn't need to flog us so hard because we were working from the base he'd laid down for us. In 2003 there were times you barely had the energy to brush your teeth before falling into bed. In 2004 we didn't need such a huge workload.

I captained the team a few times because Ben O'Connor and Newtownshandrum were on a run to the All-Ireland club title, and they got a few weeks off after that as well. We had a mixed league campaign, but at that stage losing league games wasn't the cause for panic it is now. Our focus was on the All-Ireland.

And we had a shot of adrenalin along the way. The word went around the dressing-room that Corcoran might be coming back. He'd come to the banquet after we lost in 2003, and I'd say he must have been plagued by fellas saying he had something to offer, though he had been out of action for almost two years.

I had a club football game against Bishopstown in Páirc Uí Rinn on a Wednesday night and afterwards I headed for Páirc Uí Chaoimh where Cork were training. I wanted a rub, but I'd also heard that Corcoran was coming back that night, and I wanted to be there. It was great – a lift to everyone.

The older lads had played with him and he'd been the younger guys' hero. He was Michael Jordan to them when they were in their early teens, and then to have him back . . . I respect what Christy Ring did for Cork, but I never saw him play. Corcoran was Ring to me: I saw what he did when I was a kid and I saw what he did when I was his team-mate.

He was the catalyst that year. Not in a vocal way in the dressing-room, necessarily; he mainly led by example, and other fellas followed. Of course, when he did speak fellas listened. That's the value of a guy who doesn't talk that often.

If I had to single out the best Cork players I lined out alongside, I'd pick himself and Dónal Óg. Corcoran was even more impressive as an individual than he was as a player. When I came on to the panel in 1996 there were strong characters there from the 1980s team, but Corcoran was the one who made me feel at home. He was the first to welcome me, which means a lot when you're questioning whether you should be in the dressing-room at all.

Before our Munster semi-final against Limerick, we played Clare in a challenge in Ennis. It was an intense game, with Clare playing on the edge. Corcoran, playing as a forward, was marked by Brian Lohan. Lohan gave Corcoran fair stick, but he just dismissed it and racked up 2-4 or something. He dominated him. That underlined it: he was back. I shouldn't have doubted it, I knew that as an under-age player he'd played as a forward, but I felt it was a huge ask to come back after two years of doing nothing at all and to reinvent yourself.

Limerick were ready for us the way we'd been ready for Clare the previous year, and they were in their fortress, the Gaelic Grounds. It was touch and go. Corcoran got a point from his knees, forty yards out.

We got over them and faced Waterford. The rivalry with them was beginning to bubble, and it intensified as a result of that Munster final. Our attitude was always that, no matter how good Waterford would be, we'd find a way to beat them. We'd have based that on beating them at minor and U-21 levels. We certainly didn't see the juggernaut coming down the tracks.

I was central to one of the main plays in the game. I was penalized for fouling Dan Shanahan in the second half and it was never a free – I'd been putting in similar tackles all day without being blown.

The free was a long way out and I went back in on Dan in front of the goal, and he kept saying, 'He's going for it lads, he's going for it.'

And Dan was right. He was going for it. Paul Flynn dipped the ball in over us and got his goal. That was typical Flynn, putting top-spin on the ball and finding the corner of the net from forty yards. And it was typical Dan, chatting away on the field, getting into your head and distracting you. It was the first time he'd predicted a goal, mind.

That set us back and drove them on, and we couldn't quite close the gap.

There were plenty of questions going around after we lost to Waterford. Plenty of blame. We were scrutinized, players and management alike, because we'd lost a Munster final after playing nearly an entire half against fourteen men, John Mullane having been sent off.

O'Grady put it to bed, though. We went back training down in Páirc Uí Rinn and he told us to forget about it. The game was gone. History.

'The real championship starts now,' he said.

Against Tipperary, in Killarney.

That was a tense encounter. It was a humid, close day in Killarney. For both ourselves and Tipp, the prospect of going out of the championship was terrifying, plain and simple.

Just before half-time, Jerry O'Connor was shepherding a ball over the sideline when he was pushed by a Tipperary player needlessly. It happened close to the subs' bench and there was a brief melee – we piled in to protect Jerry, and the Tipp lads responded in kind. Nothing savage – no suspensions were handed out afterwards – but it livened up the game.

The other significant event was the introduction of Timmy McCarthy off the bench. He'd come in for more than his fair share of criticism after the Munster final, and he'd been dropped, but he came in and gave an outstanding display, notching a crucial goal that turned the game our way.

If you want to know how fickle supporters can be, the response to Timmy's performance was a perfect example. The people who had been baying for his blood a couple of weeks before were chanting Timmy's name towards the end of the game. Figure that one out.

I didn't have a chance to enjoy the win. After the final whistle, a guy with a yellow vest pulled me and Dónal Óg for a drugs test. Dehydrated from playing, we spent two hours in a small room, trying to produce a sample. Eventually O'Grady came in and expressed his dissatisfaction, to put it mildly. But we were not released into the general population until we'd produced our samples.

We got past Antrim and Wexford easily enough in the All-Ireland quarter-final and semi-final. Next up, Kilkenny.

We were confident. The spirit was good, the Munster final was forgotten, we were playing well and we felt we'd be too good for Kilkenny, no matter what they'd throw at us. We had momentum on our side, while they'd come through tougher games than they were used to, including a replay against Clare.

And we wanted to play Kilkenny, too. Wanting to match yourself against the best isn't a cliché: it's the truth. If you win a title having beaten the top sides along the way, then no one can question your credentials: there's nobody who can say, 'Hey, you never played X.'

Management had learned from 2003. You don't have a lot of time the day of the All-Ireland to get your warm-up sorted, to get everything that you want done, because an official is over to you, saying to get over to the parade. And that can knock some lads out of their stride. That's not why you lose a game, but it doesn't help, and in an All-Ireland final you need all those percentage points in your favour. So, approaching the final, O'Grady insisted on rehearsing the lead-in to the start of the game: leaving the dressing-room, warming up, going in for the photograph, meeting the President (Dónal was Mary McAleese, walking down the carpet, shaking hands), the parade . . .

We were ready.

It was tight until half-time, but we took over in the second half. If we'd played until midnight Kilkenny wouldn't have beaten us that day, and there aren't too many days you can say that about the Cats.

The game turned our way decisively when Dónal Óg made a great save from Henry Shefflin, and we worked the ball upfield, where Joe Deane took a loose challenge to win a vital free.

That Joe would suffer for the sake of the team was a given, by the way. He was known to most of us as 'Wizard', and he came up with me from U-14 through the minor and U-21 ranks. A match-winner for us so many times – if we ever needed a score he was the go-to man – but his guts were, for me, his hallmark.

That was true from early on. In 1995 he was badly split playing minor against Limerick – his lip was half hanging off. Dr Con stitched him up and he played on through the second half. Never mind the skill and the accuracy: his guts in Kilmallock that night were what I remember above all. When he fought off testicular cancer and resumed his hurling career it wasn't surprising, because even though he was coming up against bigger corner-backs, he read the game well, was very quick over the first couple of yards and had a razor-sharp touch.

It was the sweetest win, probably. It was redemption for the previous year, and the fact that we won emphatically meant we couldn't be accused of being lucky. Winning by nearly double scores – 0-17 to 0-9 – underlined our superiority.

Afterwards O'Grady suggested that they put Henry on me specifically: I don't know about that. Our attitude was that we were going to line out as planned, and no matter who was assigned to us, we'd stick to our formation and structure.

The feeling in the dressing-room was more relief than anything else. We'd expended a lot of energy to get back there. That was the year when a lot of the guys were at the peak of their powers. The training was top class, all the players were healthy . . . it all came together. If we hadn't won that day we'd have started thinking that beating Kilkenny was impossible.

Looking around the dressing-room, it was good to see the lads enjoying the win. Honest guys like Timmy McCarthy, who'd gotten huge stick from people over the years. Anyone in the camp knew he deserved better than that. One year we were going to a Munster final and he got on the bus in Fermoy and sat next to me. The city slicker here asked if he'd had a good night's sleep.

'I was up at six to milk the cows,' he said.

That went totally against what we were trying to do – to rest up ahead of a big game, to chill the morning of a game – but here was Timmy with probably a day's work done before going out to perform in front of 50,000 people. That's why it drove me mad when people criticized him; they hadn't a clue what the man put in to perform for Cork.

His namesake was across the room. Niall McCarthy, the Roberto Duran of the team, collected the man-of-the-match award for that final. He and I got on well because we were always the last two to sit down for the grub after training, which was a bone of contention for the caterers down the Páirc. We'd rock in near ten o'clock for our dinner, and the cooks, Marie and Peter, would ask if we were playing with rubber ducks in those ice baths or what? Ironically enough, myself and Niall ended up building a good relationship with Marie and Peter: they had to wait around until we had finished eating, so we had interesting chats with them up to 11 p.m. on some nights!

Sitting down to talk with guys over your dinner, you get to know them. Niall, to me, was the classic case of a player who needed his manager to know him well in order to get the best out of him, and Dónal O'Grady knew exactly how to do that.

Niall is a hard man. If you told him running up Mount Everest twice would help win the All-Ireland, he'd do it in a heartbeat.

We started to use ice baths to aid recovery after training sessions around 2003, 2004. Niall being Niall, he'd outlast everyone.

One evening after training everyone had cleared off when Jim McEvoy heard someone calling for help from the shower area. There was Niall, still in his ice bath.

'Niall, are you OK?'

'I can't get out, Jim. I can't feel my legs.'

'How long are you in there?'

'Don't know. Watch stopped after ten minutes.'

That summed Niall up.

One of the other lads didn't have quite the same level of preparation under his belt for that final. John Browne missed most of the 2003 campaign because he was studying dentistry in London. He came back in 2004, around March, and fell back in with us as a panellist.

Brian Murphy got a migraine in the All-Ireland final very early on, and Browner, Cian O'Connor of Erin's Own and Pat Mulcahy were told to warm up. They went down to the old Canal End to warm up, and when they came back O'Grady told Browner to go on. He played without a helmet, glove or gumshield because he hadn't been expecting the call. It seemed that the only items in his gearbag were a toothbrush and a pair of jeans. But he did well when he came on: he mightn't have had all the gear he wanted, but he was fully tuned in.

For the two O'Connors, it was the end of a special year: Ben had the Liam MacCarthy Cup next to him, and Jerry had joined him in Newtownshandrum's All-Ireland club victory that March.

You can't talk about one without the other. I'd have heard of them long before they played for Cork. They had an unbelievable underage reputation around. I saw them in the intermediate county final for Newtown against Cloyne in 1996, when they were seventeen, and I played against them in an U-21 county final the following year. I was well established with Cork that time and would have been expected to dominate the teenager I was on – Jerry – but it was the other way around. Whether it was push-ups, sprints, runs, or a game, Jerry was ultra-competitive.

They're identical twins, but I could always tell which one was which. Obviously it helped that Ben wore a black helmet and Jerry wore a green helmet. It got a bit trickier when they weren't wearing helmets. It annoyed them if you got the name wrong – they wouldn't answer you.

The O'Connors were living further away from Páirc Uí Chaoimh than anybody else and had to make more sacrifices to get to training – but they did it for over ten years with no complaining.

Ben was one of the most gifted players I ever met – himself and John Gardiner must have been the best stickmen we had. He was humble and unassuming, like his brother, but he had huge confidence in himself as well. The two of them had a great understanding of each other, naturally enough.

The scores Ben got for us over the years were incredible. He got a point in Thurles against Clare in the qualifiers in 2008, when we were under huge pressure; that summed him up. He was covered when a high ball came to him, he tapped it down, ran on to it, soloed through: point.

Another ultra-competitive guy. I often marked him in training games and he'd spend the hour running. Tireless.

In the middle of it all was the man who kept us healthy. The first time I saw Dr Con was on TV, attending injured players in big games Cork were involved in. When I started playing Cork minor in 1994 he was on the sideline, and I got winded at one stage so he came in to check up on me. Now here we were, ten years later, at the top of the tree. We built up a great relationship over my years as a senior. It'd be difficult to put in words all he did for us over the years. If you had anything wrong with you, day or night, you could ring him and he'd sort you out.

He's a very witty guy, a great man with a one-liner. That's been a huge part of his value to Cork over the years. In dressing-rooms before big games there's huge stress, pressure, testosterone, nervousness. Con would crack a few jokes to bring guys back down to earth. He sat at the back of the bus with us going to games, and the stories would keep you going to Thurles or Limerick or wherever you were going. His line to me always was that Vijay Singh was keeping me out of the Fijian Sports Personality of the Year award; then he'd let on to make it up to me on the bus.

'The best number seven in the world?'

I'd turn around.

'Nah, Ogie, has to be Richie McCaw.'

A great friend. He'd put the band on my wrist before every game, give me a quick kiss on the forehead and wish me the best of luck. That was the ritual.

The year got better when we won the Cork county championship with Na Piarsaigh. What made it better again was the number of familiar faces in the dressing-room.

Aisake growing up never had the same interest in watching me and Teu play that Setanta had, and at underage he didn't show the same drive as the rest of us. The serious stuff of playing hurling seemed to go against the grain of his nature, but there was an expectation that he'd follow us, and he did.

Aisake showed glimpses of promise early on and would have been a standout for his team at the club. He had one downfall, though: he had a short fuse. I don't know how many times I had to intervene in arguments between himself and Setanta over petty stuff when they were growing up and I was around the place.

My most vivid memory of Aisake is from when I was about fifteen, pucking around in the garden at home in Blarney. Beautiful summer's day, taking shots into a makeshift goal Dad had built from wood and iron, the usual crack, until Aisake went in to block me, mistimed his challenge – and my hurley slashed his forehead open along the eyebrow.

Dad was at work, Mum might have been shopping in town, and here's Aisake, seven years of age, blood spouting out of his forehead. He was panicking with the blood, naturally enough, and Setanta tried to calm him down while I ran into the house and pulled out the old Rose's chocolate tin that was our first-aid container.

I got a bandage and wound it round his head – and off we went to Blarney to get the bus into town. We thought about thumbing it for a second. Then we decided that the sight of Aisake with a bandage on his head like a turban, and blood seeping out through it, mightn't be the best way for us to get a stranger to stop his car. As it was, the people on the bus weren't that keen to sit next to us on the journey.

We brought him to the Mercy Hospital and they patched him up, but they needed a parent or guardian's signature to give him stitches, so we ended up having to ring Dad's work, they had to track down the job he was on . . . I'd say Aisake didn't forgive big brother for that for a long time. But he learned to time his blockdowns after it.

I think Setanta's success at underage level spurred Aisake on to achieve a bit more himself when it came to hurling and football. He was just out of minor in 2004, but he was Na Piarsaigh's free-taker, which showed he was moving in the right direction.

And someone else was with us that season too: Setanta. He came home after his first year with Carlton, and he fell in with us. Even though he hadn't played hurling for a year, he made a huge difference, and I'm not sure we'd have won without him. He worked hard all through the final: he was pumped up because he didn't think he'd ever get another chance to play with us for the club, and he was right.

I'd won counties underage with Teu which were special, but winning the big one with the two of them really gave it that family feeling. It was the only time the three of us got to share in the winning dressing-room together, which makes it kind of a bittersweet memory.

The team we beat in that county final was Cloyne, by the way. That's the GAA: you go to war with fellas for the county and a couple of weeks later you're trying to cut their throats in the local club championship. At the final whistle that day in Páirc Uí Chaoimh I tried to find Diarmuid O'Sullivan and Dónal Óg Cusack. I shook hands and commiserated. Dónal Óg, I knew, would want to be left alone, he would be in no mood for talking, but I wanted to make sure I saw him on the field.

It was a tough end to a great year for Sully in particular. The man known as 'The Rock' was the heartbeat and barometer of our team for so long. Never have I seen crowds erupt to such excitement as to his heroics on the field of play. The man was a gladiator. We had warriors in abundance around that time, but he was the ultimate warrior. For instance, when we were under pressure in the 2003 All-Ireland final, he kickstarted the revival with his cameo, flooring three Kilkenny lads. He had a reputation for taking no prisoners and he was a big man, but by god could he hurl. He was well up there alongside John Gardiner and Ben O'Connor in the skill department. For me he was hurling's Robert DiPierdomenico.

I remember one year when we got to the All-Ireland series we had a quiz on the train going up to Dublin. We'd divided up into teams of four, and I was with Sully when John Allen gave out the quiz sheets. Tricky questions.

I asked my team-mate for his contribution: 'Do you know any of these answers, Sully?'

'Are we here to win All-Irelands or fucking quizzes?'

That was the end of our chance of winning the quiz, right there.

Around that time there were rumours cracking around Cork that I was off for the AFL as well. People were putting two and two together but they weren't coming up with four.

Larry Tompkins was an Ireland selector for the Compromise Rules team, and he invited me to train with them. I was a bit embarrassed, because I hadn't played intercounty football for a couple of years, but Setanta was in the Irish squad and I liked the idea of playing with him.

'You'll never get this opportunity again and you might regret it if you don't take it up,' Setanta said. He convinced me to come out.

At the same time, Carlton had expressed an interest in bringing Aisake out to play for them. Because I was suddenly playing Compromise Rules, people jumped to the conclusion that I was going to Australia. The reality was that I was twenty-seven by then, and recruiting a guy who'd never played the game at that age was never a runner. When the news broke that it was Aisake, and not me, I could almost hear people saying to themselves, 'Ah, it's the other brother . . .'

14

In those days the county champions had the right to nominate the captain of the intercounty team. Paddy Connery, the Na Piarsaigh chairman, rang me to say they wanted to put me forward but needed to know if I'd be interested.

'This is humbling for me, Paddy,' I said. 'I'd be delighted.'

I was being honest. They could have nominated John Gardiner as easily, and I'd have been grand with that. I'm not into individual glory, more the team effort, and I'd have been happy to row in behind John as captain, absolutely. It was a chance in a million, the way things fell – winning the county, getting the armband, and then the way 2005 unfolded.

There's pressure associated with being captain. It's a subtle thing: you're leading the troops, so you've got to perform. That's a pressure you put on yourself anyway when you're playing, but as captain you feel players are looking to you to set an example.

And if you're talking to players and trying to get them to measure up, then you've got to back that up with your own play. If you tell players you want more out of them, then you've got to show them the only way they'll respect: with what you do on the field.

There are other calls on your time, more responsibilities than simply going up to the halfway line before the game and saying heads or tails to a referee. You're involved more with the management of the team. At that time we had five player reps, and as captain I met them regularly to discuss what was going on: how training was going, what management needed to know from the players, did this guy need more training, that guy need less.

You're the first person at press nights or after games that the media wants to speak to, and the media commitments could be exhausting. It was important not to let those outside responsibilities diminish my own preparation. For me, that meant going out, sometimes, on nights when we didn't train as a team, and doing some more work. I wouldn't have missed a lot of sessions, but I was always conscious that I needed to ensure my own preparations weren't compromised, for instance, and that I could meet the standard required and make the contribution I needed to make.

Some of the outside commitments came totally out of left field.

We'd just started back, early in 2005, when Jerry Wallace, our trainer, rang me. He'd trained a youngster called Robert Holohan with the Midleton GAA club, and now Robert was missing. Jerry asked me to go on television to make an appeal for Robert's return, because he was a big GAA fan and a Cork hurling supporter, and they were hoping the appeal might prompt him to contact his family.

Obviously I was keen to help. A missing child is the kind of real-life emergency that puts sport in its proper place. In addition, Jerry was an integral part of our backroom team and went above and beyond the call of duty in terms of extra training sessions for me over the years. So, anything he wanted from me, I was happy to help.

The case had a terrible end when Robert's body was discovered in east Cork. I went to the funeral down in Midleton and read a prayer, and it was heartbreaking.

I'd planned to hit the gym that evening, but I couldn't face it and just went home. It's a cliché to say that certain events put sport into perspective, but that day put life into perspective for me, never mind the game of hurling.

We also had a new manager, of course. John Allen was now in charge, having been promoted from selector to replace Dónal O'Grady.

By the end of 2004 we had huge respect for Dónal as a manager and a person, and I remember saying to some of the senior players that we'd have to double that respect for John. It wasn't going to be easy for him to move from selector to manager, and some people would have questioned his credentials; there were a few nasty cracks about the fact that he'd been a team masseur with us back in the late nineties. That got under my skin, I have to admit. Those comments didn't recognize the fact that John had played senior hurling and football with Cork, which was more than any of the comedians repeating the wisecracks had done. In addition, they didn't know how good he was in management; as I've said, he'd facilitated those goal-setting sessions we had as a team, independently of his selectorial duties. (He's since gone on to show, with the Limerick hurlers, just how good a manager he is with a totally different group of players.)

The first night back in training was down in Carrigtwohill. Before we went out on the field I called for the players' attention and said: 'Lads, we have a new manager. We know him from his time in the backroom team but he's the main man now, and if he asks you to jump, your answer is "How high?"'

That was the message I wanted to get to the team: that we'd row in with him one hundred per cent. There was no big formal meeting about it, so much as getting that point across to the lads: this guy's the boss now.

That was about standard for my speech length, too. I wouldn't have given lengthy pre-game talks so much as backing up what management had said, to remember our game-plan and to stick to our structures. Very game-specific, rather than the old *Braveheart* orations and smashing hurleys in the dressing-room.

I had another interesting development in my career as captain ahead of the Munster final with Tipperary that year.

People may have forgotten, but that year there was a lot of tension between the GPA and RTÉ because the latter had an issue with GAA players drinking Club Energise, the energy drink which had a sponsorship tie-in with the GPA, when those players were being filmed giving post-game interviews. Alan Brogan of Dublin had refused one interview as a result.

Brian O'Driscoll had recently been interviewed by RTÉ drinking an energy drink he endorsed, so we felt there were double standards involved. (People might not remember that, Brian refuelling live on camera, but they probably recall George Hook and the RTÉ panel taking the piss out of him by drinking water with 'Hook's Hooch' labelled on it.) In the run-up to our press evening, myself and John Allen spoke a lot about the issue, and he backed us when we informed RTÉ we wouldn't be making ourselves available for interview before or after the game.

Of course, yours truly nearly cocked things up. We had our usual press night in the Maryborough House Hotel ahead of the game – myself, John Allen and John Gardiner at the top table – and I spoke briefly before we started, saying that we wouldn't be taking questions from RTÉ, which was represented by Paschal Sheehy. Fair enough.

Then the questions started from the other journalists – any injuries, what did we make of Tipp and so forth – and Paschal slipped in a question.

Without thinking, I started to answer, but then I got an almighty kick under the table: 'Sorry, Paschal, that's it.' John Gardiner nearly blew the foot off me, and he was right. I was the one announcing the lack of co-operation with RTÉ, and there I was answering their questions.

We should have withdrawn co-operation a bit more often, maybe. We led Tipperary by twelve points at half-time in the Munster final, and although they rallied we won comfortably enough in the end.

In the All-Ireland semi-final we were up against Clare. They were huge underdogs but we knew well they'd put it up to us. Anthony Daly was in charge of them and he always prepares his teams well – as is obvious with the current Dublin outfit. At that time he was using the Gaelic football blanket defence by deploying a forward to the back line.

I was confident ahead of the game, though. That was based on us having the wherewithal to find a way: the hallmark of the team around that time was that we'd always find a way. No matter what the challenge, we'd find some way to overcome it. That doesn't happen by accident. We prepared properly, we had great physical trainers, we were well organized – and that all went along with good hurling ability. What happens then is all of that strengthens you when you're under pressure on the pitch. It fortifies you: you're less likely to give up because you know that work has been done by everyone, that everyone is part of the same plan, and that it was all done to make sure you passed the test you were facing.

We needed that against Clare in 2005. They outclassed us for most of that game. They came to play, and by God they imposed themselves on us. They pulled us out of position and got their men into great positions, and more than once in the game they hit points they had no right to attempt. When that happens you can feel the doubt start to creep into your mind: maybe it's not going to be our day. Maybe it's all meant for them.

But that's where the belief came in. The faith in the structures. We were going to stick to the game-plan no matter what, no matter if we were ten points up with a minute on the clock or ten points down.

For instance, our mantra was 'Support the guy, support the guy': make yourself available at all times, give the man on the ball an option.

At one stage in the first half Jerry O'Connor was in midfield but was hemmed in, so I offered myself for the outlet pass if he needed me. He popped the ball to me and I had oceans of space, so I put it over from long range. If I'd missed I'd have been shot, and rightly so, but it shows the faith in the game-plan, in the instructions we got. I wouldn't have been a big scorer, but by following those instructions, by supporting the man when it might have been easier to hang back and just mind the house, I was available to Jerry as a target, and the point followed.

We hung in there and just about kept them in sight, and in the closing stages we went into overdrive. Our game clicked into gear and we finished very well. But we were able to finish that well only because of that faith in the structures keeping us going when we were under the gun. We always felt we'd have a good run against Clare at some stage of the game, and that happened in the last ten minutes. Space opened up. Tom Kenny and Jerry O'Connor started to drive forward. Clare wobbled.

And John made two huge calls. He took off Brian Corcoran and Ronan Curran and made a few positional switches, and they worked like a charm. We burned Clare off towards the end with a sensational finish. There weren't many questions asked about John's credentials after that.

After the game I was pulled out for a TV interview as captain and, as always, I tried to be honest. I said we'd been dead and buried, but that we'd gotten out of the game through divine inspiration. I think I said Jesus Christ himself came down off the cross to help us over the line.

I'd say Clare look back on that game with nightmares, the way we'd look at the 2003 All-Ireland final.

On the Thursday night before the All-Ireland final I addressed the players because there was a story I wanted to share with them. I'd been watching a DVD of an AFL Grand Final between Carlton and Geelong in 1995. At the start it was rip-roaring stuff: guys flying into each other, all-out combat.

One of the match commentators remarked about a Geelong player, 'Isn't Garry Hocking fired up today?'

And the co-commentator replied, 'And so he should be, Sandy. This is a grand final. There is no room for second best today.'

I relayed that story to the lads. The point I wanted to make was that we were facing into our third All-Ireland final in a row. The danger is that the more times you get there, the more you take it for granted. I stressed that Sunday might be the last time this group played in an All-Ireland final together. There were no guarantees that we'd be there next year, or the year after that. We had to put our bodies on the line because, as we learned to our cost from 2003, once it's gone it's gone.

In the dressing-room before the game itself I would have reiterated sticking to the game-plan, and I would have stressed that we had to make it count when we were on top. In any game you have periods of supremacy and periods when you're under pressure, and exploiting your supremacy is the key.

I was talking to mature players, though. They were all leaders, guys who'd played in the previous two All-Ireland finals, and some of them had been there in 1999 as well. Any of them could have given the few words before the throw-in. They had as much experience as I had – some of them more – so it wasn't much of a chore to fire them up for the game.

It wasn't a lengthy speech, either. I know from experience that players are in their own space just before a game, preparing themselves. You're not going to absorb a detailed message twenty minutes before you play an All-Ireland final; your attention span is probably half a minute at most in those circumstances. I just stressed the point that we should rely on the organization that had served us so well all year and that we weren't to waver from that.

And then it was out on to the field.

We'd expected Kilkenny. They played Galway the week after our win over Clare, and it came as a shock when Galway turned them over.

We had to rethink our strategy immediately. They were a different team, obviously, and we were going to treat them with the utmost respect. They had game-breakers in Alan Kerins and Niall Healy, who got three goals against Kilkenny in the semi-final. Richie Murray and Ger Farragher were also on our radar. But we felt we had a more mature team by then – that we were probably a couple of years ahead of Galway in terms of development.

We had a great start in the game, which always helps against an inexperienced team. I think we caught Galway on the hop a little. By then we were well known for the support game, short passes and backing each other up, but we decided to mix it up a little bit against Galway. They had a young full-back line, apart from Ollie Canning, and we felt they might be a bit nervous in their first senior All-

Ireland, so we decided to test them by going long more often. It worked, too. Corcoran got an outrageous point over his shoulder early on and we were on our way.

Galway rallied late on in the game, and we weren't as good in the second half, but we were confident we'd done enough to keep them at bay. They got a goal towards the end, but we were never in real trouble.

Going into the match there was obviously a chance I'd be giving the All-Ireland-winning speech, and I never had any doubt I'd do it in Irish, as I did after we won the Munster title.

If I regret anything, it's that I didn't put in a small bit of Rotuman. My Irish heritage is hugely important to me, but I also come from another culture which is a very important part of me. It would have been nice to mix the two cultures with a few words of Rotuman, but I probably had enough to be thinking of as the All-Ireland final approached.

As for the Irish, well, I didn't go to a Gaelscoil for five years wasting my time. I'd say people I went to school with, people who taught me Irish, would have been disappointed if I didn't use *Gaeilge*.

I didn't write the speech out, but I got some help from Brother Jack Beausang, who'd taught me Irish in the Mon. He'd retired from teaching at that stage but he was living in the Brothers' house on the school property, so I dropped up to see him.

'I've an idea of what I want to say,' I said. 'Can you just put a bit of a *snas* on it for me?'

And he was excellent, too. He polished it up nicely. Why wouldn't he? His family were founder members of Na Piarsaigh, after all.

15

In early 2006 we all went on a well-deserved holiday to South Africa. During the second week of the trip there were a lot of rumours, originating back home, about Dónal Óg being gay.

'Has anyone spoken to him about it?' I asked.

'No' was the reply. Myself and Siobhán had arranged to meet up with him for dinner that evening, so I rang his room to confirm that it was still on and to ask if I could have a quick chat with him.

I told him that rumours were going around about him being gay and aked whether it was true or not.

He told me that he had had gay relationships. Having heard that, I told him to say no more. I gave him a hug and said, 'You know this doesn't change a thing,' and that I'd see him down in the foyer at eight o'clock for dinner.

I killed myself training on that trip. There were team sessions organized, but I was also doing sessions twice a day every day outside of that. Looking back, it was crazy. Myself and Dónal Óg had a new training companion in Kevin Hartnett. Kevin had come through the underage ranks with Cork, playing with Setanta, and John Allen had drafted him on to the panel in 2005. He had a good underage boxing pedigree so he was tough, very committed to training and an endurance freak.

No sooner had we come back from holidays than official team training started in earnest. I underestimated how hard the training was going to be, and by the end of the first week I pulled my hamstring. Out for four weeks minimum. In the third week of my rehab programme I got a recurrence. Out for a further four weeks. I get freaked out at the smallest of things – just ask Siobhán – so an injury like this is a 10 on the 'freakster' scale.

I've pulled hamstrings in the past but I've recovered pretty quickly from them. Not this one. I missed out big-time on the good quality hurling sessions with the team. Of all years, this was not a year to be on the sidelines, injured. We were chasing the three-in-a-row.

The three-in-a-row? Much as we tried not to talk about it, as a topic it had a habit of popping up.

We'd shown nothing in the league and had a few weeks' hard training before the Clare game, our first game in the Munster championship. That was billed as a grudge match because Clare had put it up to us the previous year, but we blew them away. Not physically, but we were just flying. Humming.

Because we were so good in that game the three-in-a-row talk cranked up in earnest, particularly with the supporters. As it turned out, the Clare game was our best performance of the year.

In the Munster final we faced Tipperary, and Eoin Kelly in particular. He'd been unmarkable against Limerick and Waterford. Outstanding.

What a player he has been for Tipperary over the journey. For me – and no disrespect to his team-mates – he carried Tipp on his own during a lean period for them from 2003 to 2008. He reminded me of Brian Corcoran, who singlehandedly carried Cork from 1993 to 1999. If Kelly didn't perform, then Tipp didn't win.

Henry Shefflin is as good a player as I've seen, but he's had a fair supporting cast over the years – Eddie Brennan, Richie Power, Martin Comerford, Eoin Larkin, DJ Carey, Charlie Carter, John Power . . . Eoin Kelly wouldn't have had the same calibre of player with him over the years, but he never hid behind that. That's the way it seems to me with hindsight. At the time, Eoin was just a threat, not someone to stand back and admire.

In the game I played deeper than usual. Management hadn't given me explicit instructions ahead of the match to play a little deeper; they didn't have to. Any time I felt the ball might go to Eoin's corner, any time a Tipp man out the field got the sliotar in his hand and they glanced at Eoin, I headed back to try to cut out the supply.

Dónal Óg would have been stressing that anyway: 'If you're not going to be involved in the play, then you know where you need to be, you need to funnel back into that space.'

It worked pretty well, but you have to remember he had a tasty defender for company, too. Brian Murphy is one of the top markers in the game and would have been keeping a tight rein on Eoin anyway.

The longer the season went on, the more the three-in-a-row stuff got to the team, I felt. The Limerick game crystallized that.

We were haunted. They came with aggression, there was plenty of squaring up to each other – and it worked, because it put us off. We seemed to be reacting to that rather than playing our own game and keeping the scoreboard pressure on them.

It's a cliché to say you get drawn into a dogfight, but that's what happened. You could expand on that and say we played the game on Limerick's terms, because they wanted a scrappy encounter. (Scrappy might be generous – a spectator confronted Tom Kenny and Jerry O'Connor in the middle of the field before the start of the second half.)

It was a strange one – the longer it went on, it looked like they might get something out of it. I never felt comfortable in it. There was a rain shower and Limerick thrived on it; there was one passage of play when a ball ricocheted off Pat Mulcahy's boots and went sailing over the bar for a score . . . it looked like one of those days when they were getting all the breaks.

Ben O'Connor helped us over the line, not for the first time. We had plenty to think about on the bus home: we accepted that the display wasn't good enough, that in previous years we'd have dealt with the situation better. But now, looking back, I think maybe our finishing power was ebbing away. We'd been known for our strong finishes, for coming with a flourish in the final quarter, and that wasn't happening any more. I know Sean McGrath felt it was getting harder and harder to keep twenty-five, twenty-six guys fully fit as the year rolled on. Guys were breaking down with soft-tissue injuries – myself included.

We refocused for Waterford in the All-Ireland semi-final, where I got a specific job: Dan Shanahan.

Dan was having a terrific season. He'd killed it against Tipperary in their quarter-final meeting and was hurling with incredible confidence.

By 2006 he was a different animal. He'd transformed himself. What was scary was not his aerial ability, which everyone knew about, but his running game. I struggled to cope with his runs on and off the ball. He complained in the media afterwards that I'd been hanging on to his jersey, and he was right.

Myself and Dan go as far back as 1990, when his club Lismore competed in an U-13 tournament at my club. He was gangly, but could he play! He was a player that needed minding, and when his dander was up you might as well take an early shower. Dan, Shefflin and Setanta, when he played his only season in 2003, reinforced to me the value of tall players. The game of hurling has changed so much, but the one thing you can't buy is tall guys. There is a saying in Aussie Rules: 'When the small men get tired, the tall men don't get smaller.' Tall target-men cause consternation to defences around the square. How many times have we seen Dan ghost in around the square and latch on to a long high ball; before you knew it, his two arms were in the air celebrating.

Another feature of Waterford's play was the rotation of their forwards, which was done cleverly. It wasn't overt – forwards swapping places during play. They'd just drift into space, as subtly as possible. The question then was to stick or twist: do you follow your man or hold your position? I know this system caused a lot of headaches for us to defend.

There was a distinct sense in the country that it was Waterford's time. Those were the vibes coming out of Waterford, that they were going to do it, and much of the game bore that out. They weren't destroying us, but they were ahead, winning key match-ups, and it was going to take something monumental to turn the tide.

That something was Cathal Naughton, who came on for us in the second half. We tried a pre-planned move from a free and Cathal hit a point; and then he got a goal. Advantage Cork.

It was willpower that sustained us that day. If we weren't so experienced, I say we'd have buckled, but we kept going. We needed a break or two, and when we got them the momentum switched.

Everyone remembers the end of that game. Waterford had a late, late free to equalize from the middle of the field and Ken McGrath caught it well, but Dónal Óg not only saved it going over for a point, he flicked it out to the wing and away from danger. Myself and Brian Corcoran descended on the ball and Corcoran cleared it. Game over.

Dónal Óg deserved to influence the game like that. His goalkeeping had gone up to another level. He'd done savage work to improve his flexibility, his puck-outs, the way he organized the defenders around the square – he practically lived in the ball alley.

Because of all that work he would have been dreaming of that moment, of getting the chance to make a save like that. And when the chance came, he took it. John Allen said that at that time he had the best touch in hurling. I'd believe that.

The mood was high in the camp after beating Waterford. We'd been aware of how confident they were, and on the way home we were saying, 'All talk again,' and so forth. We thought that that loss would break them – how wrong we were!

It had taken a huge effort to beat them. We didn't have the power to kill teams off any more. Was that down to individuals? I know that I wasn't at my best. Was that team just at the end of its natural life-cycle? Or was it that other teams knew us? Maybe we weren't fully aware of it at the time, but as All-Ireland champions you're constantly being analysed and scrutinized by the opposition. Maybe teams had figured out how to beat us.

I watched the All-Ireland semi-final in Siobhán's house in Innishannon. Kilkenny were impressive in dismantling Clare.

A week and a half out, I pulled up with a sore hamstring after a series of flat-out forty-metre sprints. I dropped out and looked for Declan O'Sullivan, the physio. He ran some tests and said I hadn't torn the hamstring, which was a huge relief. He gave me a rehab programme that I'd have to follow all the way to the All-Ireland final, and he said I wouldn't be able to train with the main group.

Again John Allen handled the situation admirably. He had noticed me pulling out of the sprint and he asked me, 'Everything OK?' I told him what had happened, and what Deccie had said. I was expecting him to raise his eyebrows, but his response was, 'Deccie is the expert. You do what he tells you to do.'

The final was no classic. Kilkenny had the game won a long time before the final whistle. They were so dominant they could afford to hit plenty of wides. Even Henry hit very scoreable frees wide that day, which was not typical of him.

We were beaten by a better side on the day because we couldn't win primary possession all over the field. It was noticeable that from our puck-outs their full-forward line dropped back, their half-forwards clogged up midfield. When the ball broke to the ground, they were winning the rucks and dirty ball.

When we did get on the ball, we were being harried into positions we were uncomfortable with. The grass didn't help. It was very long, and the lads who'd gone out to watch the minor curtain-raiser earlier in the day had come in and said, 'Long cogs today, lads.' Walking around in the parade, we left visible footprints behind us in the long grass.

But it was the same for them, unless they were training in ankle-high grass down in Nowlan Park. No excuses. The better side won.

What was alarming was the level of heat and intensity they brought to the game and the structural zoning they had for our puck-outs. This was to be a familiar feature for the next six years as they trounced teams at will. Although we couldn't know it, this Kilkenny victory was the start of the most impressive period of dominance by any hurling team in history.

The order of things had changed.

16

Our feeling after John departed as manager was that it was vital to maintain the structures that had been introduced by him and by Dónal O'Grady. The system needed to evolve, it needed tweaking, but we felt that would be done best by someone who was already part of the set-up – someone who knew what was involved, who knew what was needed, and who knew the players.

There's a vital point here: 'knowing the players' isn't a matter of meeting them on a Saturday night for a drink. It's a matter of knowing their strengths and weaknesses as players. The ideal man would have been Ger Cunningham, who knew the players inside out – as players, not as drinking buddies.

As well as being a selector, he'd also have been doing a lot of the on-field drills anyway. He worked hard with the goalkeepers in particular, and in general he was excellent on the technical side of things, in preparing and improving players. I'm sure he would have had ambitions to manage Cork if he'd been asked.

The age profile of the players was good. Hardly any key members of the squad were in their thirties, apart from Brian Corcoran and Pat Mulcahy, so a big clear-out wasn't required. All things considered, the window of opportunity was still there for us. We felt an All-Ireland wasn't out of reach, all things going well. The crucial thing was the new man accepting the template which had brought us to four All-Ireland finals in a row.

Gerald McCarthy was appointed manager. We were on the team holiday in Cancún, Mexico, when he gave an interview to a paper back home, in which he said he wasn't a fan of 'their' game, i.e. our game, the game as played by his new players. To us that wasn't a good sign, a manager telling the media that he didn't favour the way his team played.

Early on, though, the other signals were largely positive. Gerald told us when we all met up that things wouldn't be changed – that the structures that were there wouldn't be thrown out. (There were a lot of references back to those comments later among the panel when things went sour.)

I remembered Gerald managing Waterford, of course. When I worked in Cork City centre, I'd often bump into him on the street and we'd salute and say hello. I'd always give him that respect as a former Cork great.

In mid-January of 2007 a TV documentary on the family, *Tall, Dark and Ó hAilpín*, was aired. At the following training session, Gerald came over to me and congratulated me on the documentary, saying his son Alan had been out in Australia travelling and had met up with Setanta, who'd been very good to him.

All hunky-dory.

Jerry Wallace had stayed on as the physical trainer, and hard physical work was the main focus early in the year, as usual. Everything rolled on without a hitch until we started playing pre-season games.

Before playing Waterford, down in Dungarvan, the pre-match meal consisted of sandwiches with coleslaw, which was going back to the bad old days before the strike. In addition, we were eating in the same place as the Waterford team, which meant we were eyeballing our opponents for an hour before the game. No disrespect to the Waterford players and camp, but we felt it wasn't ideal to be sharing a pre-match meal with the opposition. Maybe it's a small thing, but could you imagine any pro team worth their salt eating their grub in the same room as their opponents?

During the first half, Dónal Óg tried a short puck-out and the ball was intercepted. At half-time Gerald told him to cut out the short puck-outs, and Dónal Óg said he'd go short again if the opportunity presented itself. After the game Dónal Óg was summoned to a meeting by Gerald and his selectors, who were unhappy with his response. I was also asked to attend the meeting as a playing colleague of Dónal Óg's.

We found ourselves in a meeting room in the Grand Hotel in Fermoy before a training session on a Tuesday night. Management said that they felt Dónal Óg had overstepped the mark, and they wanted to drop him for the next game. We felt that this was severe, and tried to explain that the short puck-out was a tactic that we'd been encouraged to employ by previous regimes. They took this on board, but still insisted that Dónal Óg sit out the next game. He did so.

The whole exercise gave us reason to believe that there was more than just short puck-outs at issue. It appeared that the continuity we had hoped for was not favoured by management, and Gerald was going to do his own thing.

This was early in 2007. We had no appetite for going back on a war footing. Not a bit of it.

People would have asked – particularly when the whole thing fell apart – how we were able to work with Gerald if things were bad, but you have to remember that it's like work: you have to be professional and get on with it. You may not like or agree with the boss, but you get on with the job as best you can.

Fellas had serious reservations about Gerald's appointment, and the feeling amongst us was that he had been appointed by the Board to put manners on us. Yes, in the aftermath of the 2006 All-Ireland defeat, things needed tweaking, but we didn't feel we'd be best served by a person who hadn't coached intercounty in seven years. At training, you had goalkeepers doing the work outfield players were doing, corner-backs doing overhead pulling . . . we felt the game had moved on and that we'd experienced better training under previous regimes.

For me, the most significant sign of the unrest in the camp was the walking away of one of Cork's greatest corner-backs, Wayne Sherlock. It was a midweek training session down in Páirc Uí Rinn. During a water break Wayne approached Gerald. They spoke briefly, and then Wayne strolled off the pitch in disgust. That was the last time we would see Wayne as a team-mate. It was such a shame, because he still had plenty to offer.

Wayne had injured his groin badly in 2004, then spent all of 2005 in rehab after a recurrence of the injury. By 2006 Pat Mulcahy had established himself as an All-Star corner-back in Wayne's absence. When 2007 came around it looked like Wayne was back on track, with the injury fully healed. Although he was busting a gut in training to get back, he was seeing very little game time in the National League and was becoming very disillusioned.

When they spoke, Gerald wasn't giving him any comfort as to his future on the panel. Between that and weighing up if it was worth hanging around in the current set-up as a bit player, I'd say he reckoned his time would be better spent elsewhere. It was a privilege to know him and to play alongside him for ten seasons between U-21 level and senior. Wayne was our number-one tagger, getting big shut-down roles on the best forwards from opposing teams. Our own forwards dreaded getting him in training games.

But Gerald was the boss. There is a perception that we downed tools in a huff because we didn't like what Gerald was doing. That's not true at all. We trained his way for a couple of years, and anything he wanted done, we did it as best we could.

For many people Semplegate was the defining incident of 2007. And Gerald backed us to the hilt on that. We saw the other side of him in that episode and we appreciated that support.

What caused it? Poor Niall McCarthy gets the blame for Semplegate because he spoke last in the dressing-room. That wouldn't have been unusual: over the years Niall would have chipped in the odd time just when we'd be ready to head out, and you wouldn't be expecting it; but invariably there was value to what he said. Fellas in every team in every sport will tell you that: if a guy doesn't speak before games all the time, then the odd interjection carries a lot of weight. You listen.

Niall spoke from the heart that day and we headed out. The last thing you think of is the schedule – Cork out at 3.04 – and you go when the knock comes.

I'd usually be the last out because I like to tap everyone on the shoulder going out – 'Best of luck, best of luck' – and I let a couple of subs go past as well to make them feel a part of it. You head down the tunnel in Semple Stadium and you can see all the way down to the far end, where the other dressing-room is, and I saw the Clare players coming out. It didn't occur to me that there could be trouble. I thought the GAA had introduced a Champions League-style entry to the pitch, where both teams come out together.

At the end of the tunnel from the dressing-room we turned left towards the pitch and Clare turned right, coming from the opposite direction. By the time I made my left turn, there were hurleys flying everywhere. Holy shit. I saw one of the Clare players hit Dónal Óg a belt of a hurley across the back and run off. I thought, 'Fuck that, you sneaky fuck!' If you're going to strike someone, have the *liathróidi* to do it in front of him and be a man about it. Don't do it behind his back and run off.

I went after him and tried to wrestle him to the ground. 'You're a brave man, running away,' I said as we struggled. After about thirty seconds, an eternity for an amateur wrestler like myself, we finally went to ground. There were no punches thrown, and soon some Cork and Clare players were pulling us off. While our mini rumble was happening, the main rumble had been going on behind us.

The referee warned the two captains that the next player who stepped out of line would get the line, but it was over even at that stage. We'd regained our focus on the game and won it well in the end.

On the bus home we tried to dissect it – 'What happened to you when you got a belt?' – that kind of thing; but we weren't expecting much of a reaction. The referee hadn't taken any action, remember.

I didn't see *The Sunday Game* that night, but I heard later that they'd made a big deal out of the row, pointing to the fact that there were primary schoolkids in the guard of honour and that it had been scandalous to let the children witness this.

*

I got a phone call from Gerald at midnight on Monday, which didn't bode well. Nobody ever got good news in a midnight phone call.

'Look, Seán Óg, I've some disturbing news. We've been contacted about yesterday's incidents and they want to suspend some players for contributing to a melee. You're one of them.'

We needed to meet in Frank's office to discuss our approach, and the next evening we found ourselves in the room with the table topped in green baize: Frank, Gerald and his selectors, John Gardiner, Dónal Óg, Diarmuid O'Sullivan and me.

Frank said Croke Park had been on to him: the Competitions Control Committee had cited the four of us for contributing to a melee. He asked if they were right in their view, and we said no – we gave our version of what had happened and Frank noted what we said, then asked if we wanted to appeal it, as we'd miss the next game if we accepted it.

Gerald said we'd have to appeal. We all agreed. We felt hard done by because there'd been a couple of dozen guys involved. The players who'd been singled out on the Cork side had been the very guys who'd been front and centre in the strikes, and that seemed a strange coincidence.

We went to Croke Park for our hearing: me, Dónal Óg, Diarmuid, John, Gerald, Frank, Dr Con and Jerry Wallace, our trainer. We wore our 2006 All-Ireland suits to try to make a good impression, and Frank had his briefcase bulging with notes: ready for road.

Frank was good company on the way up on the train. Much as I've given out about him, he was excellent in that whole period. I've always felt that Frank has Cork's interest at heart. We were four players that were facing suspension and we needed him in our corner. On his own he can be very good and interesting company. He certainly made the train journey short with funny stories and yarns of Cork teams and players of the past.

As we pulled into Heuston Station, Frank's game face was back on.

He was a man who meant business and a man who was well used to committee-room fights. He knew GAA case law going back decades.

We went in one at a time – Sully was first, I was last – and each player spent about twenty minutes with the Central Competitions Control Committee. The CCCC made its case with the support of a video projector in the room, playing back the relevant incidents. We knew the footage well, because we'd all gone to Donie Collins' house one evening and spent hours dissecting it. Then Frank offered a counter-argument and added on a glowing character reference: he was very strong for me and I've no doubt he was as strong for the other three.

It was midnight when we finished and the last train home was long gone. We were raw with hunger, not having eaten since 3 p.m.

Frank to the rescue: 'I'll ring my good friend Oliver Barry, he'll get us a good place to eat.'

He rang Oliver, who recommended Jury's in Ballsbridge and rang ahead to sort us out. We went over, got some food and headed back to Cork in hired cars. Sully drove our car and all I remember is waking up and asking him where we were: 'Near Watergrasshill, Seán Óg. We're almost home. Thanks for keeping me company, though.'

Next day Frank had news. John Gardiner escaped, but the rest of us were suspended. Our next option was the Central Appeals Committee.

Bear in mind that the team was training away all the time – Gerald and the management were trying to keep the show on the road and concentrate on the next match, against Waterford. The other lads didn't know if we'd be playing or not, and we didn't know ourselves. Not ideal preparation for a championship game.

Back to Frank's office, where he explained that the approach would have to be different if we decided to pursue an appeal. We wouldn't be appealing the substantive issue of whether or not we'd done what we were accused of; we'd be going to the Appeals Committee with a flaw in the ruling or with a technicality. We didn't know what Frank had in mind and he wasn't inclined to share, but we all agreed on one thing: we wanted to appeal. We needed to move fast. The CAC would meet on a Friday, so it was decided we'd have to get a helicopter to Portlaoise.

Don't ask me who paid for it, but there we were in *Airwolf* mode, the three of us and Frank, in the chopper up to the Killenard Hotel helipad, and we were driven to the Heritage Hotel in Portlaoise for the appeal. The only member of the Appeals Committee I recognized was Mick Curley, the football referee.

Again, each player went in one at a time with Frank, who had a different argument prepared for each of us. He gave me another glowing reference, focusing on my exemplary disciplinary record and so forth.

We waited for the verdict in the hotel, and Frank got the phone call: unsuccessful.

We asked what options were left. He said the Disputes Resolution Authority was the only avenue, but it'd be tight if we wanted to keep alive any chance of playing against Waterford; he'd have to request a hearing by mail and lodge money to cover it within the next twenty-four hours; and it was all subject to DRA panellists being available to meet the next day. This was a Friday, remember, with the Waterford game due to be played the following Sunday.

We drove back to Cork and convened at a hotel up near the airport – this was at 2 a.m. – to discuss whether or not to go ahead. We decided to go for it and Frank, in fairness, was gung-ho. He still had to go down to Páirc Uí Chaoimh to send the email and lodge the money.

'Go home and rest,' he told us. 'We'll meet at 8 a.m. at Silver Springs and head up.'

Crazy stuff.

★

The Disputes Resolution Authority hearing was at the Heritage Hotel's establishment outside Portlaoise rather than the one in town. Eddie Keher from Kilkenny was one of the adjudicators.

There was a representative from Croke Park putting the GAA's case forward – that the evidence was damning and the previous committees had done their job and applied correct procedures. It wasn't looking promising for us, but Frank tore into the Croke Park representative with his counter-arguments. You could see he had him rattled. As well as Frank performed, we were clutching at straws because cases that end up with the DRA rarely get overturned.

Afterwards we all had grub together while waiting for the verdict. I remember looking at Frank at one stage and he was cooked. His top shirt button was opened and his tie at half mast. After he'd left us at the airport hotel I've no doubt he stayed up all night doing his homework.

Again his company during the meal was enjoyable. I don't think myself, Cusack and Sully had ever laughed so much. We started asking him questions about his days as an intercounty referee. He came out with some beauties of stories about the knacks players would get up to in order to con referees. You could see this was right down Sully's alley! It was probably the last genuine crack we would all share in each other's company.

Eventually the DRA gave its verdict to Frank. Our last appeal had been unsuccessful. We got word back to Gerald that we wouldn't be available for the match the following day. Donie Collins had travelled up with us for the hearing instead of Gerald. Myself and Frank travelled with Donie. On the way back one could sense that Frank was pissed off about the outcome, but by the time we hit Abbeyleix the conversation had turned to Blackrock players in the seventies. Donie, who represented Cork in his time, would have been one of them. For a northsider, the conversation was fascinating.

By the time we passed Horse and Jockey, there was just snoring.

The next day was the Waterford game. It was a blessing in disguise that our appeal had failed, because if we had been cleared to play we'd have been in no shape to do so. We'd missed training sessions, and for the three or four days coming into the game itself we hadn't been sleeping or eating properly. We were all over the place.

Dónal Óg, Diarmuid and I were with the team in the dressing-room in Semple Stadium, and Gerald suggested coming out together after the team and sitting with the subs. He felt it would be a strong gesture, so we did. And the reception we got from the Cork supporters was great when we did so.

The game went to the wire but we lost, which sent us into the qualifiers. We came out of the qualifiers and as fate should have it we ended up drawing Waterford in the quarter-final.

Towards the end of an epic game, we were up by a point when Dónal Óg made an unbelievable save from a close-range shot by Eoin McGrath. Brian Gavin, the ref, whistled him for lying on the ball after the save and gave them an unmissable free. Eoin Kelly landed the ball in Dawson Street, almost, to level it.

In the replay, a week after, there were to be no excuses. Waterford dominated us from start to finish and Dan Shanahan continued his Jairzinho season, scoring goals in every game. Gerald took Joe Deane off in the second half, which I thought was a bad call. For me, Joe was the kind of player you'd always leave on because there was always a chance he'd get a goal.

It was a most peculiar year. We'd seen the departure of Wayne in sad circumstances. And we didn't know quite where we stood with Gerald. He'd supported us during 'Semplegate', but we weren't sure he understood what was required to take us back to glory.

17

In Gerald's first year in charge, there was a meeting between player reps and management to discuss various team issues. Gerald brought up the perception that he was a Board man – he wanted to dispel that perception. He mentioned that he'd had plenty of run-ins with Frank in the past.

He gave us the evidence, recounting the story of a time when he was chairman of the Barrs and they were involved in a stand-off with the Board because of a suspension. He also told us of the time he managed the Barrs and had a blazing row with Frank, who was refereeing a game they were playing; in the end, Frank sent him to sit in the stands.

We hadn't been aware of that background. Some of the lads hadn't even been born when Gerald was playing for Cork; I was in Sydney as his career was winding down. Stories like that gave us reason to hope that we might be singing from the same hymn sheet after all. Then, in late 2007, Gerald was unwilling to go along with the Board's plans to remove the manager's right to choose his own selectors – an issue that caused us to join a winter strike that was driven by the footballers. That was another indication that he mightn't have been as pro-Board as we thought. Yet by the end of 2008 the players and Gerald were at daggers drawn.

How did that happen?

The Tipperary game in the 2008 Munster championship was a turning point. There was a lot of criticism of the management afterwards for various decisions – letting Paudie O'Sullivan take a penalty, taking off Timmy McCarthy when he'd been one of our best forwards on the day, bringing Niall McCarthy on and taking him off again, and throwing Joe Deane on when it was too late to do anything.

At half-time in the dressing-room Gerald and Sully had heated words. Gerald told Sully to tighten up on Lar Corbett and to follow him wherever he went. Sully retorted by saying he'd been told to stay in his full-back position. That wouldn't have been the cause of any grudge, but the defeat left a mark. We felt we'd lost the game more than Tipperary winning it – and that the decisions made on the line that day were a major contributing factor to the loss.

We had a sticky outing against Dublin in the qualifiers down in Páirc Uí Chaoimh, one which hinged on the Dubs hitting the post with a good goal chance. We went downfield after that for the decisive score, but morale wasn't great and more doubts were seeping into players' minds about the capabilities of the management.

We put some suggestions to Gerald at that point, and in fairness to him he took them on board. It would have been easy for him to say, 'Fuck off, this is my show and I'll run it how I want,' but he didn't. He said, 'If it means getting the best out of fellas, we'll do it.'

One consequence of this was a bonding session for the entire squad and management, run by Cathal O'Reilly, who worked in HR for Johnson & Johnson. Some of us had played against Cathal years before – he was involved with the Galway minor team in 1995 when we beat them in Thurles in a thriller. The session took place upstairs in the boardroom in Páirc Uí Chaoimh. Gerald introduced Cathal, saying that he felt there might have been a breakdown in communications between the team and the management, and that Cathal was going to facilitate a few exercises to bridge that gap. One of them was to go home and write something positive – had to be positive – about everybody else in the room. It was fairly stand-ard corporate team-building, stuff that a lot of readers will be familiar with.

We did that, and Cathal collated the material – each player got a one-pager back which showed what other players had said about them, and it was inspiring stuff. Very positive.

We played Galway next. Deano gave us a highlight for the ages in the first half: a ball came to him unexpectedly and he was able to hit a point with the bas upside down on the hurley. That was Joe's greatness in a snapshot. The game seemed winnable right up until half-time; but by then Dónal Óg had been sent off, we were a couple of points down and we were facing a strong breeze in the second half.

At half-time Dónal Óg was asked to speak, and he spoke well. He inspired us.

During the second half he made a suggestion to Gerald and the management team about changing the approach – to get the two men in the full-forward line to stay out of the middle in order to stretch the Galway defence. If Galway had a spare corner-back he could roam and cover his team-mates, but if the man in the centre was free we could keep the ball going up the wings and keep him out of the play to some extent.

The suggestion was acted upon, and it worked a treat. We ground out one of the sweetest wins of Gerald's reign. It seemed to galvanize the whole group and bring everyone together. We all woke up on the Sunday morning to a text from Gerald, sent in the small hours, telling us he couldn't sleep with the emotion from the win.

We had a meeting on the Monday in the Rochestown Park Hotel. Cathal O'Reilly went around the room and asked every player, including substitutes, what the win over Galway had meant to them as individuals (which must have been torture for him as a Galwayman). When it was my turn I said that it was one of the best victories we'd ever had, and that the elation I felt reminded me of Marco Tardelli when Italy won the World Cup in 1982, when he ran to the camera.

Cathal spoke about Stephen Roche's Tour de France win in 1987, and he mentioned a stage in the mountains where he'd made up time on Delgado as they climbed to La Plagne. Cathal said that evening the other riders came to Roche and congratulated him on a great effort. Roche took their good wishes as congratulations on a moral victory, so he was even more determined to win the following day's stage and to go on to take the overall title.

Cathal's point was that the victory over Galway would be worthless if we bowed out of the championship the next day out.

People have forgotten the Clare game that followed the win over Galway, but we were hanging on in that one. Niall Gilligan tormented us in the first half, they were nine points ahead at the break, and we were being beaten all over the field. I had my hands full with Tony Griffin, who was tall, strong and fast, and I wasn't the only one trying to keep the head above water.

We needed something to put us back in the game, and Timmy McCarthy, on as a substitute, got a goal just after half-time, just what we needed.

Ben O'Connor, meanwhile, gave an exhibition of hurling. He pulled some amazing things out of the bag in the second half. At one stage there was a high ball dropping to him and you could see the Clare defender coming behind him, about to munch him; Ben was leaning back, hurley extended backwards, and he tilted the stick slightly to deflect the ball down and past the Clare guy. He was away and on to the ball before the Clare defender could react, soloed up the middle of Semple Stadium and hit a superb point.

Beating Clare got us a date with Kilkenny in the semi-final.

I was asked to attend a press night in the build-up the Kilkenny game. I did an interview for the *Sunday Tribune* and was asked to give my thoughts on Gerald as manager. My response would come back to haunt me. I gave him a glowing report, of course. As much as I wanted to tell it as it was, I couldn't do it to the team and management. Last thing we needed was guys picking up the *Sunday Tribune* on the morning of the game and saying, 'What the hell is going on here?' I found myself in the classic case of 'you're damned if you do and you're damned if you don't'.

I've played in some unbelievably intense games, but the first twenty minutes of that match against Kilkenny was the most absorbing contest I've ever been involved in. It was a rip-roaring affair, with ferocious intensity. Players on both sides were throwing themselves into everything. It was a warm day and at one stage I thought my lungs were going to explode. It reminded me of the world middle-weight championship fight between Marvelous Marvin Hagler and Thomas 'The Hit Man' Hearns in 1985 in Las Vegas. The fight lasted only three rounds but they absolutely killed each other.

We had a good period of dominance in that first twenty minutes, but unfortunately we didn't show it on the scoreboard. Then Kil-kenny lifted it up a gear and that was that. It was one-way traffic in the second half, and it got embarrassing. What was most disappoint-ing was the level of resistance, or the lack of same. The towel was thrown in quickly. In the past we'd been beaten, but there'd always been a sense that we'd made the opposition earn their win. There'd been fight against Galway and fight against Clare, but Kilkenny was one fight beyond our class. To be fair, we were fighting against a Sugar Ray Leonard or a Marvin Hagler: an all-time great.

That game summed up for me the gulf in standards between the two teams. We'd gone so far backwards it was frightening. A lot of the Cork supporters must have been passing Portlaoise on the way home by the time the final whistle went.

Gerald thanked us for our efforts afterwards. The standard stuff. There was no 'Well, it's been great,' no formal farewell, but we assumed that was that. He'd had two years, the same as Dónal O'Grady and John Allen, and they'd won an All-Ireland each.

The Board asked for two player representatives to attend a meeting to discuss the manager for 2009, as provided for in the resolution of the 2007 strike. John Gardiner and Dónal Óg were the two player representatives. I ended up standing in for John, who was away on holidays. We met the County Board representatives in Páirc Uí Chaoimh and after the pleasantries we got down to business. No sandwiches this time.

The general theme from the Board men was that we weren't that far away from Kilkenny, that we'd stayed with them for twenty minutes, and that they were happy with the work that Gerald had done. Funnily enough, the continuity that hadn't appealed to them when Ger Cunningham was a possibility at the end of 2006 now seemed to be a prime qualification for Gerald.

We asked if there wasn't a responsibility to explore other options, but it was clear from their attitude that they wanted Gerald; we came to believe that they'd probably already offered him the job. They asked us to go back and consider the possibility of Gerald staying on, which was where we left it.

There was a meeting of the panel after we met the Board, and we conveyed to the other players the Board's enthusiasm for retaining Gerald as manager. The consensus among the panel was that we were falling behind other counties and the basic question was this: was Gerald the man to take us forward? When we discussed it, nobody favoured Gerald staying on. It was a measured discussion, not a matter of personal attacks on Gerald; but we were unanimous.

John Gardiner was back for the next meeting with Dónal Óg, and they told the Board reps that Gerald wouldn't be accepted, that the players didn't want him. After that meeting with the Board, John and Dónal Óg had a meeting with Gerald at selector Donie Collins' house. They told him the panel didn't want him. He said he found that hard to believe and wanted to continue. We were surprised to hear that, because a member of Gerald's management team had told us he was going to finish up, that it had been a stressful two years. And Gerald himself had told Niall McCarthy that he wouldn't be back if the players didn't want him.

We couldn't understand the apparent change of mind, but we were certain that we weren't going to play under him. We felt that continuing to work under Gerald would be a backward step. Panellists who could make it, myself included, met him in the Imperial Hotel and told him as much. I kicked off the meeting by saying that the purpose of the players in meeting him was to convey that John and Dónal Óg weren't on a solo run, and that the panel didn't have confidence in him. I asked, 'Do you really need this hassle at your age?'

He didn't flip when I said that, though it was obviously hard for him to hear; but it was used against me later in the court of public opinion: 'Who does Seán Óg think he is – that's ageist.'

Cue World War Three.

A lot of it was played out in the media, and the Board had us on the back foot from early on. They'd learned a lot since the first strike in 2002 and they were ahead of us early on. We took a while to get up to speed.

I wouldn't inflict a re-run of the entire saga on anyone – it was bad enough at the time. In a nutshell, we were trying to get out the message that the Board weren't adhering to the process they'd agreed to; but that was lost in the narrative of poor Gerald and the bolshy players.

In November I attended an Adidas gig in Westmanstown along with a few other GAA players. The Cork dispute was the hot topic, obviously. November isn't a month in which GAA writers normally have a lot to write about, so I found myself surrounded by reporters looking for material. The likes of Alan Brogan and Joe Canning got off lightly while I faced the scrum, but the reporters wanted my opinion and I offered it.

I said: 'Players are not going to be playing under Ger, they are not going back . . . we have no confidence in him as a coach.'

The response was immediate. Gerald issued a statement on me to the media, and he didn't hold back: 'I accept that Seán Óg has a very busy life. His substantial commercial interests arising from his Cork hurling career, dealing with his agent, his membership of the GPA, his job with Ulster Bank and his on-off role with Cork, must make it difficult to find time to reflect. If he did find time then perhaps he wouldn't be flip-flopping around the place and changing his mind about my abilities as a coach to suit the agenda of the day.'

Gerald took my comments personally. Fair enough: I could say it wasn't intended personally, which is true, but I understand that criticizing someone's coaching ability is something they'll view as a personal attack. I accept that. But I didn't mention his business or his interests outside sport. Or concoct stories about a non-existent agent.

Was it hurtful? Of course it was. If the dispute hadn't been dirty up to that point, then it was officially dirty after that. We knew there were going to be casualties. We'd seen this from previous disputes, so we were hardened to expect the worst. However, we felt Gerald's comments had gone beyond the rules of engagement. It rocked me, for sure, so it must have rocked my own family and people who knew me. (Funnily enough, one of the criticisms we heard most during the strike was that we were causing stress to Gerald's family and the families of the players he called in to play for Cork. Evidently our own families were immune to stress.)

I got loads of support from people who disagreed with the comments. Team-mates, friends, and my own immediate family were all tremendous.

Siobhán didn't take the comments too well, obviously. She was the one who bore the brunt of the sacrifices – she'd be the one who'd say, 'We'll do something this weekend,' and I'd be saying, 'Sorry, I promised a club I'd attend their social . . .'

By the way, when Gerald issued that statement I wasn't in Cork. I was in Down, presenting medals and giving a coaching session in Ballygalget, Graham Clarke's club. Graham played in goal for Down for years and he works hard to keep hurling going in the Ards peninsula. As I drove through Tipperary on the way to Down, the texts started coming through about Gerald and his pop at my commitments and interests.

Sorry to disappoint the people who happily spread the rumour that I don't get out of bed without getting paid, but I was happy to go and help out, to spend the day training kids and encouraging them, before heading back down to Cork. Graham covered my diesel, fed me, and put me up overnight, fair enough. That's what I'd do for anyone I'd invite to Cork to help out with training or to present medals, and they wouldn't get wealthy on the back of it.

People mix that up with the work I occasionally do for big corporations, though in some cases I'd suspect it suits them to mix it up. The two are completely different. For one thing, the two or three gigs I did during the season were always on a Wednesday, and never interfered with training. For another, I was surprised to hear of Gerald's concern about my being distracted because he never once raised that with me in his two years as Cork manager.

On the other hand, if I were involved in a GAA club and I rang an intercounty hurler to get him to drive an hour or two in order to spend another two hours handing out medals and standing in for photographs, what would I say to him at the end of the night? 'Hey, that's expected of you, so enjoy the two-hour drive home now'? I'd at least feed the guy and put him up, if he wanted to stay overnight, and I'd make sure his petrol tank was full after taking a night out of his private life to come and help me out. That's not business. That's realism.

Gerald's statement hardened me further. I felt it was below the belt and trying to steer the debate away from the issues that were on the table. Once I had time to sit down and consider it, though, the more it seemed just another shot in a long PR war. I moved past it. It wasn't even the lowest point in the entire strike.

I got plenty of mail, most of it addressed to the bank or the club. Unbelievable abuse. I keep that in a box at home.

One afternoon in work my boss at the time, Sam Beamish, rang me: 'Look, one of your clients doesn't want to deal with you because of the stand you're taking in the dispute.'

That hit me for six. The last thing you wanted was the strike interfering with your work. It knocked me back, because hurling is sport but work is work. A huge difference.

Sam reassured me that my job wasn't in jeopardy and added that they were happy with what I did for the bank. It was support I'll always be grateful for.

★

Members of management rang individual players, telling them being involved wouldn't be good for their chances and their reputations: threatening them, in other words.

On top of that there was the never-ending round of meetings. After work – head straight to a hotel or in Diarmaid Falvey's office in Cloyne, trying to put out fires. The board was well ahead of us in the PR war, and we needed a strategy to make up ground.

I lost count of the number of times I rang Siobhán to tell her I wouldn't be home for 10 p.m. as promised. We'd usually leave Cloyne around 1 a.m. and I'd get home around 1.30, have something quick to eat because I hadn't had dinner. Bed for a few hours, up for work and another meeting the next night.

We'd been organizing training sessions to show we were still serious, but then the Board scored by getting a team out to contest league games. That was a blow. We knew it wouldn't fly come the championship, when you need the best players on the field, but it was disappointing that fellas were willing to play in those circumstances – and be vocal about it. Whether they genuinely thought they were good enough to be there I don't know.

I do find it hard to credit the story that some of our lads were ringing fellas to intimidate them and stop them from playing. At that point we'd have known better than to go down that route. I was lucky because there were no Na Piarsaigh players on Gerald's new team, but it was hard for lads who had clubmates playing. Maybe the likes of Kieran Murphy and Ronan Curran had conversations with those players, but I doubt there were any threats going on.

The march we organized through Cork city was a big turning point. There were more people on that march than there were at a hurling league game the following day. The Board had to be rattled, because their spin was that we had 'shoppers' going to the march. The meeting in the Rochestown Park Hotel after that was damning for them, because it was attended by members of clubs. And they couldn't be dismissed.

When we walked into that meeting we were applauded, and some people felt the strike was as good as won when that happened. Not all the club members who turned up backed us – a few of them were there to question what we were at – but the vast majority supported what we were doing. A poll in the *Examiner* showed that the vast majority of people were behind us.

Running in parallel with all of this were the defeats that Gerald's team were suffering. At one stage we considered playing a game ourselves – Anthony Daly's Dublin were a possibility as opponents, and we always respected him as a warrior – but nothing came of that.

There were still speed bumps, though. Sourcing club grounds for training among ourselves was difficult. Clubs were nervous of upsetting the Board.

Clyda Rovers were terrific and the players were hugely appreciative of their help and generosity. Their attitude was not so much that we were right or wrong, but that we were lads who wanted to train, and wasn't that what the Association was all about?

My own club, Na Piarsaigh, were also tremendous, giving us the use of club grounds, and the ladies' committee fed us afterwards. There was a backstory: during the previous strike, in support of the footballers, I was quoted in the media saying that Frank had been waiting to settle scores. That didn't go down well with Frank. At the time I was part of a delegation of players in negotiation with the board, negotiations that were organized by Kieran Mulvey of the LRC. I remember him remarking to me when that article came out: 'You certainly haven't helped things, Ó hAilpín, with your article.'

Our club came under pressure, too. The then chairman, Denis O'Neill, rang me to tell me that I had the club's support through this turmoil because I was a club member. I remember finding the timing of the call odd as I'd have assumed I had that support in any case.

Then they issued a statement distancing themselves from my comments. I rang Denis and we had heated words: I told him it was embarrassing. The incident suggested to me that the club had come under pressure from the County Board – that the Board had pushed them to make a statement when they didn't need to do that. All they had to do was say nothing.

I said to him that I wouldn't forget what had happened.

In the next strike, though, the club were very helpful, perhaps because they felt they owed it to me and to John to support us.

In the end, Gerald stepped down after receiving threatening phone calls. The strike ended, but the atmosphere was cold, and sometimes awkward. You were sitting in the same dressing-room as lads who'd walked across the line, and some of the lads who'd stood with us during the strike weren't around. The team we knew was gone, which was one of the saddest things about the whole experience.

I certainly didn't go over to shake hands with the new guys. I kept my distance. I didn't feel any loyalty to them: my loyalty was to the lads who'd toughed it out with us.

Ours was the hardest battle. We were the ones taking on City Hall. It was tough for them, getting beaten out the gate in games; it was tougher for us, getting personal abuse for five months.

18

During the strike I'd trained harder than I ever had. I knew deep down that we'd get back, but I also knew that there'd be casualties afterwards. I'd been through it all before and knew what was waiting for us at the other end: when the whole thing was over, the pressure would be on us to deliver.

The senior guys stressed that point to all the players. The training sessions on Saturday mornings wouldn't be enough and everyone had to do more on their own, because we'd be laughed out of it if we weren't ready to play when needed.

Michael Shields was drafted by Carlton to play Australian Rules, and he was given a programme by them to work on for the four weeks leading up to Christmas. I told him I'd fall in with him for that training programme to get myself in shape.

It was hard going: we'd mark out a one-kilometre run from the Kingsley Hotel out the Lee Fields and do that as hard as we could; one-minute break, then back. You'd repeat that six times, twice a week.

Towards the end of March I started to have hamstring problems, so I missed the first game back for the strikers, against Clare in the league. I got back for the Limerick game but pulled the hamstring badly going for a ball in the first half. The stress of the strike and the fanatical training during it had taken its toll. I'd been burning the candle from both ends.

Because of the injury I missed the famous game in Kilkenny, where we were destroyed. We learned afterwards that there were cheers at venues all over the country when that result came through, which taught us there wasn't much goodwill around that we could rely on.

I was rehabbing the hamstring injury for the next six weeks, which was frustrating, so I missed those initial training sessions under the new manager, Denis Walsh. He and his management team were understandably anxious to get the show on the road — they had less than three months to get the team ready for championship. Our competitors had had four months or more of training underneath their belts at that stage.

In the interests of continuity Denis retained Jerry Wallace as physical trainer. I'd played with Denis at the very end of his career. I'd shared a bench with him as our paths intersected in 1996. But I couldn't say I knew him. I imagine that, because he'd come in half-way through the season, he probably wanted to wait until the end of the year before deciding who he wanted to hang on to.

One of the players in the shop window was Aisake.

Aisake had enjoyed Australia, and Aussie Rules, but he'd come back to Cork in late 2008. Hurling wasn't on his mind at all — he fell in with the Cork footballers because, obviously, there'd be more transferable skills there from Aussie Rules. But then Denis rang him and invited him to a trial game.

He did OK. Aisake hadn't done a lot of hurling, but he did enough in that trial game to impress the management. He dropped the football and threw his lot in with the hurlers.

You could see the professional training in him. His body shape had changed, and he was much stronger. Jerry Wallace took a body-fat reading from the panel at one stage and, while most of us were at 10 per cent plus, Aisake was at something ridiculous, down around 4 per cent.

The professional approach showed in other ways. He'd take his supplements religiously after training; he'd stretch any chance he had, not just before or after training. We'd be watching the television and he'd be stretching and limbering up. And in the weight training it was obvious he was a pro. We'd do a solid conditioning session in the weights room and the following day my body would be crying with pain, but Aisake would bang out another conditioning session to the same quality. His technique when lifting weights was spot-on.

The team went to Brown's in Villamoura, Portugal, for a warm-weather training camp and it was very severe – you're training three times a day and you're shagged after two days because you're not conditioned to it. But Aisake was unbelievably consistent in all the sessions, all the days.

Denis's training drills were good – he was definitely more drills-orientated than Gerald – but the flip side was that training would go on for well over two hours. Even in the week of championship matches, when things should be winding down, he flogged us.

Sometimes in training Denis would tog out himself – boots, shorts, training top, the full works. He enjoyed having a few pucks with players and would occasionally fall in for drills if there was an odd pair. I thought it was a way of showing off that he still had it. I wasn't buying that, anyway. Another thing I wasn't buying was the couple of times he said to me, 'You know I was finished with Cork when I was your age.' I took it that he was implying that he had been wronged by the selectors and he should have stayed longer. Or maybe he was dropping me a hint!

We lost to Tipperary in the Munster championship that year, but we probably exceeded expectations, given that they had several months' preparation in hand on us. They began well but we pegged it back in the second half, before the lack of cohesive preparation counted against us in the end.

Denis got rid of Jerry Wallace at the end of the season – which I'd say Jerry is still annoyed about. He brought in Mark McManus, who I thought was excellent, but Denis didn't utilize him enough.

Mark worked us hard without killing us, and if there was a rigorous strength session in the gym, he'd tone down the running session the following night – and vice versa. The difference there is that an inexperienced guy or someone who's anxious to impress would flog you every night he could. Not Mark. His training was geared towards power and speed, the way the game had gone, and he was excellent

– as was Dónal Burke, Mark's assistant, who worked with players who required extra fitness sessions.

There was no copping out in the sessions – if you did the work properly you saw the benefits. But as the year went on, the training inclined towards longer and longer hurling sessions, and while the drills were OK, the fitness part was neglected. Mark and Dónal couldn't have been happy with this, but they said very little and played it down.

One comment from Denis at the start of 2010 certainly didn't go down well – not with me in any case. This was a good year after the strike had ended. While giving a long speech before training, he said: 'This new squad is a creation of two different teams. One team that went on strike. It mustn't have been easy taking on the establishment. I have good time for ye.

'Then you have the other team who played when the strike was on. I have more time for ye. It was harder for ye.'

I gathered my senses and thought, 'Did I hear that right? Nah, I must have been dreaming. He couldn't have said that.' Still to this day I don't know what he was trying to achieve by coming out with that. The issue was still raw enough in our minds, and just as we were trying to get over it, he brings it up again. I knew there and then that it was going to be a rough year ahead.

There was a pretence at consultation – he'd ask players in team meetings what they thought was needed – but it became a running joke within the team that if Denis pushed the glasses up his nose when you were making a suggestion, that suggestion wasn't going to be taken on board. The man didn't want to listen, full stop.

On the morning of the league final, I woke up at 5 a.m. Setanta was playing for Carlton against Collingwood that morning, and I wanted to watch the game. It's something I'm ashamed of, that I've never seen him play Australian Rules in the flesh, so any time a game of his is televised I religiously get up to see it. Because of the time difference, games are on in the early hours of the morning Irish time.

So I got up early that morning, and I'm glad I did. Setanta had a break-out game, scored five goals, and I was delighted I got to see it.

But the league final we played later that day is a game I'd want to forget in a hurry. I had a stinker. There were aspects of my play which were not up to standard, and I was on a very good player, Damien Hayes, who was red hot. He towelled me up in the first half. Worse was to come. I was rightly hauled ashore in the second half.

There were plenty of people delighted to see that, I'm sure, and the word rattled around that I was gone. At the next session Denis pulled me aside and said, 'You didn't have a good game and we pulled you off last weekend.'

I said, 'Look, that's your call, I didn't do myself any favours and gave ye no choice.'

Five weeks out from championship, he told me at that training session to get my focus right because I'd be playing against Tipperary no matter what.

My relationship with Denis was never great during the two seasons I played under him. But it would be wrong of me to forget the support he gave me after my League final disaster. It meant a lot at a time when people were writing my obituary as a hurler.

We were underdogs, given how close Tipp had come to the All-Ireland title the previous year against Kilkenny. In the run-up to the game I heard plenty of times that I was past it.

As it happened, we beat them well, down the Páirc. It was sweet. Eoin Cadogan dominated at the back and saw off a few opponents. Aisake terrorized the Tipperary defence, and the other forwards fed off him. It was a sweet, sweet victory, and we thought we were set for the year.

We beat Limerick the next day – they were going through their own internal troubles – and met Waterford in the Munster final. I pulled a hamstring and had to go off early in the second half, and the game ended in a draw, thanks to a desperate call against Brian Murphy.

We thought his hurley had been played but a penalty was given and when we stopped it, Tony Browne buried the rebound. We were beaten in the replay, when Waterford won thanks to Dan Shanahan striking for a goal in extra time. I sat out that game due to injury.

We beat Antrim in the qualifiers in Croke Park. The day of that game myself and Shane O'Neill trained together down in Páirc Uí Chaoimh, rehabbing injuries.

I was fit for the next game, which was a tilt at the four-in-a-row champions, Kilkenny, in the semi-final. We went up to Dublin the day before and stayed in the Burlington, and Denis said that he had organized a guest speaker to come to talk to us that evening. We looked forward to hearing from guest speakers – it definitely beat listening to Denis rambling on – and earlier in the season we'd had a talk from the Munster and Ireland rugby player Donncha O'Callaghan, who was excellent.

We were wondering – Ronan O'Gara? Roy Keane? Sonia O'Sullivan? Then Denis said, 'This man needs no introduction. He coached me and ye all know who he is.'

Billy Morgan walked in. And proceeded to give the greatest speech I've ever heard. Without exception.

I'd never played under Billy, but Brian Corcoran had told me how impressive he was, and now I saw for myself. He was fantastic. Started off quietly, but he was unbelievably passionate by the finish.

'They're writing ye off tomorrow,' he said. 'They're writing off the Rebels. Let me tell you something, lads: no one writes off the Rebels.'

He went on to tell us he was born in Galway, but added how grateful he was that his parents moved to Cork. He said that people thought of him as a football man, but his heroes growing up were Cork hurlers. He rattled them off: Willie John Daly, Matty Fouhy, and the king of them all, Christy Ring. He told us how he noticed that Ringy would always rub his right hamstring during the pre-match parade, and that he did the same himself when he played.

'They're writing ye off tomorrow, but I'll list games in our long and proud history that we've turned the tables' – and he listed them off.

'There's passion,' he said, 'and there's Cork passion, and you can't beat Cork passion.'

A lot of things he said definitely connected, but what was most impressive was the delivery. The speech touched me, certainly, and I could see why lads would follow him into battle when he was with Cork.

Jimmy Barry-Murphy had spoken excellently in dressing-rooms and before games over the years, but Billy was on a different level altogether that night in the Burlington. We gave him a standing ovation that lasted for thirty seconds if not more. What a man.

Billy wished us the best of luck and left. Denis then said that Billy 'was the best coach he had played under and that was the reason why'.

After fourteen years playing senior hurling, you develop a pretty good sense of what a particular manager or coach might say before a big match. There is usually a consistent set of themes over the course of a season. That was never the case with Denis. He was capable of saying anything, and his speech before the 2010 semi-final was an example.

He started off by talking about a person he knew that had played for Cork. This same player had become very frustrated with being asked to play here, there and everywhere, covering for team-mates and bailing them out. This frustrated player found himself in an All-Ireland final against Kilkenny. He had reached the stage where he was so fed up that in an act of frustration he gave away a penalty just before half-time. Kilkenny scored a goal and the rest is history. The frustrated player was taken off in the second half.

A few of us in the room knew which All-Ireland he was referring to. It was the 1992 final. A needless wild stroke happened in the square and a penalty was awarded to Kilkenny. A young DJ Carey stepped up to take the shot on a wet day and buried a low strike that skidded off the wet surface. The goal brought Kilkenny within touching distance of Cork after they'd played the first half against a strong wind. They ran away with it in the second half. I remember it vividly because I was at the game as a spectator.

Denis continued, saying that that same frustrated player who gave away the penalty had waited for a chance to redeem himself. Unfortunately the chance never came for that player – until today. He'd been waiting nearly twenty years. Wait for it. That frustrated player 'was me, lads. It was me.'

I don't know if the hurling gods were punishing us for past sins, but to listen to that was pure punishment. I was thinking, 'Is this the best you got, mate?'

After Denis's inspiring entrée, we did cover some technical stuff on Kilkenny, but it was nowhere near enough. Not one mention of what we were going to do, not if, but when Kilkenny zoned for our puck-outs. What happens if Shefflin moves there? What happens if Larkin moves here? Do we pack our defence by playing an extra player in the back line and try and catch them on the counter-attack? Do we drop our midfielders back for their orthodox long puck-outs so we don't allow them to catch clean ball? Set us a goal for tackle counts, turnovers, hooks and blocks. These things would have been valuable to us, but it seemed more important to Denis to address what he felt went wrong in his own career.

We got what was coming to us.

We were pummelled by Kilkenny. The game was over at half-time, and the white flag was up long before the end. Denis took off Aisake at half-time, which I couldn't believe. Aisake was our only goal-scoring threat. Anyway, there was very little ball going in to the full-forward line in that first half because we were all chasing shadows.

I could see Aisake fuming over the decision, so I went over to him to calm him down. We were heading out for the second half and when most of the players had exited the dressing room Aisake asked politely, 'Denis, what's that about?'

'Not the time, Aisake,' Denis said.

It was immaterial. The second half was a hammering, and it's where I got a bit angry. I didn't want it to be a ritual, to be beaten out the gap every year. I was thinking, 'How are we going to face the Cork public after this?'

The dressing-room was like a morgue, as you might expect. I was wondering how we were going to bridge the gap — to what was admittedly an exceptional Kilkenny team — when Denis spoke. He told us the management team was baffled, as they'd done everything they could think of and left no stone unturned. You can imagine how well that went down with the players. He said he was going to go out and apologize to the people who'd come up from Cork for the game.

That was 2010 over and done with.

Throughout that season I was writing a column for a website, Joe.ie. Denis mentioned to me before a training session that he wasn't comfortable with me revealing team secrets. I didn't know where he was coming from on that. My pieces were bland and general and never once did I make reference to in-house secrets, tactics or strategy. Still, it was clear the he didn't like it.

The day after the Kilkenny defeat I wrote that some of the management's decisions on the day were baffling, including the substitution of our only goal threat, Aisake. I'd say that definitely didn't go down well with Denis.

The week after the All-Ireland final, in which Tipp beat Kilkenny to stop their drive for five, the management called an end-of-year debrief meeting for the entire panel. After the meeting Denis said he'd be conducting one-to-one meetings with us after the conclusion of the local county championship, and we'd get our times and dates in due course.

I started back doing pre-season work in early October, with focus on my troublesome hamstrings. Deccie O'Sullivan was eager to get me started before the panel resumed training in early December. My one-to-one appointment with Denis was on a Saturday morning in mid-October at the Rochestown Park Hotel. I decided to do a session in the Páirc before heading on to Rochestown. My own feeling while driving to the meeting was I hadn't had a good league final, but I felt the rest of the year had gone reasonably well, and my best game of the year was the semi-final against Kilkenny.

I got to the hotel as Anthony Nash was coming out of his one-on-one, and he seemed like someone who hadn't received good news. I didn't want to pump him for details of his experience in the room, but I learned later that he'd been told that his position wasn't secure for the next season.

When I went in, Denis Walsh and Jerry Ryan, one of the selectors, were sitting down. There was a bit of small talk and then Denis got to it: 'Coming to your position, Seán Óg, management have sat down and looked at your performances over the past year. We feel your performances have slipped downwards. Do we see you having the ability to turn it around for next year? We don't.

'We have other people in mind – we're looking at William Egan, or maybe bringing Shane O'Neill out from the full-back line. We have options. We don't see you in our plans.

'This is probably hard for you to hear. You've been a great servant, you've had a decorated career, your commitment to training has been second to none and you're still in great condition. I'll leave you talk now.'

When he'd said I wouldn't be part of their plans I decided that I wasn't going to cause an ugly scene or let it develop into a heated argument. I had gone past that stage. I knew well from the tone and delivery that there was no way back.

'Look, Denis, I've had a good innings,' I said. 'I'd love to stay involved, but if I'm not part of your plans there's no point in discussing this further.'

He agreed with that. He went on to say that, apart from the Tipperary match, I hadn't had a good game.

I knew that was bullshit, but I said, 'Grand, is this over so?'

He said it was. I shook his hand and Jerry's hand. Maybe they expected me to argue the toss, but I knew well if I'd said it was dry he'd have said it was raining. I said to myself that I'd keep my dignity, though in all honesty I was stunned by the decision. (At least I didn't get the 'hurling graph' – I learned later from Tom Kenny that Denis asked him was his hurling graph going upwards or was it going downwards, because Denis wasn't sure where it was at. He told Tom that he had been extremely lucky to make the cut and if there wasn't an improvement on his graph for next year, he wouldn't be around. Denis will be glad to know that Tom's hurling graph skyrocketed when he moved on as manager.)

As I was leaving the room, Denis said: 'By the way, this is going to be big news, you retiring' – *retiring?* – 'and how best we deal with it. Have a think about it and get on to me and we might discuss about issuing a joint statement. I won't say a word till you get back to me.'

I just said, 'Yeah, let me think about that one.'

Cathal Naughton was the next man in. I wished him the best as I left, headed out, and to this day I don't know how I got home. I just remember pulling up in the car outside my house: no memory of how I got there.

Despite Denis's assurances, by the Sunday night I was getting texts and calls from journalists. The news was filtering out. I spoke to Eddie O'Donnell and we decided not to wait for a statement to come from the Board or the team management. We got the GPA to release a brief statement on my behalf on the Monday: I wished the players all the best but I wanted to make my point, too – that I wanted to continue playing, but I'd been dropped.

The flood of phone calls, text messages and letters from family, friends, team-mates, former managers and hurling supporters all over the country that followed was phenomenal and truly humbling.

Aisake was supposed to have his review meeting a few days after mine, but he didn't bother going. I told him that whatever had

happened to me had happened, but if he wanted to continue playing, then he had my blessing to drive on. But he went back to
Australia with Setanta to resume playing Aussie Rules. Being taken
off against Kilkenny, with no explanation given, had turned him
off. He also said he couldn't go back and play under Denis after
what he did to me.

The lads who were retained on and off throughout 2011 weren't long
saying that 2011 was worse than 2010. That wasn't much consolation
to me, though. I was gone.

19

I brooded through 2011. Denis had said dropping me was a hurling decision, but I didn't buy that. I hadn't been stellar in 2010, but I'd been solid. I believed there was more to his decision than my on-field displays, particularly when I was the only one dropped.

At least I was club captain at Na Piarsaigh for 2011, which gave me some responsibility. It killed me not to be involved with Cork, but I kept my thoughts to myself.

Cork didn't do well in 2011 and the board didn't want to continue with Denis. Names started to float around as possible replacements, including Jimmy Barry-Murphy's, and around mid-August he gave me a call. That was out of the blue. Since he'd stepped down in 2000, we'd have rarely met or spoken. He wanted to meet for lunch and a chat, so we met in the Commons Bar with a mutual friend of ours, Mick Higgins. Not the most private of places, in retrospect, particularly when his name was floating around as Cork senior manager, but we had our sandwich and our soup and he got down to it.

'What exactly happened with you and Denis?' was his first question.

I told him, and his answer was, 'That was wrong. Jeez, I feel partly responsible because I was on the committee that appointed him.'

He went on to say that he hadn't been offered the job of Cork hurling manager – that he hadn't applied for it – but he asked if I'd still be interested in going back playing for Cork if approached. I said I would, but that I'd come back only if the set-up was good; if it was like the previous regime, I wouldn't bother. In particular I pointed out that the physical trainer would be a crucial appointment. He said fine, and that was that.

The board waited another few weeks before announcing Jimmy's appointment.

★

A couple of weeks after that, in early October, I got another call from him.

'Just following up on our talk in August,' he said. 'I'm just conscious your views might have changed. What do you think?'

I said I was still interested, and we agreed I'd call out to his house that Friday. He brought me to his study, out the back.

He said he was delighted that I was still interested in playing for Cork. The last couple of years had been disappointing, and his aim was to bring respectability back to Cork hurling. He also mentioned that he'd lined up a guy called Dave Matthews to handle physical training, and that the training programme wasn't going to be fun for the next two or three months. 'Guys are going to have to shape up or ship out,' he said.

Jimmy said there were no guarantees but that I'd be on the extended training squad for the winter ahead. They'd carry up to forty players and cut it down in the new year. Our first session was a fitness test, the October Bank Holiday weekend.

'All I want is a chance to prove myself,' I said, even though I didn't think I needed to prove myself. I felt deep down I had the goods. But that was one side-effect of the turnover in managers – Gerald, Denis, then Jimmy. Every time a new man came in, you were on trial again, no matter how many years you'd put in.

There was a meeting scheduled for the following Sunday, but I couldn't make it – I had a holiday booked with Siobhán. But I didn't need to go to that meeting to have my first encounter with the new physical trainer. I was at Ger Hartmann's book launch in the University of Limerick and a guy came over to me and introduced himself as Dave Matthews. I asked what was coming in the fitness test and he didn't tell me – understandably – but I was confident I'd be able for it. I'd have kept myself in reasonably good shape, and I'd played a good season of club hurling and football, which would certainly keep your fitness up.

The test was done out in Tyco, near CIT, where Munster Rugby do a lot of their sessions. It began with the usual strength exercises –

bench press, chin-ups, push-ups and so on. The second half was out on the track in CIT, where we did four 400-metre runs. After the testing Dónal Óg was announced as captain.

We trained out on the pitch in CIT the following Tuesday, endurance work, and we didn't touch a hurley until Christmas. The management seemed happy with my levels of fitness. Kieran Kingston, one of the selectors, said to me, 'You've kept yourself in good order.' Training was hard: two gym sessions, two endurance sessions and then, on a Saturday, a hill-running session in the old quarry out in Beaumont, a walking path at an angle that would test you when you ran it. The running sessions were competitive and I was struggling to keep pace with the top group, which consisted of Cathal Naughton, Damien Cahalane, Christopher Joyce, Billy Joyce and Daniel Kearney. The '*maillot jaune*' had well and truly been stripped off me by the new breed of hurlers that were coming through, and I was back in the *peloton*. Cathal Naughton has got to be one of the greatest athletes I've trained with. A running machine.

The player rep system that had come in with Dónal O'Grady was still in place and, after one meeting of the player reps, Dónal Óg said to me, 'Jimmy is delighted with you, he's saying you've exceeded his expectations.' After Christmas I played in challenge games and was named in the league panel.

Having played most of the pre-season games and all of the National League games at either half-back or midfield, I found myself out of contention come the championship. The first sign that I wasn't going to make the team for the first round against Tipperary was when I was assigned to the B dressing-room in an A versus B game among ourselves in Sars the weekend beforehand. Although I was hoping against hope when we went out on the field, the A team looked like the team that would figure in the actual game. John Gardiner found himself in the same boat as me.

It was the same on the Tuesday, and on Thursday the team was officially named: we were in the subs. I was naturally disappointed at not making the starting fifteen, especially having played all of the league games, but hurling is a team sport and you park your individual emotions to one side. What would have been nice was some communication from the management team, an explanation of why I was being left out, but none was forthcoming. The only people who made some acknowledgement were Ger Cunningham and Dónal Óg, who said, 'Hard luck.' I know John didn't get an explanation either.

The league had ended badly, with Kilkenny destroying us in Thurles, and my relationship with Jimmy had seemed to change after that. Until then he would have been full of jokes and chat, and would often ask me how the body felt. Now, management were keeping their distance from me; more than once, when we'd come out for training sessions, I noticed that they would walk away rather than engage in conversation. This went on pretty much all summer. I'd been around long enough to know whether one was welcomed or not.

On the field the year panned out reasonably well, despite losing to Tipperary in the Munster championship: the draw was kind to us at every turn after that.

The only conversation I had with Jimmy during the summer was after the Tipp defeat. I didn't play that day, and towards the end of a midweek weights session down in Páirc Uí Chaoimh he came up to me. I was on my own.

'I can see you're disappointed,' he said.

'I am,' I said, 'but I know you have a job to do'.

'Hang in there,' he said. 'I'll assure you you'll get a chance. I should have spoken to you before the Tipp game but I never got a chance.'

After that conversation I thought the ice had been broken and maybe things were about to improve, but they remained the same. Cork faced Offaly in the qualifiers, and because it was so soon after the Tipp game I didn't expect to start. But Offaly gave Cork enough of it and when the game was in the balance I felt they'd throw in John or myself. They didn't.

Every ten minutes the subs are sent to warm up, and towards the closing stages of the game myself and John were completing our last stint of warm-up at the corner of the covered stand and the City End terrace of Páirc Uí Chaoimh, when I turned to him and said, 'John, read the tea leaves here.'

'I know.'

After the game there was no communication, no feedback from management.

We drew Wexford, the softest draw we could have got. By that stage I had resigned myself to the fact that I definitely wasn't part of the management's plans, and I wondered if it was a huge mistake coming back.

The game went much the same way as the previous day out, with Wexford asking plenty of questions. With ten minutes remaining I was warming up in the corner of Semple Stadium, towards the Killinan end, when Matthews came over to me.

'Get ready, you're coming on,' he said.

'You're joking,' I said. I was shocked – I wasn't expecting to get a run. I got ready and came on for William Egan. We won by a comfortable margin in the end, but the scoreline was flattering: Wexford had given us a scare.

Kilkenny, Limerick and Waterford were with us in the draw for the quarter-final. We drew Waterford. A week and a half before the game I was surprised when Kieran Kingston came up to me and said, 'We have an A versus B game this Sunday morning. Get yourself focused for the game because if you show up well, you'll be in for the Waterford game.'

I said, 'Grand, thanks,' but in truth by that stage my motivation was waning. I felt I had done everything in my power to get back to the best I could be, having spent twelve months in retirement. I honestly couldn't have given it any more in terms of preparation, hand on heart. I felt I was a proven championship performer. Therefore it was frustrating to be out of the picture for the most part of the summer.

Teu and Siobhán were fantastic. They saw that I was bottling up my feelings and that this was doing me no good. They always convinced me to remain patient. My chance would come eventually. Teu's sporting career really put things into perspective for me. The man had had his fair share of setbacks in sport and never enjoyed the same level of success myself, Setanta and Aisake would have had, but he always remained positive and dignified. Here I was, facing a problem that would hardly register as a setback for most people, and I'm thinking it was the end of the world. Teu told me to knuckle down for that A versus B game. If this was going to be my last year at that level, he said, at least go out fighting and not have any regrets. I did exactly that and pulled up well in the game.

Another tower of strength for me was the fourth brother I never had, John Gardiner. John is the same age as Setanta – six years younger than me – and they played on the same teams all the way up. Like Setanta, he was destined for the big stage from an early age. I got to know him when he started playing senior hurling championship for the club at seventeen. When Setanta and Aisake departed to Australia I saw him as another brother. His family are steeped in Na Piarsaigh. Outside of Tony O'Sullivan, he has been the club's best ever hurler to represent Cork. After eleven years of putting his body on the line for the county, he too was demoted to the subs and was finding the going tough. Management weren't talking to him either. His positive attitude towards training and to the panel was exemplary. I learned an awful lot from him during this time.

I got my first start of the championship against Waterford. I had made my way back into the starting fifteen, I was anxious to prove a point and I couldn't wait to get out there. What happened? John Mullane ran me ragged in the first half, and I ended up having to be switched off him. Christ, was I filthy with myself at the half-time break. 'After all this, you put in that crap display,' I thought. 'Maybe the management were right all along.' If I'd been pulled off at half-time I wouldn't have had any complaints. Things improved in the second half, and I managed a point late on. John Gardiner came on and made a couple of vital interventions, including stopping Mullane at one point in the second half when a goal might have been on the cards for Waterford.

We'd probably exceeded expectations by getting to an All-Ireland semi-final. Our opponent was Galway. After we had played a promising first half, they took control in the second half and were too strong for us in the end.

Afterwards I don't recall any big speeches from management, though Galway manager Anthony Cunningham came in and was very humble, very articulate in his commiserations.

There's grub for the players after those games in a lounge on the fourth floor of the Hogan Stand, and I was last into it as usual. But there was a different reason this time: I sensed it was my last time in a dressing-room in Croke Park. I knew the management team was in place for another couple of years and I certainly wasn't going to figure.

Niall Mac, my old mate in dawdling in dressing-rooms, was there as well. I didn't know it at the time, but Niall was thinking of travelling, and would head off soon for Asia, so he was in a reflective mood as well.

We had a chat about the great days we'd experienced in this very dressing-room and we wondered, would we see the good days again. Then he headed off, and I was on my own. The steward who was assigned to the dressing-room for the duration of the game popped his head in. I gave him a sliotar. You'd get to know those guys from going up there, very decent guys, and he asked if everything was OK.

'Grand,' I said, and headed up to join the team.

When I came out of the dressing-room there were kids from Glenariff, in the Glens of Antrim, looking for signatures and photos to be taken. I was chatting to them for a while and then a journalist caught me for a few words. I was asked about the future and I said I'd have to think about it over the winter.

Dr Con, who had come down from the players' lounge, spotted

me, and after I finished he warned me not to make any snap decisions. He said, 'You've a lot to offer. Don't do anything rash.'

We got on the bus – no more train journeys for Cork teams, because the motorway makes the bus a quicker, more direct option – and headed south. Journeys home after a defeat are always long and this one must have been the longest. Not because of the time it took us to travel from Dublin to Cork but because my head was in constant deep thought. Mixed thoughts. I knew that today was my last day in a Cork shirt, but equally knew I was still good enough to play on. As much as I'd convinced myself that I should retire, I felt I could go on another season.

I wasn't the only player that was undecided. After coming out of the toilet in the back of the bus I sat next to Eoin Cadogan for a while. We had a good chat, dissecting what went wrong and reflecting on the year as a whole. He was to be back for football training the following night in preparation for the All-Ireland football semi-final in two weeks' time against Donegal. What a tough gig. He was finding the schedule between both codes demanding and was not sure if the body could carry on for another season or two playing both.

By the time the bus let us off at the Rochestown Park Hotel, I was steering more towards taking the Doc's advice to hang in there.

I was back in Dublin on the Tuesday with the Ulster Bank GAA Force competition, a club improvement programme. I was asked about the future again and I fobbed the question off, saying there were a few things that would need to happen for me to continue, that we'd probably talk it over during the winter. The usual.

We played club championship, the year rolled on and I didn't hear anything until I got a phone call from Dónal Óg in late October. Dónal Óg had ruptured his Achilles tendon in the spring and missed the whole playing season as a result. He was keen to get back for the following year. I'd fallen in with him for a few training sessions in Páirc Uí Chaoimh in September and early October as he rehabbed the injury, but this call came out of the blue.

'I'm meeting Jimmy tomorrow,' he said. 'I don't have a good feeling about this one. My instinct is that it's bad news.'

I'd had no contact with the management, so I didn't know the lie of the land. But it would never have occurred to me they'd want to . . .

'Get rid of you? I wouldn't think so.'

'As soon as I'm finished the meeting, I'll ring you,' he said.

He called me the next day around twelve.

'How'd the meeting go?'

'Bad.'

He said Jimmy had taken the captaincy off him and that he wouldn't be the number-one keeper next season. It was a huge blow for him.

Dónal Óg also said that myself and John would be getting phone calls from Jimmy and to brace ourselves because it wasn't going to be good news. We weren't surprised, given the way we'd been blanked all summer.

I was in all-too-familiar territory now, having gone through this before with Denis Walsh. Jimmy rang me – the same day I spoke to Dónal Óg on the phone – and said he wanted to meet as soon as possible. I asked why, and he said he wanted to discuss next year.

We arranged to meet up in the car park of the Kingsley Hotel on a Friday night. He hopped into my car, we had some small talk, and then we got to business.

'What are your intentions for next year?' he said.

'I've been thinking about it,' I said. 'But I want to hear your plans first.'

'Look, the management team sat down recently. Realistically we're not going to win anything for the next two to three years, so we're going to go a new direction next year and throw our full lot with youth, be it good, bad or indifferent. We're going to work with these guys for the next few years. We don't know if you'll be still playing around then. We don't see a place for you there.'

'A place on the team or the panel?'

'The panel,' he said. 'Look, we saw the frustration on your face during the summer when you weren't making the first fifteen.'

I was thinking to myself, wouldn't anyone who was serious about high-performance sport be unhappy?

I told Jimmy that I was very grateful for the opportunity he gave me to come back, but I hadn't come back to sit on the bench. No one wants to be dropped, and I was unhappy. 'I'm as competitive as the next man,' I said. 'I'm sure you wouldn't accept a sub being content to be on the bench and just be there for the ride.'

I asked him two questions. Firstly, I asked him to rate my year. Glowing report from Jimmy: 'I couldn't have asked for any more from you in training, you played well in the games that you played and you bailed us out towards the end of the year when other guys were struggling for form.'

'Name a half-back that's better at the moment, then?'

He couldn't name anyone, but with the youth policy they were undertaking, he was hoping 'someone might come up trumps next year,' he said.

I said that that was the one reason I felt I should be around – I felt I could offer something to the younger guys coming up. But he was having none of it, and kept going on about his 'youth policy'.

'Let me recap so,' I said. 'I'm not going to be part of the panel, you're going with young fellas.'

'But if none of them perform or progress the way we want,' he said, 'we might come back to you.'

Take whatever you want out of that, but that was curtains for me. I had well and truly played my last game for Cork. I said, 'Thanks for your time,' and he hopped out. Disappointment is disappointment, no matter which way you try to package it up. I wasn't as gutted as I had been two years previously, but I was still gutted. On the trip home I kept thinking that if I'd known it was going to end like this, I would have stayed happily retired. I felt Jimmy had called it wrong.

I'm alive to my own inconsistencies. I was the one bidding a mental farewell to Croke Park in August, then getting thick that I was being jettisoned two months later in October. But any athlete, any competitor who feels he has something to contribute, will want to continue. I'm no different.

I'm also able to hold my hand up when I'm wrong. As I write, the Cork team that Jimmy has assembled through his 'youth policy' are counting down the days to an All-Ireland hurling final with Clare, a final pairing few people would have predicted when the two teams met in a league relegation playoff in April.

On that basis Jimmy could say he was justified, certainly, in cutting me adrift. It's a results business and the team he picked got the results for him. I'm a competitor, as I say, and I'd love to have taken that journey with them. I'm also a proud Cork man and I salute them: *Corcaigh Abu*.

Myself and Siobhán were going to New York the week after the conversation in my car with Jimmy. I didn't want to create a big stir about packing it in. I went to the GPA, gave my statement to Siobhán Earley in the office there and told her to release it when I was in the air en route to JFK.

In New York we visited a friend of ours, Phil O'Shea, who comes over every summer. His wife Elizabeth gave us a great dinner and I told him I'd retired and he came back with his news – he'd retired from the NYPD as well.

'Now, two retirements,' he said. 'What are they gonna do without us?'

My mobile doesn't accept calls or messages abroad, thank God, so we had a great holiday. When I came back and switched it on, it nearly melted down with the volume of texts and voicemails, but that was immaterial. I was an ex-intercounty player and, strange as it may sound, a relieved one at that. I was finally at peace – no more dramas, no more disappointments and no more false dawns.

20

One of my old heroes, Dermot Brereton, once said that he didn't realize how good-looking he was until he put on a Hawthorn jersey.

I know what he meant. My life changed big-time when I started to play for Cork at senior level. It ascended to a whole new level when I became an All-Ireland medal-holder. For a person who came from somewhere else and picked up the game at a late age, earning respect had been bloody hard. Hurling for Cork was my gateway to acceptance.

Acceptance demands patience, though. In the early years representing Cork at senior level, Teu recalls vividly that after I had a shocker against Clare in a Munster championship game in 1998 a fan remarked, 'Is that what Cork have come to, they're giving jerseys to fucking Fijians now.' We laugh about that now, but it wasn't so funny at the time.

The amount that's expected of a GAA intercounty player, an amateur, is huge. He's expected to train almost full-time, to be a pillar of society, a role model who encourages kids. It's a pastime. A group of lads in for a year to win some silverware. I hope the fans and supporters of our great game never lose sight of that, and understand that no player ever goes out to perform poorly.

In the very same way, I never forget about the genuine fan. Supporters are a massive part of the game.

I'd have tried to interact with supporters over the years as much as I could. I can be accused of many things throughout my playing career, but I'd like to think that I always gave the supporters and public my time. Sometimes it has come to the detriment of my loved ones, but I got great enjoyment out of meeting tremendous people. I know family, friends, neighbours, workmates and schoolmates followed me closely over the years with Cork, and it was very much appreciated. It's an expensive business, and when I think of supporters I think of those people especially.

There's an odd split, these days, amongst the six Ó hAilpín siblings. Half of us have clear memories of Australia and half of us don't. Think you can work out which half are living in Australia now?

Teu was the brightest academically in the family. He was known as the 'professor' at home. He certainly got the best Leaving Cert results of all of us. After graduating from DCU, two years behind me, he went to Boston and played hurling and worked at different jobs. Then he went down to New York for a few years before moving to London.

Like his brothers, he represented Cork in football at minor and U-21 level. He'd have given his right arm to play hurling for Cork at any level but most especially at senior level, but when it didn't happen, he decided to go travelling. Teu went travelling to find himself – he'd tell you that. He had a great time. I often said to Setanta and Aisake, when we were sweating our nuts off back here with training and games and before they set sail themselves for Australia, that Teu would end up being the most rounded of us all. Travelling broadens the horizons, unlike the surreal world of hurling at home where you're caught in a bubble and never think it's going to end sometime.

Teu is an accountant now with PriceWaterhouse, living in Jersey with his lovely partner, Emily Cotter. Going to Jersey was a professional move for him, but he's keen to come back to Cork some day.

I would love it if he did. I'm closer to Teu than to anybody else in the family, and I would share more with him than with the others. That stems from the fact that only a year separates us – back in Sydney we shared the same bed, and headed off together to Roberts Park to kick footy around. Everywhere I went, Teu would have been there with me.

He's a deep guy. It takes a while for him to open up to people, and when you meet him for the first time he can come across as reserved. Serious. But he's someone whose opinion I'd value very seriously on all matters.

Teu had his fair share of setbacks and disappointments in sport. Not making the cut for teams, injuries, etc. Doors opened for us but shut for him. Only a person like that can appreciate reality, because success can make you blind. I've found that out badly to my cost over the years. That's why I've always valued his opinions. Towards the end of my playing career, when he returned to Cork, I talked to him after games. He'd give an honest assessment of how I did, good or bad, and I'd have valued that opinion more than anyone else's.

Rivalry in sport brings out the best in competitors. We were ultra-competitive growing up, and Mum had to defuse endless fights and arguments. I wouldn't have developed my character and competitiveness only for him pushing me on and vice versa. He was a great sparring partner.

Sarote is a different ball game. She is a person of strong opinions, and her personality is nearly the opposite to Teu's. Teu mightn't agree with you, but he'd take your view on board and make up his own mind in his own time. Sarote doesn't beat around the bush. She is direct.

She's a teacher now in the AG. A lot of kids at the school play for Na Piarsaigh, and if I'm up at the club I'll often have a kid say, 'Oh, you're Sarote's brother,' and I'll be thinking, 'What's coming here?'

This is very sad to admit, but I never really knew my sisters growing up because, in our household, if you were a guy playing sport, you were the only game in town. In addition, I was gone to college in Dublin for four years when I was eighteen and Sarote was fifteen, so I wasn't around that much at that time, which we sometimes refer to as her rebellious period.

Now she's a model citizen – responsible teacher, great mother to her two lovely daughters, Letiah and Kerera – but the odd time we'd say to her, 'Hey, you weren't always like this.' When she was fourteen or fifteen she'd be trying to bunk off to the discos in town, which wouldn't have been something Mum and Dad experienced with the two older kids, me and Teu, who were completely focused on sport.

I only really got to know Sarote in later years, when I finished up in DCU and she started going to my hurling games. She completed her Leaving Cert and went to college down in WIT. She did business studies there and then the H. Dip in UCC, and eventually she started teaching in the AG. And she loves it. She must be one of the few people I know who loves her job: she never complains about anything she has to do in school.

She's married to Dónal McSweeney, who lived next door to us. He's my age. You can imagine how it went down with her four brothers, going out with the next-door neighbour at seventeen, eighteen. We noticed he was around the house a bit more, then we wondered why, and when we found out it didn't sit very well. Setanta and Aisake used to throw rocks at his car, for instance, and because he was living next door it wasn't as if he could get it out of range that easily. They were eleven, twelve years of age and they'd be pegging rocks at Dónal's Toyota Corolla. Aisake in particular has a great arm, as they'd say in baseball: very accurate.

What kind of clowns were we? Dónal's a super guy. Had enough guts to walk in the front door and present himself. He would drive Sarote up and down to Waterford when she was studying there and he really took care of her. It was little signs like that which showed us how serious he was, and what a decent guy he was. We copped ourselves on.

They got married in 2008 and they have two girls now, with another one on the way. When I was playing, her house was the safe haven on the Saturday night before a big championship game with Cork. You'd head over to her place and she'd serve up a great meal without once mentioning the game. Just what you want the night before a match: good food – usually lasagne, her speciality, to get the carbs on board – and a relaxed atmosphere, good company, no worrying about what you were facing the following day.

Unlike Teu, Sarote and me, the younger trio don't remember childhood in Sydney; they wouldn't have had anything with which to compare the early years in Cork. Now they're all living in Australia. Setanta and Aisake are still playing Aussie Rules – Setanta with Greater Western Sydney, having spent eight seasons at Carlton, and Aisake with Hillside, having also been with Carlton for four years. The three of them are very close. They all went to the same primary and secondary school growing up, and would have spent a lot of time in each other's company. Étaoin is now completing a teaching course in Melbourne University. Herself and her boyfriend, Neil Waters, who is a mechanic by trade, are living with Aisake.

There is a three-year gap between Sarote and me, and if I didn't have much of a relationship with her, you can imagine what relationship I had with Étaoin, who is eleven years younger. Non-existent. There's a lot to be said for just being there, but I wasn't around for Étaoin's main events. I did make her graduation day from CIT.

It's funny – I'm probably closer to her now than I ever was, though she's Down Under, because I have more time now I've retired from intercounty.

From the steps of the City Hall in Cork, off to your right beyond the office of the Harbour Commissioners, you can almost see Kent Station, where my family and I first landed in Cork, back in 1988. That was in my mind, back in June 2011, when I came out of City Hall, because I had just been awarded the Freedom of Cork.

I couldn't think of a bigger honour. I had been asked to open the City of Culture in 2005 by striking a blazing sliotar on Merchant's Quay, and that was a great thrill, but the Freedom of the City . . . you're talking about the likes of John F. Kennedy. Jack Lynch. Unbelievable company.

After the ceremony, from the steps of the City Hall I could see other places that were significant for me and my family. The intersection of the South Mall and Parnell Place, where victorious Cork teams that I was privileged to be part of showcased the Liam Mac-Carthy Cup to fans. The office across the river where Teu used to work, and, across the street, the old Modh Scoil, now a courthouse, where Teu, Sarote, Setanta and Aisake went to school when we first arrived. A stone's throw away from the South Mall is Patrick Street, where I started working with Ulster Bank in 2004.

Being honoured in a city I'd never heard of a quarter of a century ago was special, and humbling. Twenty-five years sounds like a long time, but it feels as if it was yesterday. What was equally humbling was sharing the experience with people who have shaped my life and career. One of those has been Siobhán, my partner of twelve years and the most patient woman alive.

Siobhán's brother is Alan Quirke, the Cork senior football goalkeeper. Alan is usually credited for introducing me to Siobhán, but it's their eldest sister, Lynda, who actually made the official intro. I first met Siobhán the night of the All-Ireland football semi-final in 1999 and Lynda introduced me to her, but we didn't start going out until 2001.

Tús maith leath na hoibre: that was the summer I had badly injured my knee, and travel was a challenge, but there's still no excuse for the fact that I was late for our first date. Dónal McSweeney, Sarote's then boyfriend, gave me a lift in from Blarney in his Hiace, and I hobbled out of his van about an hour late. We got over that hiccup, though, and we've been together ever since.

It helped that, because of Alan, Siobhán understood the demands on an intercounty player in terms of training and so forth; but it wasn't always easy for her, particularly when we were first going out.

We were often out for the evening and some guys would come over and discuss a game, and she'd be pushed to one side. Literally. Or we'd be having dinner and someone I'd never met would come over and spend ten minutes dissecting Cork's attacking problems.

I'd be too nice: I wouldn't tell someone to clear off, and people know that about me. Eventually Siobhán would say to someone, 'Look, we're having a meal here,' and you could tell the person wasn't impressed – even though they might have been talking to me for so long that the food had gone cold. That was on me, though. I should have been more assertive.

It wasn't just a Saturday night thing. When I worked in Ulster Bank in Patrick Street she'd meet me for lunch the odd time. The Moderne clothes shop is five yards away and it wouldn't have been unusual for half of lunchtime to be lost to people stopping me before we got past the Moderne. Again, Siobhán would be left standing on her own.

She'd tell me to put the mobile up to my ear as soon as I left the office, to pretend I was on a call, but when I tried that I found people were willing to wait until I finished that imaginary call before talking to me.

There were other challenges for her. My commitments meant I wasn't around a lot. Some of her friends would never have met me, and they'd be slagging her about this non-existent boyfriend: 'You're not really going out with him,' that kind of thing.

We learned along the way. Both of us. When I brought Siobhán to functions I'd often be inundated and she'd be left alone; but she started to bring her sister, or a friend, for company, or else she wouldn't go.

I wouldn't just assume she didn't want to go. I'd ask, and she'd simply say, 'Is there going to be someone there I can talk to?' and if the answer was in the negative she'd stay at home.

People might be surprised by our lifestyle. We've never gone away for a weekend together in Ireland. We don't even do the shopping together. We wouldn't get it done. We spend a lot of time at home.

One crucial part of our relationship is the fact that when I'd come home after a big game she wouldn't dwell on it.

'How did the game go?'

'Grand,' or 'Not too good.'

And that'd be it. No analysis, no discussion. It's always been a pleasure to drive home after a game because I know I'm not facing the kind of analysis I faced for years at home.

Siobhán was important there, too. Her parents had always been supportive of their children rather than pointing out their failings, and when she began to come home with me to the family place, she was amazed by how harsh Dad would be.

Like any couple, we've had our ups and downs. We went to see Elton John at the Marquee in Cork in 2008, which promised to be a great night but ended up in tears. We had an argument, and it escalated. I got thick and she got thick – Elton was in full swing, probably belting out 'Saturday Night's Alright for Fighting', while we were going at each other. Hurtful things were said. I should have known that day would come, because the source of the argument was that I didn't appreciate her enough. If I did, I had a funny way of showing it. All of the pent-up anger built up over the years spilled out and Siobhán said, 'Look, maybe it wasn't meant to be.'

She stayed with a friend that night. There was a lot of soul-searching done and if the previous seven years together meant anything to me, then I owed it to Siobhán to put it right. The next day we met up, and I apologized: 'I thought about what you said, and you're right, I have to give you more time. You're right to feel that a lot of things are put in front of you and that has to change.'

It's some empty feeling when you really hurt loved-ones. It's the kind of experience that wakes you up.

Taking my preparations for games seriously has brought me honours and accolades, but other parts of your life suffer. That's a reality. When I was playing for Cork there'd be days when I'd be gone at half seven in the morning and back from training, or the gym, at eleven at night.

I haven't been the model partner in terms of availability, but our relationship is built on trust. I might not be in the house but I always have her in mind. For me the most pleasing part of the day is driving up the Whitechurch Road, to where we live, after a game, training session or a day's work. I look forward to her smile and welcome when I go through the front door.

At the time of writing Siobhán is on an international marketing fellowship with the Smurfit Business School, so she's away a bit; and when she's away, I miss her. Maybe there's a sense of the shoe being on the other foot.

Siobhán tells a story of one of her aunts, Kathleen Bevan, who went to Wales back in the sixties on holiday when she was in her early twenties. She ended up marrying a Welsh man and rearing a family. She still lives in Wales. When asked about it, to this day her reply is, 'I went to Wales on a holiday and after all these years I'm still on a holiday.'

Back in 1988 when I arrived to Cork, like Auntie Kathleen, I seriously thought I was on a holiday and that we'd return back to Sydney. Never in my wildest dreams did I think I'll be still in Cork to this day. I must say it's been some holiday. The day of the Freedom of the City ceremony, in my mind I made a phone call to the travel agent. I told them to cancel my return ticket. That I was staying put. On acceptance of the award I said, 'Although I am not of you, I have become one of you,' and I am.

Acknowledgements

I owe thanks to many people. Apologies to any I've left out.

Many people helped us when we first came to Cork: Betty and John Anderson, Jim McAllister and Maureen O'Brien, the Gardiner family, the McGregor family, John and Marion O'Sullivan, the O'Byrne family, the Hutchinson family, the Lahive family, the O'Flynn and the Shaw family. They all made a strange place more welcoming.

The teachers in the North Mon, primary and secondary, educated me and, in particular, they gave me Irish: *go raibh mile maith agaibh*.

Walking up the hill to Na Piarsaigh H&F Club was one of the best decisions I ever made. Thanks to all mentors, coaches, managers and team-mates, and especially to the late Abie Allen and the late Paddy Moore, Tony Hegarty, Billy Clifford and Christy Kidney for all their patience when I was starting off.

My Cork managers, coaches and team-mates made representing my county a special experience. *Corcaigh abú.*

My workmates and bosses in Ulster Bank were always understanding and helpful when I was playing intercounty hurling: I appreciated that help hugely. Special mention goes to Peter McKenna, Sean O'Donnell, Sam Beamish, Declan Daly, Tom Leahy and Sean Healy.

Eddie O'Donnell has been more than an adviser and a sounding board for many years. He's been a friend I trust completely.

Paul Moloney of Adidas has been generous beyond the call of duty.

Michael McLoughlin and Brendan Barrington of Penguin Ireland made writing this book a rewarding experience from start to finish. So did Michael Moynihan, who isn't just a Mon boy but an AG boy: top of the class.

Paul and Noreen Quirke have always made me welcome in their home in Innishannon since I started dating their lovely daughter. Thanks also to Lynda and Alan Quirke for their support over the years – I've always appreciated that and am glad to be able to say so in print now. To Siobhán, how can I begin to thank you in so few words? Your commitment to our relationship has at times made me feel ashamed of my own commitment to it, but rarely have you complained. You've always been there for me, no matter what. But most of all, thank you for showing me the true meaning of a relationship. I can't think of a better person to spend the rest of my life with. I love you.

Thanks to Mum and Dad for giving me the gift of life, for encouraging me to play sport and ensuring I got a very good education. What can I say of Mum? If I were to describe her, she has the poise of Corcoran, the strength of Sully, the cutting edge of Gardiner, the grace of Ben O'Connor and the patience of Deano, all in one. Above all my childhood and sporting heroes, Mum has simply been my greatest ever hero. I've always said it that if I turn out to be even a shadow of the person she is, I'd be an extremely happy man. Your endless commitment and love to each and every one of us is something we will ever be grateful for. I'm proud to say that we are part of your Rotuman culture, and for as long as we're alive it will continue to live. '*Helava Rotuma.*'

Finally, thanks to my brothers and sisters, Teu, Sarote, Setanta, Aisake and Étaoin. They are the only people who really know how tough the journey was. I have always admired every one of them for lasting the journey, and they've been the main inspiration behind my sporting achievements. Some of them are spread out across the world but I hope they all know I am always there for them.

Index

He just wanted a decent book to read ...

Not too much to ask, is it? It was in 1935 when Allen Lane, Managing Director of Bodley Head Publishers, stood on a platform at Exeter railway station looking for something good to read on his journey back to London. His choice was limited to popular magazines and poor-quality paperbacks – the same choice faced every day by the vast majority of readers, few of whom could afford hardbacks. Lane's disappointment and subsequent anger at the range of books generally available led him to found a company – and change the world.

'We believed in the existence in this country of a vast reading public for intelligent books at a low price, and staked everything on it'
Sir Allen Lane, 1902–1970, founder of Penguin Books

The quality paperback had arrived – and not just in bookshops. Lane was adamant that his Penguins should appear in chain stores and tobacconists, and should cost no more than a packet of cigarettes.

Reading habits (and cigarette prices) have changed since 1935, but Penguin still believes in publishing the best books for everybody to enjoy. We still believe that good design costs no more than bad design, and we still believe that quality books published passionately and responsibly make the world a better place.

So wherever you see the little bird – whether it's on a piece of prize-winning literary fiction or a celebrity autobiography, political tour de force or historical masterpiece, a serial-killer thriller, reference book, world classic or a piece of pure escapism – you can bet that it represents the very best that the genre has to offer.

Whatever you like to read – trust Penguin.

read more
www.penguin.co.uk